To

Geoff

Thanks for buys

Enjoy

C000274116

Jon Purdie

PURDS

BOOZE

and

FOOTY

Best Wishes

Published for Jon Purdie by Verité CM Limited,
124 Sea Place, Worthing, West Sussex BN12 4BG
+44 (0) 1903 241975

email: enquiries@veritecm.com
Web: www.veritecm.com

British Library Cataloguing in Publication Data
A record for this book is available from The British Library

ISBN: 978-1-914388-09-5

Printed in the UK

Contents

Acknowledgements

I have to thank my parents Johnny and Isabelle for always being supportive throughout my life but especially in my formative years. It's only when you become a parent yourself that you appreciate the sacrifices that are made during your childhood. I also need to express my gratitude to my ex-wife Julie for helping me adapt from being a professional footballer to life as a normal working man (although she probably won't think I'm normal at all). In regards to help with the book I am in debt to Tim Nash for encouraging me to tell my story, Jason Guy as an ally and my eldest son Charlie for proof reading and helping with the delivery of the book. Lastly for the lifelong support and friendship of my best friend Alan Wortley.

Foreword – Graham Allner

I first saw Jon Purdie play for Cheltenham Town and it took barely a few minutes to recognise his undoubted football talent. I was managing Kidderminster Harriers and in the middle of a rebuild after a brush with relegation the previous season. Subsequent research revealed a promising, but largely unfulfilled career that glittered at schoolboy level and began in earnest at Arsenal where he was part of the Adams, Rocastle, Merson, Keown, Quinn, Thomas generation at youth level. When his career at Highbury stalled a spiral through the Football League at a number of clubs landed him in non-league football by his mid-twenties.

Jon possessed an X factor that could change a game in an instant with eye catching close control and the ability to escape tight situations which allied to a deceptive turn of pace and precise crossing and finishing was perhaps reminiscent in style of Nottingham Forest's John Robertson.

In football management success and failure is largely determined by the quality of your players and ability to get the best out of them, but in a part time setting, as non-league mostly was in those days, money was tight and scouting networks non-existent. In my long career at Kidderminster in the Conference talented players that could make a difference were at a premium, but I was fortunate enough to sign many good ones over the years.

When Jon signed in January 1993 I was attempting to restructure the club by bringing in a mixture of experience and youth to gradually rebuild the team and he proved an important part of that process. Intelligent and strong minded he was generally quiet and reserved in manner, but though often accused throughout his career of lacking industry and commitment was always willing to contribute to the team cause in his own way. He knew his own strengths, craved for his team to play to them and was very confident in his own ability to produce for the communal cause given the service he required. I was braced for the challenge of succeeding where others had failed to get the best out of him and playing what is now known as a high pressing game was not going to help given his laid back approach. I knew it would not be easy.

I believed however if you took a perceived gamble in signing his type of player you signed them for what they could do, playing to their strengths not what they were poor at and with Jon the trade-off was to let him do his own thing and trust him to produce. This meant in a closing down system that had always depended on everybody working in unison, unusually I was prepared to accept Jon was not always going to join in and because of his game changing ability the other players accepted it too and compensated. In truth he was willing enough but wasn't very good at it which could cause us problems.

The gamble was to pay off for the club in spectacular fashion the following season which I will come to shortly, but an early heart to heart when I left him out four games into his Kidderminster career and didn't explain why beforehand, proved crucial. He came to see me after missing games at Wycombe Wanderers and Welling asking why I had left him out saying if he wasn't going to play he might as well move on which offered the opportunity I wanted. He was surprised when I said he was signed for problems he could cause opponents going forward and so far all he had done was make futile attempts to track overlapping full backs into his own half. I assured him that if I wanted someone to do that he would not have been high on my target list and when he replied that it was what Managers had always wanted him to do I said his request to leave was granted if that was what he continued to do. Restored to the team for the following game he scored nine goals from the left wing in the remaining 21 games including a memorable hat trick in a 5-1 win at Woking and with his Kidderminster career now fully underway he looked a player with a new lease of life.

The following season proved memorable for both the club and Jon when we won the Conference and reached the fifth round of the FA Cup, a rare achievement for a non-league club. Jon's big moment came when he grabbed national attention by scoring a fabulous winning goal of the highest quality at Birmingham City in the third round. A goal down early on with their right back Scott Hiley's incessant forward runs causing problems down our left side, Jon was torn between playing his normal game or conscientiously doing a job for the team by tracking Hiley. Given Jon's defensive limitations it was obvious changes needed to be made, so gambling, I sent a message out for him to let Hiley go and stay up field leaving left back Paul Bancroft the onerous responsibility to pick Hiley's runs up as well as dealing with their right winger.

Jon was our obvious outlet as we began to win more possession in midfield and gradually forced Hiley back. He became an ever increasing threat after we equalized and produced the defining moment of the game after breaking forward from midfield to lash a thunderous drive into the roof of the net from outside the box for the winning goal. He hit the national headlines the following day and then again when another moment of his magic set Delwyn Humphreys up for the winning goal in the next round against Preston before a Lee Chapman goal in a fifth round tie against West Ham eventually ended our cup run.

We went on to win the Conference that season and Jon would have had visions of returning to League football until a controversial ground grading decision by the Football League denied us promotion.

Injuries marred the following season for him, but he returned to the side in time to play in the FA Trophy Final against Woking at Wembley which proved to be his last full appearance after another injury hit season led to his eventual departure to Telford in March 1996.

So an eventful three years at Kidderminster came to an end for Jon where he certainly made his mark and enjoyed moments in the spotlight his talent undoubtedly warranted. He contributed greatly to one of the most successful periods in the clubs history and his goal at St Andrews guaranteed his place in club folklore. On the basis that a player's value to a club can be measured by the extent their strengths outweigh their weaknesses determining their part in any subsequent success, I think Jon can be more than satisfied with his contribution at Kidderminster and I certainly enjoyed my time managing him.

Jon's story is an interesting one that will resonate with many who in their youth thought they were destined for great things in football and wondered where it went wrong. It should make for an excellent read.

CHAPTER ONE

FOREST, CORBY AND SCRAPS

Football was my life from being a toddler. I would kick a ball around with my dad as soon as I could walk. At the beginning I suppose this was the same as millions of other lads with their fathers – all done for a bit of fun and to bond together. However it soon became apparent that I was born with a natural ability to kick a bag of wind around much better than most kids. I just loved football, playing any time I wasn't made to do something else such as school or eating and washing. At the age of seven I was selected for the school team, playing with 10-year-olds. Although they were bigger than me, I was still quick enough to get away from them and score goals.

Loving kicking a ball with my dad.

School photo with the Man Utd kit on at Kingswood Primary School.

This continued and when I went to secondary school I represented the district and the county, before being spotted by a scout from Nottingham Forest. I was invited for trials and I would attend training during school holidays, staying for a week and training alongside the river Trent on adjoining pitches to the first team. It was a great time to be involved with Forest as it was the golden period of their history when they won the League and back-to-back European Cups. Forest's legendary manager Brian Clough would appear occasionally on a Friday to watch his team of international stars such as Peter Shilton, Viv Anderson, Frank Gray, Kenny Burns, Martin O'Neill, John Robertson, Garry Birtles, Tony Woodcock and Trevor Francis, which was an extra thrill.

During one such week, there weren't many first-team players training as I think they were away playing international fixtures. A few of the senior lads such as Ian Bowyer and John McGovern – good pros who were probably training voluntarily – joined in training with us kids. I was about 14 at the time and during the customary seven-a-side at the end of training I was playing particularly well. John McGovern, who had clearly had enough of my dribbling and nutmegs, decided to welcome me to professional football by unceremoniously kicking me up in the air and telling me to stop trying to take the piss! It was a lesson learned.

I think the sporty lads of my generation were all the same – we played football in the winter and sometimes rugby at school, and then in the summer cricket and tennis took over and we would pretend to be Derek Underwood or Geoff Boycott in a Test match, and copy Jimmy Connors or John McEnroe at Wimbledon. My poor dad would get in from a hard day grafting as a plumber and I would drag him outside on the drive so I could practise whichever sport was my favourite at the time until he was totally knackered! We didn't have computers, Playstations or X-Boxes so we played outside all the time all year round. I do think kids miss out on that these days in the UK, all sporting activities seem to be organised and any natural flair and ability is coached out of them. I used to play in the park which was about 100 metres long, and depending on the numbers, the pitch would be adjusted to suit. On a Sunday afternoon there would be kids from my age – 11 or 12 – to adults having just left the pub a few pints deep. Throwing out time was about 3.30pm after last orders, so the pitch would be extended to full size and the game would develop into about 20-a-side. This made you either get rid of the ball quickly when needed or have to use some skill in tight areas – I think it's called 'decision making' now but it was just called survival then! Alongside this I would play on the street in small sided games – 1 v 1 or 2 v 2 with jumpers for goalposts and I would learn to dribble and play one two's off the kerb which was great practise. This, along with 'Murderball' at school lunch

Corby & Kettering district U11s captain.

and playtimes taught you think on your feet and run like hell at times. Murderball was a game played in the school playground and if you kicked the ball out of the cage or were caught in possession then basically you got seven bells kicked out of you by everyone else! The more confident of us would see how close we could kick the ball to the top of the cage without it going out and risk getting beaten up – but obviously this would occasionally go wrong and you had run out of the cage or take a beating!

All this helped me in training with professional clubs, and I loved it at Forest. I was also training at Leicester City around this time, but I always thought I would join Forest. Indeed I was due to, and I was invited to sign for the club after watching a European Cup game against Ajax. My parents and I were invited to the game and it was first experience of live European Cup football, I remember Rudi Krol being majestic. The plan was to meet Brian Clough afterwards to seal the deal and my mind was on that meeting through most of the game. Unfortunately for some unknown reason Cloughie refused to speak to anyone afterwards. The poor youth development officer – Alan Hill, had to tell us the meeting was off! My father was not impressed on a matter of principle and the incident put doubt in our minds.

So it was back to my home town of Corby. It's a unique place in the rural county of Northamptonshire, where the majority of the population were of Irish or Scottish origin. My mum Isabelle and her family migrated from Newtonards near Belfast and my grandad on my father John's side migrated from Belshill in Scotland. I was the second born after my sister Joanne was born 18 months prior to me. Thousands of Celts moved to Corby and settled there, working in the old British steelworks. The steelworks are long since closed and have now been replaced with new industry after a long period of unemployment for many. This 'difference' in Corby people created a bond and feeling of not being liked or wanted in Northamptonshire and meant we closed ranks when visiting or playing football against neighbouring towns like Kettering, Wellingborough and Northampton. I think we intimidated lads from other towns due to our closeness. This rarely progressed to fighting, but if it got to that stage, there were plenty of willing lads from Corby to ensure there was never a step backwards. This was fortunate for me as I was never one to step forward in the hope and confidence that others willingly would!

Such was the case at one end-of-season presentation in Leicester after the team I was involved in, Corby Gainsborough had won the Leicestershire League. A convoy of cars got all the lads and parents there to witness us 14 year olds collect our prizes, but we were 'welcomed' with sneers and some derisory comments from some of the Leicester based boys. My mate Gez Goodall had had a bit of a ding-dong during the season against

Corby Gainsborough u13s.

a big lad from Syston who apparently was a Leicester boxing champion. Gez turned to me, handing me his jacket and just said 'watch this'. He proceeded to go straight into the middle of the Syston team, tap his target on the shoulder and whisper something in his ear – at which point the lad started to put his fists up. But before he got them above his waist Gez had headbutted him about six times and he collapsed to the floor, leaving us to make a great escape back to Corby without our medals or trophy! Despite the fighting Gez was a great lad and a good pal of mine who sadly died in a tragedy in his early twenties and he's still missed terribly by all that knew him.

Tragically, some years later another great lad from Corby who I was brought up with was to leave us far too young. David Longhurst was a striker who was a couple of years older than me and also spent time coming through the ranks at Nottingham Forest before turning pro. After being released from the City Ground, he went on to play for Halifax, Northampton and Peterborough before joining York City in 1990. In September, in just his sixth game for York he died on the pitch in a game against Lincoln at the age of 25. He had suffered a heart attack and an inquest later found he had suffered from a rare heart defect. Both tragedies made me think that you have to enjoy your life while you can as you never know what's around the corner.

At this time in secondary school I was playing sport of any sort every day without fail – football for both my year and the one above, rugby, basketball and athletics in the summer. The only sport I didn't enjoy was cross country running so I didn't put myself forward for that and my dislike for running never really went away especially during the torturous pre-seasons that were to come!

Village Victors my first Sunday team, I didn't know how to sit obviously.

I think this volume of sport was regarded as normal back then but with hindsight I think that I was doing too much and I honestly think it affected my knees in the long run. At the time I loved it all because sport was the only thing that I knew I was good at and it would have been difficult for anyone to have stopped me. I was also playing on a Sunday for a team called Village Victors but I soon moved to Corby Gainsborough who had formed a second youth team a year above me. We entered the Leicestershire league to challenge us a bit more as the local Sunday league standard had become too easy for our talented group of lads. It was in this league that I was first spotted by Forest and Leicester.

Throughout my childhood my dad John was involved in everything to do with Corby Gainsborough. He played and managed the team, he ran the line and later became the club secretary. Before I was considered old enough to play, I would go with him every Saturday to the games. I would play behind the goals or on the side of the pitch with other lads in the same situation and get covered in mud, pretending to be Kenny Dalglish or John Robertson until there was no-one left to play with, or it got dark. If the team were playing away we would stay in the bar for an hour and then listen to the football results on the way home. If we were at home it would be a case of how the 'craic' went as to what time we would get home and I'm sure my dad was in the doghouse on more than one occasion! Although I was just a boy, this was my first experience of men enjoying playing a game of football and then unwinding by having a good drink on a Saturday night. It was the first time I heard the saying 'win, draw or lose – hit the booze!' But it certainly wasn't the last.

* * *

FOCUS ON CORBY'S BRIGHT YOUNG THINGS

● The Corby Town youth team squad which faces Bedworth United in the first qualifying round of the FA Youth Cup at Occupation Road on Monday. Back row (left to right): Neil Addy, Alan Reid, Chris White, Ian Sibbald, Tony Hutchison, Ricky Muir, David Alderson, Ronnie Borland. Middle: Tommy Mann, coach Richard Paterson, Tony Gallacher, Sean McCabe, Graeme Wooley, Alex Hughes, Mark Davis, Jon Purdie, Dennis Robertson, director Tom Haworth, Dale Robertson. Front: coach Mick Addy. Jimmy Connor, Mick Morrisey, Adrian Sheerin, Andy Girvan, David McHutchison, Paul Garfitt, scout David McNish.

A very talented Corby U18s at 15 years old.

Mark Dibs Davis (Kingswood Secondary School, District & County)

I first came across Jon in junior school football he was the small but stocky centre forward for Kingswood Juniors and me, from memory standing a good foot taller as the centre-half for Danesholme Juniors. I recall being briefed by our team manager to watch the "little-un" up front as he was described as a bit quick. It was also in the era where "getting one in early" was an option. Oh how I tried. I couldn't get near the little bugger, not only was he a good footballer he could run like the wind as well.

We then made our way to "The big senior school" where new friendships were made with those coming from other feeder schools. Much to my delight "The little-un" had moved up to the same school. We had, over the next 5 years a really close knit and well drilled side managed by Dave "Master" Bates as he was known. JP would score with great regularity and I think the regular winning convinced many of us we were better players than we actually were, that said we could all play and all had that little bit to bring to the team but JP really did turn a good side into a great one.

As we moved through school I was also fortunate to play with Jon at both District and County level, going on some amazing runs in national competitions for such a small county. Even at these higher standards where you would expect a degree of levelling out on the ability front JP still stood out. His ability was recognised by the school and district teams as Jon would regularly play and represent those age groups above our own school year. He was always playing football somewhere and it came as no surprise when we heard he had been selected for the England Schoolboys team. It was apparent from early on that he had the ability to chase every schoolboy's dream of being a professional footballer and much with the England news it was no surprise when we heard he had signed for Arsenal.

Had he not made it in football I have no doubt that JP could just have easily made it in other sporting arenas, he was lightning quick as a scrum half and/or fly half in the rugby team. Athletics, over 100m and 200m you couldn't get near him... he did get a bit puffed out though if the distance got any longer!! Basketball was another sport where he excelled. All said, he always remained level headed, there was no ego, and there was no frustration if others around him did not reach his levels.

* * *

Lee Glover (Corby boy and Nottingham Forest)

Being brought up in Corby in the 70s and 80s, was interesting and lively to say the least. As my interest in football developed, I started to hear of someone a couple of years older than me, from the other end of town who was making quite a name for himself. 'He's in the England schools team and Arsenal and Man Utd are chasing him, he could do 100 keepie ups at 8. Wow that's quality! But I was not surprised, Jon was a street player, kicking balls off fences, garage doors, annoying neighbours – that's how footballers start. When he signed for Arsenal our playground was buzzing with it. The local paper had a write up about it too. All the lads and teachers at school thought this was brilliant, although none of us knew him then. One of our own, had signed for one of the biggest clubs in the land. That spurred me on. Our paths had not crossed yet, but Jon's achievement helped me and others. Signing got him respect and it's a respect that he still has within our home town.

* * *

CHAPTER TWO

ENGLAND

At the age of 14 I was progressing well with the Corby and Kettering district side, and for a small district we did well, progressing to the semi-finals of the national competition where we narrowly lost out to Newham from East London. This was a real eye opener as their lads looked more like 18 than 14, and in hindsight some may have been! I was then selected to play for the Northamptonshire county team, which was mainly made up of my district team as we were pretty good to be honest.

On the back of that exposure I was invited to attend trials for the England Schoolboys team. I progressed through the various stages, although waiting for the letter to drop through the door was excruciating and opening them more than a little nerve wracking. When I first got invited, the Corby schools representative, Mr Eccles, who was a PE teacher at the Catholic school next door to my school, Kingswood, told my dad that it was unlikely I would be selected as they tended to favour boys from the big cities and that the names of a lot of the squad had already been decided upon. Whether this was true or he was just trying to stop me getting my hopes up I don't know, but regardless it proved a great motivation to me, and the kind I could have done with later in my career.

My dad would take me anywhere to trials without question. He drove me the 180 mile round trip to Lilleshall in Shropshire for the England Schoolboys last 32 trial even though it was snowing heavily. When we arrived I was one of only about three lads who had made it there through the treacherous conditions and the trial was called off. Who knows, this may have done me a favour in the eyes of the selectors. Another thing which might have swung things further my way was an incident which happened on a train from London to some of the other players. Six of them were travelling to Lilleshall from the capital for the weekend and one of the lads gave a passenger a bit of lip on the train. Somehow this got reported back to the selectors and all six were eliminated from selection, including some lads who went on to become huge names. Tony Adams was one of them and I think Dennis Wise and Darren Anderson a central defender who went on to play for Charlton and Aldershot were two of the others, although for the record I heard none of these three was the actual culprit.

Walking out at Wembley looking focused.

Waiting for the National Anthem.

Talking of Dennis, he was to soon make an impression which became a bit of a trademark of his. I had my first glimpse of him at one of the trials when he was playing table tennis against the goalkeeper Tim Flowers. Dennis must have had a disagreement with Tim because in a flash the red mist descended and he was suddenly being restrained from clambering over the table to get at Tim! It was a bit of an eye-opener but also slightly funny as Tim was almost a foot taller than Dennis who was about five foot four then – but Dennis had that madness in his eyes which no-one would want to face and I don't think the huge height difference bothered him at all.

I eventually got selected for the squad and was in the company of some lads who made a good living at football and others who didn't do quite as well, like myself. Darren Heyes, Fraser Digby, John Beresford, Michael Thomas, Mark Seagraves, Simon Ratcliffe, Darren Beckford and Iain Sankey all made it and had careers in the game. Goalkeeper Heyes came through the

In the zone at Wembley.

Escaping the attentions of the Holland right back at Wembley.

● Corby youngster Jon Purdie pulls on an international shirt for the second time after being retained for England Schools' match with Wales at Reading tomorrow night.

Purdie burst on to the England scene in style against Northern Ireland at Barnsley after a quiet first half in which goals from Kevin Keen — son of former Northampton manager Mike Keen — and Darren Beckford put the home team 2-0 ahead.

Sporting my England cap.

ranks at Nottingham Forest before spells with Scunthorpe, Wrexham and Halifax Town and has been a goalkeeper coach at both Nottingham clubs and Derby County. Digby, another keeper, enjoyed a long career with Swindon and Manchester City. Beresford was part of Kevin Keegan's hugely entertaining Newcastle team in the 1990s after leaving Portsmouth. Centre back Seagraves started at Liverpool and went on to play for Manchester City, Bolton and Swindon. Michael Thomas went right to the top with Arsenal, winning two League titles and appeared for England. Ratcliffe, was a record signing for Brentford after being released by Manchester United and a spell at Norwich. Striker Beckford began at Manchester City and was a prolific scorer for Port Vale, Norwich and Oldham. Iain Sankey, who went on to play for Telford United after leaving Ipswich, is now doing well in the PFA coaching set-up.

John Beresford was always a chirpy, energetic lad. He was full of fun but on one of the trips his boundless energy backfired on him and stopped him in his tracks — with painful consequences. Staying away from home, it was never long before the boredom set in once training was over and we were looking for something to do. 'Bez' spotted what I can only describe as a human hamster wheel and decided to have a go on it. Unfortunately for Bez – who was even smaller than the five foot eight inches he eventually scaled – his feet didn't quite reach where they needed to. As the wheel started spinning around he came flying off, splitting his eye open and breaking his wrist!

Michael Thomas was earmarked as a bit special and he was a year younger than our age group for that England team – he was playing at left back for us which he wasn't happy about because he wanted to play in midfield. This may have been because I played on the left wing – which I'd never done before – and didn't realise I was expected to defend as well as attack! I had always played as a striker – or what would be called a number 10 these days – but the England manager Jim Morrow liked to play a 4-3-3 system, so I got into the team on the left wing as they liked a big number nine target man to lead the line and I was pretty small then. My dad had always encouraged me to practise with my left foot religiously and said it would give me an advantage to be confident on either side. As a result I became truly two-footed – even to the point where I could take in-swinging corners with my left foot. Growing up, my dad would pass a ball with me and encourage me to pass it back to him, alternating which foot I used. This became a habit and if he wasn't around, I would find a wall and practise volleys and half volleys against it for hours. During the winter I had a sponge ball so I could play indoors too. The furniture in the lounge would get moved and I would half volley the ball against the wall over and over again. How my mum and dad put up with it I don't know! At the time I was ecstatic just to be included in the England

Schoolboys squad so I wasn't going to complain about playing wide, but unfortunately being able to play on the left wing stuck with me, something which I will come back to later on.

Darren Beckford and I roomed together once at a trial and I soon found out he was quite religious. He would tell me about his beliefs, but even though I wasn't in the slightest bit interested it certainly helped get me off to sleep and stopped the nerves about the England trial! This didn't turn out to be one of those long-standing room-mate partnerships you hear about in football however. Darren went on to have a good career in the game and I believe he is doing good work in the community now in his native North West.

I also got to know Kevin Keen, another member of the squad. Kevin was a small, thin lad who was very quiet at the time and seemed very focused on his football. He has gone on to have a high-profile career in coaching with several clubs including Liverpool and West Brom after playing with West Ham, Wolves, Stoke and Macclesfield. But the armies of backroom staff would go white at his diet at the time – back in those days he basically lived off chips and very little else, no matter where we were! But he remained on the straight and narrow and I imagine having a father who had been in the game – his dad Mike had been a midfielder with Queens Park Rangers, Luton Town and Watford, who he also managed – might have helped him to avoid the pitfalls that exist for a young footballer.

Football wasn't the only sport I was excelling in. I was a decent scrum half at school which was first encouraged by Mr Thomas, my Welsh PE Teacher who was convinced I could become the next Gareth Edwards. He tried to convince my dad for me to focus on rugby and I progressed to get selected to play for the County. I was offered a place at Millfield sports school to play rugby when I was 13, but football was my first love and my mum didn't want me to leave home at that age. I was determined to be a professional footballer and rugby was purely an amateur sport back then so it wasn't too difficult a decision to make. My dad thought it was a great opportunity for me, perhaps so he could put his furniture back where he wanted and not have to listen to a ball banging against the wall constantly! Due to all this sport I suffered with Osgood-Schlatters disease in my left knee at 13. This is a common complaint in young sportspeople where the join between the knee and the shin bone becomes inflamed when you start growing and it's really painful. I was beside myself when I had to have six weeks in plaster, but I had no choice but to rest. I thought it was the end of the world but it did the trick. However problems with my knees sadly didn't end there – knee trouble plagued me for the rest of my career and I have had nine operations on them so far!

By the time I made my debut for England Schoolboys against Northern Ireland at Barnsley's Oakwell ground, my knee had recovered. To make it even more of a memorable occasion, I scored once in our 4-0 win. That wasn't just special for me but also for my mum Isabelle, being Northern Irish. Some of the family travelled over from Ireland and there were some divided loyalties! Now that I have two sons of my own I can imagine how proud my parents must have been. Next came Wales at Reading's old Elm Park ground and I scored two more in a comfortable win. The next game was probably the match of my life against Holland at Wembley. We ran out 7-0 winners and we were far too good and strong physically for them on the day. I scored another two and got brought down for a penalty but for some reason I wasn't allowed to take it to get my hat-trick! Oh well, I wasn't bothered as I had just had a blinder at Wembley playing for England!

This football lark all seemed so easy – I felt it was just a case of 'give me the ball' and I could beat a couple of players and shoot or cross for someone else. It all came naturally and I couldn't put a foot wrong, but things were soon to change.

We played Scotland at Raith Rovers and lost 2-0 when a lad called Lewis Muirhead gave our back four the run around. Next up was Switzerland at York City where we won 1-0 but I didn't play too well, and then we had a trip to Germany to play them twice, first in the Berlin stadium where Adolf Hitler and Jesse Owens appeared at the 1936 Olympic Games and then at Eintracht Frankfurt. Those games were tight affairs. They were a match for us physically and they also had home advantage with a full stadium of Germans behind them, but we managed a draw in the first game. The match at Eintracht Frankfurt was difficult and I experienced man marking for the first time – I was marked so tightly I thought my 'shadow' was going to accompany me into our dressing room at half-time! I put up with being pushed, shoved, kicked, pinched and man handled for about an hour and then the Corby boy in me came out. When the ball was up the other end of the pitch I turned and kicked the lad square in the unmentionables and ran away to hear him squealing on the floor! I thought nobody had seen it, but apparently someone important did. We lost that game and there was only one more match left of the international season – Scotland at Wembley.

On a personal level my form had dipped – I stopped getting the ball and I had lost the sharpness that was there for the first three games. As I discovered later on, playing wide means you are in the hands of other players to feed you the ball, and if a couple of things go wrong, the wide players are always the first to be criticised and confidence can drain quickly. Around this time I suffered my first real low in football. I received a letter in the

Telegraphic Address: 'STADIUM' Manchester
Telephone: 061-872 1661/2 (Office)
061-872 7771 (Ticket and Match Enquiries)

MANCHESTER UNITED Football Club Ltd

OLD TRAFFORD, MANCHESTER, M16 ORA

Manager:
R. ATKINSON.

Secretary:
L. OLIVE.

Date as Postmark.

Dear Mr & Mrs Purdie,

Easter Holiday Visits
Travelling to us Tuesday 13th April 1982
Returning Home Friday 16th April 1982

You will, no doubt have already received a verbal invitation for *John* to visit us on the above dates. This is a formal invitation and confirmation as to dates etc.

I should be glad if you would detach and return the section below for my file and for reference purposes. The section "comments" is to allow acceptance together with any date variation, travel suggestions, school commitments etc. which may be helpful to know. A S.A.E. is enclosed.

As normal football boots, training shoes and plimsolls will be the only items of football equipment necessary. We supply the rest.

We are looking forward to having *John* with us.

Kind regards,

Yours sincerely,

J.Brown,
Youth Development Officer.

Invitation to Manchester United.

post telling me I wasn't being selected for the game at Wembley. Being dropped from the team was one thing but to be excluded from the entire squad was awful. As a 15 year old boy having no face-to-face explanation and no phone call was devastating. I cried for days and I was embarrassed to go to school, because I knew I'd have to explain to everyone why I wasn't playing. To be fair they dropped another lad Paul Hutchings who played on the other wing and replaced us with Dale Gordon and Tony Daws who were both decent players. Dale went on to achieve hall of fame status at Norwich City before doing well with Glasgow

Rangers, while Tony did well primarily with Scunthorpe United. Whether my omission from the England Schools squad was down to loss of form or how I dealt with the man marking, I never got told so I don't know. What I do know is that sending a letter can't be the correct way of telling someone they're dropped, let alone a teenager. Apart from that, playing for England hadn't done me any harm and my performances on that platform had alerted a host of clubs to my ability and potential. As a result I had invites to sign for the majority of English league clubs including Manchester United, Liverpool, Everton, Aston Villa, Southampton, West Ham – and Arsenal.

This change in circumstances proved to be more of a burden than a blessing and I was totally overawed and confused about where to go or what to do. I relied heavily on advice from my mum and dad, who I would imagine in hindsight were also unsure about dealing with all this attention. I visited Manchester United and trained at their famous old training ground The Cliff for a few days, but at the time it felt like a cattle market with seemingly hundreds of lads all vying for a game and I didn't feel like it was for me. I also went to Aston Villa, West Brom, Norwich and Southampton.

Then my parents received a letter, followed by a telephone call, from Arsenal, one of the top clubs in the country. Steve Burtenshaw, who was the chief scout, and a smooth-talking but genuine gentleman invited us to visit London where he would show us around Highbury and put us up for a couple of days. My dad had always had a soft spot for Arsenal and I was excited about visiting London and 'the bright lights'. We travelled to the capital and were met by Steve, who drove us to Highbury to give us a tour of the famous old ground. Highbury was special and had an aura about it even when it was empty – I was gobsmacked and I know my parents were equally impressed. From the marble floors to the superb reception area with the bust of legendary manager Herbert Chapman, and the fact all the office workers were immaculately turned out, it just made you want to be part of the place.

That sense of being made to feel special continued. We were then checked in to a swanky hotel in the West End of London and handed tickets to the theatre to watch the musical 'Cats' in the evening. The way we were treated, you would have to be royalty not to have had your head turned. Following this it was arranged for me to travel with the first team to their game away to Brighton, who were in the top division and reached the FA Cup final in 1983. I was on a luxury bus complete with card tables travelling with some of the most famous players in the game and got treated like one of them, apart from the most important bit – getting to pull on the Gunners shirt for the game. When we got to Brighton, we stopped for a walk on the beach and on the way home we were treated to a three-course meal with prawn cocktail and steak on the menu, all served by a waiter in full evening dress. Who wouldn't want some of this life? So, without any money changing hands, Steve Burtenshaw had done his job and above all, made me feel wanted, and I agreed to join.

From then on my dad would drive me the hour and a half from Corby on Saturday mornings to Arsenal's training ground at London Colney to get some game time with the youth team. After spending the mandatory spell on the bench, I soon started getting in the side. I loved it and the set-up at their training ground was as impressive as anything I had seen. I was so excited with the idea of being a pro with Arsenal, I couldn't wait to leave school and get started full time at this great club. But little did I know what was around the corner....

* * *

Michael Thomas (England Schoolboys & Arsenal)

I am privileged & honoured to be asked to write a little piece for my old teammate as we both started our football journey at the same time from England Schoolboys to Arsenal. I remember meeting Jon at England Schoolboy trials and was amazed by his ability of ghosting past players like they weren't there. Off the pitch he could be quiet or jovial but great to be around, which I liked… as I'm a quiet person and preferred to be in the background. The big disappointment for me is that he didn't stay at Arsenal long enough to come through together with the rest of our group… Jon was special just like David Rocastle. Can you imagine Rocky on the right and Jon on the left – mind blowing artistry.

* * *

Arsenal Youth at 15.

CHAPTER THREE

SHOOTING MYSELF IN THE FOOT WITH MY OWN ARSENAL

This proved a very difficult chapter for me to write as I believe I made a lot of poor decisions in my teenage years. I didn't feel qualified or mature enough to know what I was doing. In the six-month period leading up to joining Arsenal at 16, I had started to go out a bit with my school pals. It was nothing too heavy – just a few drinks at the local cricket club that held discos for us youngsters. I really enjoyed it there and felt I just wanted to do what many teenagers do. I guess I couldn't see what harm it was doing, despite concerns from my mum and dad. This was the first time in my life that football wasn't the only thing on my mind. I know my parents were very concerned about this change in me and they were naturally worried about my impending move to London and all the temptations that lay ahead.

With that in mind, my dad spoke to Steve Burtenshaw at Arsenal and I imagine he requested that wherever I was going to stay, he wanted a close eye kept on me. So it was decided I would live with Tommy Coleman, who was the youth team manager, along with his wife and their young daughter. From the outset this proved really difficult, for several reasons. Tommy was an east ender lived in Chingford, Essex, which was a 90-minute tube and overground train journey to Highbury. As an apprentice I had to be at the ground at 8.30am to help get the training kit ready and then we would have to load the bus and make our way to London Colney, picking up some of the young pros on route in Southgate, and get to the training ground before 10am. After training we had to take the kit back to the laundry at Highbury to be prepared for the next day and I would then return to Chingford. This routine, along with the pre-season training which was traditionally murderous, soon started to take its toll and I hated it. Occasionally Tommy would give me a lift if his journey coincided with mine, but this didn't happen very often and we didn't really hit it off to say the least.

All the other apprentices who were northern or non Londoners lived around the Southgate and Barnet areas, as did a lot of the first-team players. I soon found this was where everyone met up and socialised. Living so far away in Chingford, I was lonely and felt cut off and here came my first major mistake. I requested a move to the Southgate area to cut down on the travelling, or at least that was the reason I gave. That was partly true but I also wanted to be closer to my new pals to socialise.

Looking back it is natural that Mr Coleman wasn't impressed and I guess he took it personally. He was a bit of a sergeant major type character, barking at us throughout training, and it was a rarity to see him smile. Part of his duties included ensuring we were doing our jobs correctly around Highbury. We would be allocated areas to clean and he would check on the work – even running his finger over doorframes checking for dust etc. He always found something wrong with whatever I did, and he would shout my name constantly to do extra work. It got to the point where I would find hiding places so he couldn't find me, which just made him dislike me more.

To add to our problem, during a training session in the indoor AstroTurf dome we used, he was coaching a session of attack against defence. I got the ball on the left wing, and he was encouraging the opposing right back to show me inside to allow him to have support from central areas. Naturally I jinked inside and bent a shot into the far corner of the net. I was too advanced to be shown inside and playing on the left meant I was only being shown inside to my stronger side. He just looked at me with daggers and our relationship continued to deteriorate from there.

Things went from bad to worse when I was included in an under-21 squad for a tournament in Amsterdam, playing against other top European teams. I was generally a squad player but got some game time which I was more than happy with, mixing with much older lads such as Colin Hill, Danny O'Shea, Paul Gorman, David Cork, Rhys Wilmot and John Kay amongst others. Gary Campbell and Tony Rees joined me on the trip and I was happy about that as I had become mates with them very quickly.

We progressed through the tournament and were given some time off to allow for some rest and recreation. Naturally being inquisitive young men, we had a look around Amsterdam during the day which was very enlightening for a naive 16 year old! I remember one of the lads deciding he wanted to lose his virginity to one of the prostitutes and he worked up the courage to go through the door. He came back out again so quickly we thought he had bottled it or forgotten something, but the first thing he said was "can you all chip in with some more money so I can go back again!" We all fell about laughing, but after constant begging we indeed gave him the cash to revisit the new love of his life!

Later on in the evening we were allowed out but under strict instruction to report back to reception for 11pm, where we would be met by Tommy Coleman and the reserve team manager Terry Burton. That evening I got talking to Scottish striker Ally McCoist,

I found him dressed in a checked suit stood at the bar looking like the world was going to end. It turned out he had recently signed for Sunderland and things weren't going too well for him there, hence why he was on this trip. Despite his very loud suits he obviously turned his career around and became a great success and legendary goal scorer north of the border with Rangers.

I soon found out there was a bit of a north-south divide among my young team-mates at Arsenal, and being a non-Londoner, I was in the group with Rhys, Dribble (John Kay), Corky, Gary Campbell and Tony Rees. All these lads liked a beer or two, and Rhys and Dribble enjoyed a fair few more at times. Gary and I were shandy drinkers at the time but we didn't want to be left out of the group, so we would tag along. That particularly evening we all checked in at 11pm as ordered and were told to go to bed, but as soon as Tommy and Terry disappeared, Rhys and Dribble rounded our group up to go to a nightclub about five minutes away from the hotel. I knew it was wrong but I felt under pressure from the group to go and went hoping they knew what they were doing.

We only spent about half an hour in the club before the doors opened and, to all the lads' dismay, in walked Tommy and Terry. In my mind they were the Kray twins – Ronnie and Reggie. I'm not sure if they were just having a night out themselves or had been tipped off about us being there, but we got told in no uncertain terms to return to the hotel and that we would be dealt with in the morning! As we got out into the fresh air, fear was written all over Tony Rees' face and he turned to the rest of us and said 'shall we run?' As if running back to the hotel was going to make the situation any better!

The next morning the older lads were sent home but Tony, Gary and I were allowed to stay but only after we were given the biggest bollocking you can imagine. My 'favourite' coach Mr Coleman had yet another reason to dislike me, not that he needed one. On the bright side I started getting more minutes on the pitch because the squad was now depleted. We progressed to the final, so I was thinking maybe the nightclub incident would be forgotten if I played well. My optimism didn't last long though when the final went to penalties. There were very few volunteers from the older lads, so being young and daft I put my hand up to take one. As I got to the penalty spot the keeper looked like Gulliver of Gulliver's Travels, and the goal seemed like it was a Subbuteo part. He saved my shot, we lost and I wasn't looking forward to going back to London.

To make matters worse my mum and dad had travelled over to watch the final with some friends and I only managed a quick chat before we had to pack and leave. When we got back to Arsenal I was given another talking to. I was warned to get on the straight and narrow, but in hindsight I think the die had been cast with my poor relationship with Tommy. Despite this, things were going reasonably well on the pitch and I was part of a strong team, with my year group consisting of Tony Adams, David Rocastle, Michael Thomas, Ken Veysey, Jonathan Woods and me. Among the second years were Martin Keown, Martin Hayes, Gus Caesar, Gary Campbell, Niall Quinn and Tony Rees. Terry Burton went on to describe our group as the best he had come across in 40 years and seven of them, if you include Paul Merson, who came through a year later, went on to become full internationals.

We played on Saturday mornings in the South East Counties League against all the other London clubs and then midweek in cup matches. As you might imagine, it was very rare we didn't win, but I think we perhaps got over confident. We progressed well in the FA Youth Cup in 1983-84 and after beating Carshalton,

Bristol Rovers, Cambridge United and Aston Villa, we drew Stoke City in the semi-final. The first leg was away and we played poorly and lost 3-2. No problem, we thought, we will hammer them at home – surely we couldn't play as poorly again? We did play well at Highbury, despite the pitch consisting of sand and mud sprayed green to look like grass from the stand, and peppered their goal. But we had one of those nights where we just couldn't score. They had some decent players who went on to have good careers such as their captain Steve Parkin, Ian Painter and Chris Hemming, plus Jonathan Chapman, the younger brother of Lee, who was in the first-team squad at Arsenal at the time. Unbelievably to us we lost 3-0 (6-2 on aggregate), with Steve, Chris and Jonathan scoring at our place. Stoke went on to lose 4-2 on aggregate to Everton in the final. We were a very strong team but success is often measured by how a team fares in the biggest youth competition in England and I'm still disappointed not to have done better.

On tour with Arsenal.

* * *

Alan Wortley (Lifelong friend from Corby) Chapter 3

Jon and I became friends about 35 years ago before he became a pro and I have followed his journey since then. In my opinion he is the most talented footballer ever to come out of our home town of Corby. Perhaps, in hindsight – Arsenal and the bright lights of London wasn't the best option for him with a lot of time on his hands. Jon would probably agree that he never reached his full potential and wasn't helped in his early years by a few managers. Nevertheless he comes away from it all with many memories and stories which you will enjoy in the book. Jon has always been a top man and we have a lifelong friendship.

* * *

Arsenal Youth at 15.

Player profile for the Arsenal fanzine.

CHAPTER FOUR

Rejecting England and Arsenal!

Early in that first season I was selected in a 25 man squad for England U16s after a couple of trials at Lilleshall under the watchful eye of Charles Hughes – a funny looking little chap in glasses who couldn't be further removed from the young, suave modern coaches leading the game today. This was the first time I heard the expression POMO (position of maximum opportunity) which was used to describe crosses put across the six yard box just far enough away from the keeper for a forward to attack.

During one of these trips I linked up with one of my new Arsenal team mates – Tony Adams who was very highly regarded by everyone at Arsenal and seemed to be earmarked for quick progression. During one of these squad sessions we had some fitness work and we had races over different distances, I was always quick off the mark and always held my own up to 50 metres but the bigger, longer legged lads would start eating up the ground and this was the case with Tony – it may surprise some but he won the 100 metres comfortably beating some very quick lads including Franz Carr whom we all expected to win.

I have to admit I didn't really enjoy the England sessions and I may have still been wounded from being dropped so hurtfully the previous year. I was also mixing with the Irish and Welsh lads at Arsenal, and with my Irish and Scottish heritage I wasn't sure I wanted to commit to England, so I spoke to Tommy Coleman and pulled out of the squad. He probably thought I was nuts already and this confirmed it in his head I'm sure! I was totally confused at this time and I guess as a teenager my hormones were all over the place. I was bouncing from one disastrous decision to the next.

I had played a few reserve games for Arsenal the previous season as a 15 year old and remember making my debut at Swansea away at the old Vetch, with the likes of John Hollins and George Wood the Scottish international Goalkeeper. We travelled by train and everything was laid on for us, as you can imagine I was a little nervous but John Hollins was brilliant and talked to me all throughout the game. I played well despite the torrential rain and was chuffed when Holly took the time to congratulate me on my performance. John was always immaculately dressed and was a perfect gentleman upholding the image Arsenal wanted to portray. He was coming towards the end of his playing days but behaved professionally at all times. He was also still a very good player and was one of the best penalty takers I've ever seen. He would place the ball on the spot, walk away facing away from the keeper, turn and never taking his eyes off the ball, would smash it as hard as he could straight down the middle – if the keeper had ever stood still the ball would have carried him into the back of the net such was the power he generated. He gave 100% commitment all of the time and I wished I could have followed his lead rather than some of the others.

During my first season Terry Neill was sacked and Don Howe his coach was appointed to hold the fort until the end of the season. Terry Burton was running the reserves and helping Mr Howe with the first team and Tommy Coleman was helping Terry when necessary. At the end of the season, Don Howe was given the job permanently and it was obvious that somebody new would be coming in somewhere.

News filtered through that the new addition to the coaching staff was Mr Arsenal himself – Pat Rice, who I believe was joining from Watford. To my horror they promoted Tommy Coleman to reserve team manager and Pat got the youth team job. Although I had another year at youth team level, my aim was to progress to become a regular in the reserves.

During close season while I was back home in Corby I was determined to do everything in my power to give a good impression and was hoping for a fresh start with Tommy.

I would run twice a day – a quick 3 miles in the morning and a 5 miler in the afternoon – as well as playing squash with my dad who was a decent local player. I was 17 and as fit as a fiddle although I was still enjoying a few beers in the evening with some Corby pals.

When I went back for pre-season I was winning all the races on a regular basis from sprints to a long cross country race in and around London Colney, and I know I was making the right impression. This fitness and sharpness ensured I got the best out of my ability and I was on top form. I was soon elevated to the reserves where my good form continued with a memorable highlight beating Tottenham at Highbury 5-2 where I scored and had a hand in a couple of the other goals. They had a strong team out and we just blitzed them. However, to put a dampener on one of my best games Tommy Coleman had a dig at me for not tracking back on one occasion – and never mentioned all the good stuff I'd done in the game!

My dad and my best mate from Corby – Alan Wortley had travelled to watch and I met them afterwards with them both beaming, for me to tell them that I'd just had a bollocking – unbelievable Jeff!

At around this time I was called into the impressive manager's office at Highbury with David Rocastle and Michael Thomas. Don Howe wasted no time in offering us all a 2 season deal at £150 per week. Obviously in hindsight I should have snapped their hands off and been the happiest boy in the world but oh no, not me!

I knew that the lads a year older than me were offered the first season at £150 and the second season at £175 (I was living with Gary Campbell and we spoke before I went to the meeting). At the time I thought it was wrong out of principle and I was the only one paying 'digs' out of the three of us, although in hindsight I imagine Dave and Mickey were contributing to their family's household. So Don Howe agreed that if I was doing well enough he would give me an increase for the second season and I signed a one season deal. What an absolute idiot I was!

Looking back I wasn't particularly happy at Arsenal and made these decisions with the misguided confidence that I would be able to find another good club without much of a problem.

FOOTBALL LEAGUE CONTRACT

AN AGREEMENT made the THIRTY FIRST day of DECEMBER 19 84

between (name) KENNETH JOHN FRIAR

of (address) ARSENAL STADIUM HIGHBURY LONDON N5

the Secretary/Manager/Chairman of and acting pursuant to Resolution and Authority for and on behalf of

ARSENAL FOOTBALL CLUB

Football Club Limited (hereinafter referred to as "the Club") of the one part and

(name) JON PURDIE

of (address) 48 ROUNDHILL DRIVE ENFIELD MIDDX

a Registered Association Football Player (hereinafter referred to as "the Player")

Arsenal youth team.

Tony Adams was dealt with separately as he had made it into the first team squad and made his debut against Sunderland at Highbury where he was given a baptism of fire by Colin West, a big old fashioned centre forward. I think Tony would probably admit he wasn't quite ready and it was a while before he featured again.

I had cemented a place in the reserve team and if I kept up my form I would stay there. Sadly disaster struck at Crystal Palace away – I was playing well on the right wing when all of a sudden I was tackled knee high on my standing left leg and my knee collapsed, I was carried off and had seriously damaged my medial ligaments. The following six weeks were spent in plaster and all that hard work and fitness was lost. I had to start all over again in the youth team.

Pat Rice was great, a proper old school, hard but fair bloke. In the mornings after we had sorted the kit out for the trip to London Colney for training he would take all of the apprentices up to the small gym adjoining the laundry where we would do our 'bodies'. 200 sit ups and 100 press ups and Pat would do them with us – I don't think he had finished playing long before and he was still very fit.

So I was back in the youth team again, but we weren't as strong as the year before as we had lost Gus Ceasar, Martin Hayes, Martin Keown, Niall Quinn and Gary Campbell due to age, and Tony Adams had become a regular in the reserves, plus Tony Rees had been released along with Jonathan Woods from my year.

The new apprentices included Paul Merson who I first met underneath the main stand at Highbury where he was having a cup of tea with one of the groundsmen – I think he was a relative or family friend. He seemed quite a confident lad – it seemed all Londoners like to give this impression but I think a lot of it is 'front', obviously I had no idea what the future held for him but even that day he was talking about betting. I never really got to know Merse that well as I think he had a long journey home from Highbury after training and our duties. He didn't play much in that first year as he hadn't developed physically and was quite slight, but it was obvious that he had a good touch and an eye for goal when he got a chance. I do think he is good entertainment on Sky Sports Soccer Saturday and enjoy his humour and his attempts at pronouncing the names of the foreign players – who wouldn't struggle?

I played in the youth team on the left wing for a month or so and was lucky to get the ball a couple of times each half, I was getting increasingly frustrated and frankly bored which eventually came to a head. I called a meeting with Pat Rice, Tommy Coleman, Terry Burton and Steve Burtenshaw to tell them how frustrated I was at playing on the wing and not really getting much involvement. I asked if I could play in central midfield or as a striker, but I was told that playing wide was my best position, the other positions were filled and if I wanted to play more central I would have to wait for an opportunity. So be it then! I was sub for the youth team at the next game and after about 20 minutes Dave Rocastle went down with an injury and had to come off, Pat Rice gave me a look and said 'go on then – show me!'

Without meaning to sound arrogant, I went on and ran the show from the centre of the park. Pat walked off the pitch with me and said "You're right, you can play there son".

From then on I played central midfield, forming a great partnership with Dave Rocastle – 'Rocky' went on to become known as a skilful wide player but he also loved a tackle and worked his socks off.

You know as a footballer when you're playing well and I was waiting to be recalled to the reserves but it wasn't happening! In those days the first team, reserves and youth team squads were put up on a notice board at Highbury on a Friday after training which is when you would find out which squad you would be in. One particular Friday the squads went up and a first year apprentice called Greg Allen got selected ahead of me in the reserves. I knew at that moment that the writing was on the wall – literally!

I played the next day for the youth team and went home to Corby for the weekend and when the time came for me to catch the train back to St. Pancras I refused to go back. I couldn't see the point as it was obvious to me that I was going to be released. Steve Burtenshaw called my dad to find out what was going on and after a couple of days I went back with assurances that I still had a future at Arsenal.

I carried on playing well for the youth team and was tapped up after playing at Norwich City by the scout who tried to sign me as a schoolboy. I was very receptive telling him that I thought I was going to be released. I genuinely thought that this was going to be my next club the following season but fate played its hand.

Tommy Coleman picked me once more for the reserves when he was short of options through injuries and gave me the 'experience' of playing centre forward against a strong Chelsea team, which included Mickey Droy and Joey Jones as centre halves. I hardly got a kick and was fed long balls which were meat and drink for the aforementioned – Micky was a man mountain and Joey kicked anything that moved! I wonder in hindsight if I had been set up – who knows?!

Shortly afterwards in the London Colney dining room I was called into a quiet corner by Don Howe (the second time he had spoken to me in 2 years) and he told me I was being released after a vote by the coaching staff. I found out later that Steve Burtenshaw and Pat Rice voted to keep me with Tommy Coleman (shock!) and Terry Burton voting to release me. Don Howe had the casting vote and I guess he probably thought I might give him some headaches in the future and he may have been right!

A few weeks later I was getting a lift back to Southgate from Pat Rice. He told me he didn't think I should be released and was going to speak to the others to try and keep me. I really appreciated his effort, but it didn't work, it was over.

I felt confident that I would be going to Norwich and I was told Mel Machin was coming to watch me in the last midweek game of the season at Highbury. Unfortunately I went over on my ankle a couple of days before the game and although I got strapped up and played I was pretty much a passenger and the phone stayed quiet.

I take my share of responsibility for not making the most of the opportunity that I had at Arsenal but I do think that the 'sink or swim' treatment was very disappointing looking back.

I know that I won't be the only player who didn't make the most of their ability and could have done with some help and guidance living in one of the biggest cities in the world aged 16 – 18.

My roommate at Arsenal, Gary Campbell, for example, was one of the most talented footballers you could imagine but he lost his way and was a great talent that never reached the heights he was capable of.

In my view, things have actually changed to the other degree. I think boys are being taken away from their friends into academies at far too young an age. Their instincts are coached out of them and ultimately only a very small percentage become scholars and even fewer become professionals.

Nevertheless, I wish that there had been more duty of care and an interest shown in our general welfare and in the hours not specifically at Arsenal FC. Basically if you turned up for training on time you could do what you liked in your free time as long as they didn't hear about any trouble.

I guess these days there are agents who would be involved but obviously they have a vested interest and the majority are only interested in feathering their own nest.

Mel Eves who I have got to know well through playing for Wolves All Stars for charity a few times a year has started the Football Parents Alliance (FPA) which is an independent body for parents to talk to about any problems their sons may be having regarding football.

In hindsight, I believe that I was a victim of bullying which was defined as character testing, but I couldn't find a way out of the situation I was in on my own and my parents had no idea how to help me. Ultimately, their fears about me moving to London at 16 were correct and unfortunately I wasn't looked after. However, this did lead to some interesting incidents and stories off the pitch...

TELEGRAMS : GUNNERETIC LONDON N.5

TELEPHONE : 01-226 0304

ARSENAL FOOTBALL CLUB LTD

Company Registration
Number 109244
England

Registered Office
ARSENAL STADIUM
HIGHBURY
LONDON N5 1BU

FOOTBALL COMBINATION
ARSENAL v. OXFORD UNITED
MONDAY 9th MAY 1983
KICK-OFF 2.00 p.m.

A R S E N A L   O X F O R D

Colours: Red/White   Yellow/Blue

GEORGE WOOD	1	JOHN BUTCHER
JOHN HOLLINS	2	MARK JONES
GUS CAESAR	3	DAVID GRANT
MARTIN KEOWN	4	RAY TRAIN
TONY ADAMS	5	STEVE BIGGINS
GARY CAMPBELL	6	DAVID FOGG
JOHN McNEIL	7	STEVEN ARIES
MARTIN HAYES	8	GARY BARNETT
TERRY LEE	9	GEORGE LAWRENCE
TONY REES	10	ANDY THOMAS
JON PURDIE	11	KEVIN BROCK
NICKY BEAUMONT	12	PAUL SPITTLE

Officials: REFEREE MR. P. COX (Coventry)

Linesmen MR. R. CRAMPTON (Cambs)
MR. M.J. HOPKINS (Herts)

Next match at Highbury
FOOTBALL COMBINATION v. BIRMINGHAM - 11th MAY - K.O. 2 p.m.

OFFICIAL PROGRAMME - F R E E

Secretary : K. J. FRIAR   Manager : W. J. T. NEILL

Arsenal Reserves at 16 years old.

CHAPTER FIVE

Stars and Stories

Signing for Arsenal during the summer of '83 coincided with a big signing for the first team – Charlie Nicholas.

Charlie had scored a lot of goals for Celtic prior to signing at the age of 21 and came to London with big expectations on his shoulders – but had also earned himself a reputation for being a bit of a playboy due to his liking of a night out, a drink and a pretty lady.

I always found Charlie to be a good bloke and he looked after me on more than one occasion and in different ways.

He was sponsored by Nike and fortunately I shared the same foot size with both him and Graham Rix who was sponsored by Patrick, both of whom gave me their boots whenever they were given new ones. I tried them both in training and in games but ultimately always preferred Puma Kings which I generally wore throughout my career. I still think mainly black boots are the best – old fashioned I guess!

Charlie was also sponsored by Topman clothing and on one occasion when I stayed in the spare room at his house after a night out, he gave me a pair of Chelsea boots which I was chuffed with at the time. However he couldn't have paid me to wear the leather trousers or suede tops he often went out in!

During the brief period when I was a professional and no longer had to report to Highbury to sort the kit out, Charlie started picking me up in the morning and dropping me off after training in his Mercedes Sports, which was a great experience. Unfortunately this was short lived as Charlie quickly lost his licence through drink driving!

During one evening when us young pros got together for a night in the Chase Tavern in Southgate, Charlie and Rixy came in and joined our company. They were always generous with the young lads, very often they would give me a £20 note and ask me to go to the bar to get the round and told me to keep the change – on more than one occasion I went home with more money than I went out with! That night, one thing led to another and they decided to go to Stringfellows nightclub (this was long before it became a lap dancing club for the record!) which was regarded as one of the top nightclubs in London. They asked us to go with them and most of the lads turned it down because we couldn't afford it and, to be honest, didn't think we would get in. I was wearing faded jeans cut up the side, trainers and a Fila tracksuit top – I think it must have been fashionable then!

I explained this to Charlie and he insisted I went and that he would look after me. So I jumped in the car with him, Rixy and his driver for the night and headed off to the West End.

We walked past a long queue of people and although I got a good look up and down from the bouncers, Charlie who was a regular just said 'he's with me' and in I went.

Charlie took me to the bar, bought the round and said to the barman that I could put my drinks for the night on his tab – what a bloke!

During the evening, I spotted Rixy with a massive cigar and I thought I'd try one. So I walked over to the young lady who was selling them, similar to the way that they used to sell ice cream at the cinema, and said "can I have the same as he's got" pointing at Rixy – "sure that will be £35" – I soon changed my mind as I was earning £150 a week and paying £30 a week in digs! Plus I've never smoked and it would probably have made me sick.

We ended up having a full English breakfast at 4am with Peter Stringfellow and his lady at the time!

Graham Rix was very good with the young players and would often come to the youth team games and give advice regarding football, he was a pretty down to earth bloke from Doncaster and he mixed with most of us 'Northerners' probably more comfortably than the Londoners.

He would also do some extra training with us occasionally and I learned more from watching his movement and one touch play than from any coach at Arsenal.

In fact the best education a young player can have is to play with experienced professionals who will talk to them during the game and demand they do things properly. I do think that modern football is missing a trick nowadays as there are no longer any 'reserve' leagues in which young players can learn the trade from older professionals. Rixy was good mates with Glenn Hoddle at the time and this obviously helped him get involved with Chelsea later on. Rixy has had his problems, but I'm just saying he was good to us back in the day.

While I was at Arsenal it was arranged for us to watch Spurs play in the UEFA Cup while Glenn Hoddle was playing at his peak. I have to say he was brilliant and his passing range and appreciation for the receiver of his pass was the best I have ever seen – during this game he played a 40+ yard pass over the top of the opposing defence and it looked like it would run through to the goalkeeper, but on the second bounce it spun back into Garth Crooks' path perfectly, so not only had he executed the pass he had put backspin on it too!

Another great midfielder was Liam Brady who had left Arsenal but used to train with us when Juventus were on their mid-season break. He was a very quiet, genial man who had no pretentions or arrogance about him and he just trained like he was one of us. He had a lovely left foot and kind of cajoled and caressed the ball in a very natural manner.

Another Irishman who had a tremendous career was David O'leary, although I never warmed to him as a person or as a player. He called all of the young players 'mate' because he couldn't be bothered to learn our names and he rarely mixed with anyone socially. I thought he was quite ponderous and heavy legged and during one training session when he was coming back from injury we had some 1 v 1's and I couldn't believe how easy it was to turn him inside out! Anyway – what do I know, he had a great career and earned fortunes as a player and manager so I'm sure my opinion won't concern him too much!

Alan Sunderland, who also played for Wolves, was a great bloke and also a very underrated player in my opinion, he was clever with his touch and movement, and quicker than I thought. He trained with us once and he wanted to some extra fitness work at the end, so about six of us did some laps of a pitch at London Colney and with one lap left he said to us "if any of you can beat me I will give you a £100 each" – well on the last bend he put the turbo on and left us all trailing. He was quite dry and witty, his favourite line when being given a cup of tea in the canteen was "there's nothing like a nice cup of tea… and this is nothing like a nice cup of tea".

'Sunday' played up front with Tony Woodcock who was a regular England international and also a good chap, in fact he was the only player to try and give me some really good advice.

Rixy had joined up with the England squad and brought the team to the White Hart in Southgate for a few beers, most of these lads would be married I guess and probably used the opportunity to have a night out with the lads. Along with Rixy were Tony Woodcock, Kenny Sansom, Bryan Robson, Peter Shilton, Terry Butcher, Mick Mills, Paul Mariner and a few others. We ended up going to the Middlesex and Herts Golf and Country Club which I was going to anyway with a couple of local mates so we shared some taxis.

As we were walking towards the club, Tony Woodcock pulled me to one side and said that I shouldn't be going to the club and to make sure that I made it in football first.

Obviously as an 18 year old I thought I knew everything and didn't take a blind bit of notice, but it does mean something to me that he tried – nobody else cared, certainly no-one from the club itself.

Football is very much like that – dog eat dog and cut throat. You can be best mates one day and if you move on to another club that friendship ends, especially back then as there were no mobile phones or social media which made it even more difficult to stay in touch – not that I imagine most would bother anyway.

Paul Mariner was a larger than life character who always seemed happy and you would hear him singing to himself on the way to the changing rooms. He had the appearance of someone who was successful and I think he was probably investing his money even then – perhaps a bit cleverer with his money than most! Before a first team game at Highbury, I happened to be sweeping the marble corridor just outside the first team dressing room when the swing doors opened up and there 'Marrers' was standing proud in just his jockstrap! "Purds come here" he boomed – well you were only really allowed in the first team dressing room to clean it so I was a little wary but I shuffled in anyway "right" he said "I've got £500 quid here from all the lads and I want you to put it on a horse and then bring me the winnings after the game".

Well, I'd never put a bet on before but didn't have the courage to tell him that "ok no problem – I'll see you after the game – good luck!" "I don't need luck son" he said "er I meant with the game Marrers" – "oh ok cheers Purds"

With that I left the dressing room with more money than I'd ever seen before – remember I was an apprentice earning £30 a week at that time, now I had the devil on one shoulder and an angel on the other, especially when I got to the bookies and asked about the horse to one of the punters.

The horse was called Faraway Grey and it was a 25-1 outsider, I didn't want to let anyone know that I had £500 in my pocket so I asked "how much would it win if I put £50 on?" "£1250 – it won't win though pal" he replied. So if I put £500 on and it wins it will bring in £12,500!

Or do I keep the £500 quid and hope to god it loses?

In the end I hadn't got the bottle to keep it and put the bet on, and guess what, it came nowhere! Sods law, I just couldn't see how I would have managed to scrape £12,500 together if it had won and I hadn't put the bet on!

Anyway it put me off betting and other than the odd bet on Cheltenham races, gambling has never been a problem for me.

I met Paul Mariner in the tunnel when he was coming off the pitch, he looked at me hopefully but I told him "it came nowhere mate". He looked unbothered – "no worries son"

What a weekend I could have enjoyed! I'm really glad that Paul seems to have recovered from a recent brain tumour operation.

I had another incident involving money which again might have benefitted me to have been sharper or more dishonest, whichever way you look at it.

Back in those days there were no debit cards and cash points to use, so on pay day at the end of each month we used to walk 15 minutes to Barclays in Islington from Highbury to withdraw our wages.

On one particular Friday when I reached the front of the queue I asked the young girl behind the screen if I could withdraw my wages and whispered 'I'm with Arsenal'. She proceeded to give me the full list of employees of Arsenal with all their financial details in full view and asked which one I was.

At the top of the list there was a figure of £2,400 per week for a young international and to take a full month's wages would have been like winning the pools – but I just kept looking down the list and withdrew my apprentice monthly wage of £120. It was only after leaving the bank that the thought came into my head about withdrawing someone else's wages but I was brought up to know right from wrong and I couldn't have done it anyway.

Can you imagine the trouble that young girl could have got into and knowing my luck I would have been caught anyway – did CCTV even exist then?

One day I was sweeping the famous marble corridor outside the dressing rooms when I heard a very heated conversation going on from the payphone outside of the home dressing room, between a married international first team player and what transpired to be a News of the World journalist – who was threatening to publish a story about his affair with a very voluptuous blonde who was at that time one of the top Page 3 girls in the country. He came off the phone distraught and it took a few phone calls and eventually a fair amount of money to stop the story getting to print!

All in a day's work as an apprentice professional footballer!

Kenny Sansom was a very friendly, easy going bloke and he

did a great Norman Wisdom impression. We were injured together at one point and when you're injured you had to be in both morning and afternoon for treatment. During the lunch break Kenny decided he was going to the pub and insisted about 3 other injured players went with him. Again he was very generous and wouldn't let anyone else buy a drink, we played some pool and had about four beers before reporting back for afternoon treatment but not before stopping at the shop for chewing gum and mints!

It was very sad to hear of his troubles recently and I do think there may be many more ex-players who have had problems adjusting to life after football. It's difficult to explain but when you're a part of it as a young man it's difficult to imagine not being able to play, even though it's logical that the day will come.

There was definitely a booze culture throughout football and it was regarded as normal then, when you are young and fit hangovers rarely occur and there was a culture of being able to sweat it out. Tales of Bryan Robson being the last one in the bar and then being first in the running at training are legendary and if it was good enough for the captain of England then we should be ok!

Tommy Caton was at Arsenal then and was a team mate again at Oxford a few years later. He was definitely part of the booze squad and it is so sad to hear of his death when he was so young of a heart attack at 30 I believe.

Unfortunately I think there are lots of less high profile ex-players than Kenny, Tony Adams and Paul Merson who are struggling with alcohol addiction added to the difficulty of adjusting to normal life. The money, fame and adulation disappears and there is a big void to be filled and alcohol seems to be the choice of many.

CHAPTER SIX

Didn't They Do Well!

Without the benefit of a crystal ball or hindsight, I didn't realise how well some of my Arsenal team mates were destined to do following our formative years together. To me it was just normal to be part of a group of the best young players in England at the time – as that was all I had known since I had been at Highbury. We all had strengths and weaknesses and I guess some improved more than others over time. But some seemed destined for success.

Despite his tender years at the time – he made his debut in November 1983, four weeks after his 17th birthday – Tony Adams was always outwardly a very confident person and certainly gave the impression of being extremely sure of himself. In those early days there were no signs of his later problems with alcohol. One night we arrived at a nightclub early as it cost less to get in and Tony headed straight for the dance floor where he entertained the lads with his moves – and he was only drinking orange juice! Tall and gangly, Tony quickly earned the nickname 'Rodders' after TV's Rodney Trotter from Only Fools and Horses and it was quite amusing watching him 'throwing shapes'. I got on well with Tony and used to go out with him and another of our team mates Martin Hayes. Back then, Tony wasn't the best footballer technically but finished up looking very comfortable on the ball in his later years. However, he was always a very good organiser on the pitch and an effective defender. I think he developed his game under the influence of Arsene Wenger. When he was jailed for four months in December 1990 for drink driving after crashing his car into a wall, I wrote to Tony during his time in prison to offer my support and try to keep his spirits up, and I was delighted to receive a letter in return. He gave me his parents' home address to keep in touch, even asking me to go and see him when he got out, but unfortunately I lost the letter and didn't remain in contact. He does seem a very different person the last time I heard him interviewed and I wish him the best of luck in his battle with alcoholism.

Quick with an eye for goal, back then Martin Hayes mainly played on the right wing. Ironically he did well for Arsenal on the left wing for a short successful period, which is where I had played with him. I got on well with Hayesy, and he, Tony Adams and I used to go to Tots nightclub in Southend quite regularly. It wasn't far from where Tony grew up in Dagenham, while Hayesy, a nice lad that was pretty focused and rarely had a beer, used to drive.

Another wide player, David Rocastle, was a lovely lad who always had a smile on his face. He was always rushing back home to look after his mum, who wasn't very well. We used to pair up for running drills as we were of similar speed. On Friday mornings, we normally trained on the indoor surface at the ground and then finished off with sprints and shuttles on the red gravel around the famous Highbury pitch. 'Rocky' of course went on to become a firm favourite with the Arsenal faithful and the adulation he received couldn't have happened to a nicer lad, although on the pitch he had a bit of steel about him too. It was devastating to hear about his illness and ultimately his awful premature death. It just goes to show that life's not fair.

Michael Thomas, or Mickey as we knew him then, was pretty quiet and just got on with his football. To be honest he used to talk really quickly and mumbled a bit so I struggled to understand him. I don't think he was a particularly confident talker at the time. I've mentioned earlier that we played together in the England schoolboy team and he didn't seem too comfortable playing at full back, which is where he stayed throughout my time there. I have spoken to him recently and apparently he was also very unhappy at the club and wanted to leave during our time together, however he had signed the contract that was offered to us. It was only later when he was switched to the centre of the park that he came into his own and forged a great career with Arsenal, Liverpool and England. For all his achievements, I think he will always be best remembered for the goal that won Arsenal the League title in 1989. Arsenal had to win by two goals or more in a title decider at Anfield to wrestle the crown from Liverpool, and his cool finish for the second goal in their 2-0 win will never be forgotten by Arsenal fans.

Gus Caesar was totally committed to making a career out of football. Determined to succeed, Gus would be lifting weights after training to make himself as strong as he could be. To be honest I never thought he was technically good enough but hard work and a positive attitude prevailed over ability and he did it, enjoying several seasons with Airdrie in Scotland then Colchester before settling in Hong Kong, so fair play to him.

Niall Quinn was always a little bit different – and I don't just mean because of his gangly physique. Coming from Ireland at 17, he bypassed the traditional apprenticeship to sign as a professional and moved straight into his own flat – no digs with families for him. I think he must have had a good agent in the days before most of us knew they existed! Niall lived just up the road from me and we became good pals for a while. A talented sportsman, he was sought after in Ireland for hurling and was

Arsenal Youth team 1983 with Adams, Hayes, Keown, Caesar, Thomas and Rocastle.

also a scratch golfer. I guess he could turn his hand to anything he wanted. I used to play snooker with him in the afternoons after he had been to the bookies, but I soon realised I was paying for half the light above the table and was just putting the balls back on the green baize for him to pot! I ended up asking him to buy me some white gloves! Quinny introduced me to Guinness but he drank two pints to my one – well, there was a lot more of him than me! Most nights we would have a few pints and on Saturdays we would take it in turns to piggy back each other home from our favourite pub – the Chase Tavern. Unfortunately the route home was uphill and he was a big lump, so whenever I tried to pick him up we used to end up rolling back down the hill in fits of laughter. The comedy duo Smith and Jones were popular on TV at the time and we used to do our version of the sketch where they sat opposite each other and said random words – we thought we were hilarious, but probably nobody else did! Niall had a few Irish pals and would often head to Kilburn to meet up with them and I tagged along occasionally. Unfortunately after a few beers he would forget where he was supposed to meet them and we would end up wandering around Kilburn aimlessly. He wouldn't give up trying to locate them but I got fed up and would jump on the tube while he carried on searching for a party. I kept in touch with Quinny for a while after I left and went to visit him after he had broken into the Arsenal first team. On one occasion I went to watch him at Crystal Palace in a game which I think Arsenal won and then went out with him afterwards in Southgate.

His world had changed and by this time he was revelling in the attention of Arsenal fans. Although I stayed the night with him it was never going to be the same as our old times rolling down the hill and he seemed to have been a little affected by his success. But who wouldn't I guess? As a player there was little evidence to suggest he was going to be a big success as a centre forward. In the early days he struggled with his timing and I would take the mickey out of him, saying he was six foot seven

Arsenal Youth team 1984 with Adams, Merson, Quinn, Thomas and Rocastle.

inches tall but when he jumped he could only reach five foot nine! He played centre half quite a lot then too and looked far more comfortable there than with his back to goal. Clearly he improved significantly though and became a big success, first with Arsenal then at Manchester City, Sunderland and with the Republic of Ireland. I still have a little smile to myself when I see him on Sky TV appearing so eloquent and smart. When I knew him, he dressed more like the character 'Wolfie' of the late 1970s sitcom Citizen Smith (he of the catchphrase 'power to the people'). Some of the gear he wore was truly scruffy, but he has clearly smartened up his act. I'm pleased he has become a big success and it's no surprise to me he's involved in horses as he always loved a flutter.

Martin Keown was – and probably still is – quite a complex character and it's fair to say we didn't get on particularly well. He had a bit of paranoia about him and thought everyone was talking about him all of the time. I soon picked up on this and would pretend to whisper to whoever was next to me and he would bite straight away, which obviously encouraged even more mickey taking. He had this odd habit of having to wear the same colour socks as his polo shirt, which again was good sport as I would tell him they weren't quite matching and he would insist they were. I can't resist gifts like that! On one occasion we were playing Norwich away in a double header and both the youth team and reserves travelled together. As luck had it Martin was sat in the seat in front of me, and after flicking his ears a couple of times he threatened to punch me so I left him alone for a while. Then I took things up a notch. I had a cup of tea, and having seen someone do it before, after stirring the tea I placed the spoon on the back of his neck. But I think I miscalculated how hot the spoon was. It sizzled a little and then all hell broke loose and he was swinging punches and trying to kill me. Fortunately Rhys Wilmot and Dribble (John Kay) jumped in between us and pinned him down until he calmed down. Martin was really quick and aggressive as a player but didn't like being in the shadow of Tony Adams and I think he left the club due to this. To be honest at that time I thought Martin should have been ahead of him when Tony broke through because he was definitely technically better, but Tony had the backing of everyone at Arsenal perhaps due to his more assured personality. At our training ground London Colney during pre – season we were all sitting on the grass during lunch and as usual, there was some banter flying around. I bet Martin that I would be at Arsenal longer than him. I got that one wrong! Fair play to Martin – he made the most of his pace and aggression and had a great career with Arsenal and England after spells with Villa and Everton. I now have to watch him being all deep and serious on TV. I wish he'd lighten up a little – but again he won't give a monkey's about my opinion!

Some of the other top players at Arsenal during my time there included Pat Jennings, Brian Talbot, Brian Mcdermott, Viv Anderson, Stewart Robson, John Lukic and Chris Whyte.

Pat Jennings was a very easy going, laid back gentleman with the deepest voice you can imagine although he was very quiet and I think he only ever said 'Alright son' to me! I am honoured to have played a few times with him in the reserves. During shooting practice in training he could be impossible to beat if he was in the mood for it.

Brian Talbot was in the David O'Leary bracket, keeping himself to himself, doing what he had to do and didn't really show any interest in us younger players. I presume he lived out of London because he never hung around after training.

I did cheekily try and contact him when I was released from Wolves when he was manager of West Bromwich Albion as I saw he was giving my old mate Gary Campbell a trial but to no avail!

Brian Mcdermott was a little wary of me as I think he probably saw me as a potential threat to his position at the time as another wide left player. He was generally a reserve team player who got involved in the first team when there were injuries and suspensions. We did play together in the reserves a few times as I played on the right side too. Brian used to take his guitar with him to away games and he was really good at entertaining the lads with a sing song on the way home.

Years later I played against his Slough team for Kidderminster and although we won comfortably he was a lot friendlier towards me, I guess my threat to him never came to fruition. He has gone on to do well as a manager in the league since then.

Viv Anderson was another player that I saw previously with Forest, he was always friendly enough but again didn't get too involved with us. He was always bubbly around the place and enjoyed the occasional night out.

Stewart Robson was a rising star when I joined Arsenal and he was very much part of the first team squad. He was a very energetic, wholehearted player who gave 100% commitment – very much a modern midfield player before his time. Unfortunately his career was blighted by injury and he never reached the heights expected of him. He was a little aloof with us slightly younger players and had a touch of arrogance about him, although he dressed like a 40 year old playing golf with Farah trousers and diamond patterned V-neck jumpers!

John Lukic was a lovely big lad from Yorkshire and he used to hang around with Charlie Nicholas a bit as they were roughly the same age I think. He was a decent keeper and was vying with Pat Jennings for the number 1 jersey having replaced George Wood at the club. He used to drive a 3 litre Gold Ford Capri which he loved to bits and was obviously very proud of, I thought it was really cool.

Chris Whyte was a lovely lad who always had a big smile on his face and was affectionately known as Huggy Bear after the character in Starsky and Hutch. Chris was a good footballer but was never given enough opportunity with O'Leary and Tommy Caton generally chosen first, and was then overtaken by Tony Adams and Martin Keown. I was to see Chris later in my career when he was at Leeds and Birmingham.

The physios at Arsenal were Fred Street who was also the England physio and generally looked after the first team lads, and Roy Johnson who was a nice enough chap who I became reunited with later in life. There was also a young man called Gary Lewin who had been released as a goalkeeper a couple of years before but was bright enough to retrain as a qualified physiotherapist, he was combining studying and working at Guy's Hospital with helping out at Arsenal, learning his trade. Gary was a good lad and on one occasion he invited some of us to a party at Guy's Hospital with the promise of lots of young nurses attending. Although a good night was had by all, the reality of the nurses failed to live up to the fantasy in our deluded minds!

Gary was one of the rare players who after being released was helped by a football club, I don't know how or why but he certainly made the most of his opportunity subsequently becoming both Arsenal and England's physio.

In contradiction to Gary's story, I have one last memory from my time at Arsenal which should have been a message that things can change very quickly in football.

There was a midweek first team game at Highbury and this big scruffy lad came into the dressing room area and was saying hello to a few of the players very loudly. I hadn't got a clue who it was at the time and had to ask one of the lads, it turned out to be Paul Vaessen who had been released the previous year with a chronic knee injury which he never recovered from. Anyway, he had asked for a ticket to the match but was caught during the game in the home dressing room stealing from all the players' wallets and after a fair bit of commotion he was thrown out of the ground. I never knew Vas but was soon told that he had become a drug addict after his career was cruelly ended and he was stealing to feed his habit. He had scored against Juventus against Dino Zoff in a European semi-final only two years before. Sadly he lived the rest of his life as a drug addict and finally died from an overdose at the age of just 39.

Tony Adams has started 'The Sporting Chance' charity for sports people with addiction issues and thinks Paul Vaessen would still be alive if it had happened today.

Who knows if that's true but I think it's fair to say that not enough was or probably is done when a club releases a player and that was certainly the case when I was released.

There is very much a culture of "thanks, good luck and goodbye"

CHAPTER SEVEN

Dances with Wolves…

So less than three years after being feted by every club in England I was on the scrapheap with a free transfer.

Arsenal didn't offer to help me find another club and I was wrongly under the impression that I would still have plenty of offers. In this situation the PFA are notified of all free transfers and a list is circulated with names and phone numbers to all the clubs in the league and conference. The phone (there were no mobile phones then) at my mum and dad's house remained very quiet for the first month after the season ended. I presumed this was because most football people go on holiday as soon as they can before the new pre-season preparations begin.

Eventually the first call came, which my dad took and was from Barry Fry at Barnet who always picked up players from the North London clubs. I spoke to Mr Fry and explained that I really didn't want to stay in London or want to drop out of League football either. He was very understanding and wished me well. I was to come across Barry Fry later in my career when he was at Birmingham and I was with Kidderminster. He was certainly a lively old school character and I don't think the modern player would take some of the 'team talks' he dished out.

The next call was out of the blue from Jimmy Sirrell of Notts County inviting me to go on a pre-season trip to Holland which was leaving imminently. I felt that I couldn't turn the opportunity down so agreed to go. The only problem was that I had been recovering from my ankle problem and hadn't been doing much training so I wasn't really fit to play. I went anyway and we weren't a particularly strong team and I didn't play particularly well. This was the first time I got to know Keith Downing who I was to become team mates with at Wolves a couple of years later.

The most memorable thing about that trip was watching the Nottingham Forest team play. Brian Clough was running up and down the side of the pitch shouting and bawling like a raving banshee! At the time I just thought he was a raving lunatic but it may have been after a long liquid lunch knowing what we know now.

Notts County said they would be in touch but unsurprisingly I never heard from then again. Fortunately while I was on the trip Sammy Chapman from Wolves had been on the phone and I think the smooth talking Northern Irishman hit it off with my mum and dad – they could relate to his background I think. I called Sammy and he was very enthusiastic for me to join Wolves for pre-season training on an initial trial basis. He had seen me play at Arsenal and I must have played well because he was very keen. I knew I had to take this opportunity because there weren't a lot of options available to me. So I started training really hard to ensure I was in great condition and could hit the ground running – literally!

I remember getting the train and a taxi to Wolves' ground, the Molineux, the day before pre-season started and nobody seemed to be expecting me! Sammy had been held up somewhere and hadn't told anyone else I was coming – he eventually turned up and within minutes he made me feel really welcome. You couldn't help but like Sammy, he had charisma in bucket loads and I think his contribution to keeping Wolves alive in that dark period is totally underestimated. I didn't really know how bad the situation was and Sammy wasn't likely to tell me!

It was only after starting to train, I overheard some of the lads talking about not getting paid and I realised the club had major problems.

Prior to playing Walsall away early in my first season, Sammy held a player's meeting and after naming the team and generally telling us what he expected, he then proceeded to tell us 'Boys we're really close to being a good team – there's something missing and I can't quite put my finger on it – we're like Dolly Parton with just one tit!

We all doubled up with laughter but he was being quite serious!

One day, Sammy called a meeting and it soon turned out someone had been in touch with him about the Tuesday club antics, and after giving us all a bollocking he came out with the classic line ' If this was the Heineken league we'd have it wrapped up by Christmas!

He was a lovely fella and while I have been writing this book he has passed away while I was coaching in Koh Samui, Thailand and I sadly couldn't get back in time for his funeral.

Anyway, Sammy took me to some digs in Codsall (which is just outside Wolverhampton) to stay with a lovely old couple called Jack and Olive Carr who were Wolves through and through. Jack and Olive always watched training at the Castlecroft training ground and they made tea and provided biscuits for the lads after training which I believe they paid for.

Jack and Olive gave me a lift to Molineux to report for training the next day and I was a little nervous as is normal as I didn't know anyone. Fortunately Danny Crainie spoke to me and we hit it off immediately as he was a good friend of Charlie Nicholas so we had something to talk about.

The difference between Highbury and the Molineux in those days was vast, the old ground obviously wasn't being maintained properly due to lack of funds and it looked very tired. There were even occasions when cockroaches would appear from under the seating in the changing room. I was also shown a pile of kit and told to get two shirts, two shorts, two pairs of socks and a sweatshirt and to look after them as they were my responsibility – this was very different from Arsenal! Nevertheless, it was obvious that there was still a good sense of humour around the dressing room despite the desperate situation of the club owned by the Bhatti brothers.

The routine to start with consisted of running from Molineux to the Castlecroft training ground and then more running mixed in with a little ball work. Obviously I was keen to impress and usually ran with Danny to Castlecroft, chatting along the way. However it was obvious that some of the other lads weren't taking it as seriously! We were just arriving at Castlecroft, finishing the first part of the running, when a bus pulled in front of us and about a dozen of the lads got off led by Dave Barnes and Scott Barrett! I couldn't believe it and they were all laughing at us – me and Danny just looked at each other and burst out laughing!

On another day shortly afterwards we were doing laps in small groups around Castlecroft, and after a fair few laps I was running past the bottom corner when I saw Ray Hankin being sick on all fours. After another lap he was flat out on his back. It's fair to say Ray had enjoyed the summer and hadn't got the motivation to impress that I had. I didn't see Ray again after that and his departure opened the door for me to play in the pre-season fixtures.

Before the pre-season games got underway I was called into see Sammy in the manager's office and was offered a contract to sign for Wolverhampton Wanderers. I was relieved to have some pay for my work but the offer was hardly lucrative! £100 per week plus £100 per appearance and £80 a win and £40 a draw. Not having any other option and before the days of agents working for you I agreed to sign.

The appearance bonus was certainly an incentive to make sure I was selected for the team and it did make me determined to play, but this was a double edged sword. The motivation to play well and work hard was there on the one hand but playing when injured and having cortisone injections to try and be fit enough to play was a major downside. This was regarded as normal then though, you soon realised that in football if you weren't available to be selected to play out on the pitch you were of no value at all. Being injured was no good to a manager and nor was being suspended.

I am sure I wasn't alone in playing when injured or coming back from an injury too quickly when not really ready fitness wise. It seems to be different these days where players go through rigorous fitness tests to evaluate their readiness to be selected. Also, if you are being paid a fortune or even good money on your basic wage why would you rush back to play when not 100% fit?

Tim Flowers was also lodging at Jack and Olive's and although we knew each other vaguely from England Schoolboy trials we got to know each other a little better for the couple of weeks we lodged together. Tim was a nice, outgoing, big lad – he hated being beaten in shooting practice and if you chipped him he would turn purple and chase you threatening all sorts of violence! I'm sure that, like me, Tim wasn't on great money then (but probably more than me!), but I soon realised that he was 'careful' with his money. On quite a few occasions we would have some dinner at the digs and then walk around the corner to the local pub – The Bentlands for a couple of pints to kill some time. I would get the first round, he would get the second, and after I got the third he wouldn't have enough money for the fourth! After a few nights like this I asked him why he didn't withdraw a bit more money and he told me that he would only withdraw £5 at a time otherwise he would spend it! To be fair I think he was saving up for a house with his girlfriend, but I thought I would be best finding another drinking partner. Not too long after I arrived, Tim got a great move to Southampton and eventually did well there and went on to have a great career. I hope he took more than a fiver out with him when he was going out with Alan Shearer, etc!

As I was staying in Wolverhampton I had to move to more permanent digs and Sammy found me lodgings in Clark Road, Tettenhall. This was quite handy in good weather as I could walk to the Molineux across West Park for training and for home fixtures. Very often I would be walking amongst Wolves fans towards the ground and no-one knew they would soon be watching me play. I guess it wasn't expected for a professional player to walk to a match before playing.

These new digs were quite eye opening as the landlady Verna and her two teenage daughters, Julie and Janina, were to be my housemates. The first time I walked into the house it was full of 18 year old girls and they took great delight in teasing me. I was a shy lad and hadn't really had a proper serious girlfriend to build my confidence with the female persuasion. One of the girls asked me what I did and didn't like to eat and I said I liked everything but cheese and tomatoes, and she said "that's a shame it's cheese and tomatoes on toast for tea tonight!" I wasn't sure at the time but found out later that she successfully pulling my leg!

FOOTBALL LEAGUE CONTRACT

AN AGREEMENT made the ..*FIRST*.... day of *AUGUST*.. 19 *85*...........

between (name) .. *KEITH DAVID PEARSON*.................................

of (address) ...... *MOLINEUX GROUND WATERLOO ROAD*.......

.... *WOLVERHAMPTON WEST MIDLANDS*........

the Secretary/~~Manager~~/~~Chairman~~ of and acting pursuant to Resolution and Authority for and on behalf of

.... *WOLVERHAMPTON WANDERERS*

Football Club Limited (hereinafter referred to as "the Club") of the one part and

(name) .... *JOHN PURDIE*...

of (address) ...... *40, SOUTHBROOK*.................................

.... *CORBY NORTHANTS*..........................

a Registered Association Football Player (hereinafter referred to as "the Player")

My non lucrative contract with Wolves.

On the ball for Wolves with Geoff Palmer in the background.

As time went by I settled in and once they got to know me we all became friends and we started mixing socially at places like Rocky's, The Mermaid and Eves nightclub. Before long Julie and I took a shine to each other and we ended up seeing each other, which led to a 27 year relationship and a 20 year marriage which produced two great sons of ours, Charlie and Jack, who we're both very proud of.

The landlady Verna, wasn't aware of our relationship for a while and I don't know if we thought she wouldn't approve so we tried to keep it quiet for a while. I would get up to go to the loo about an hour after going to bed, flush the toilet and then sneak into Julie's room so we could spend the night together. I would then get up early in the morning and do the same manoeuvre in reverse in an attempt to make it seem like I was just going back to my own bed. However, we slept in one morning and Verna brought Julie a cup of tea to find me in her daughter's bed. "Oh I see" she said! Going downstairs for breakfast that day was probably the most nervous I've ever been but it wasn't mentioned and our relationship soon became accepted thankfully.

Although I was going out with Julie I still liked a night out with the lads. It was normal for us to go out separately with our friends, then meet up in Eves and end up going home together. I found the people of Wolverhampton very friendly and welcoming and although quite a big place everyone seemed to know each other. I got to know the bouncers at Eves and always felt pretty safe there in our own regular group.

At the time I usually went out with Danny Crainie, Campbell and Cavan Chapman, and Jim Carty who was the brother of Danny's girlfriend Fiona. On one occasion we decided to have a change of scenery and went to a club called Christopher's which was about 5 miles outside of Wolverhampton. We were a little wary and very much out of our comfort zone, and had the feeling of being strangers in town or walking into the wrong saloon in the wild west! Julie and her friend Melanie came to meet us and after a while we decided to leave in Melanie's little yellow Mini.

Eyes on the ball for Wolves.

As we made our way to the car I noticed Cavan and Campbell being surrounded by 4 lads who wanted trouble. Now, Cav and Campbell really weren't fighters and I couldn't stand by and watch them get beat up, so I told Jim to go and get the bouncers and went over to try and diffuse the situation. Well as soon as I got close the lads turned on me and Cav and Campbell ran off!

I was once told that, if I had no choice but to fight, to get the first punch in and hit the biggest one in the hope that the others would back off. So I took a deep breath and hit the biggest lad with a right hook and he went down like a sack of spuds – so far so good! Unfortunately the other three lads hadn't read the script and they all jumped on me and I ended up scrapping on the floor with them. Somehow I got free and managed to get up and start running towards Julie and Melanie who were in a bit of a state. "Get the car started!" I was shouting before jumping in – with the other lads chasing me. Well, Melanie stalled the car about 3 times before eventually firing it up by which time the four lads were jumping on the car, kicking and punching it but Melanie put her foot down and we escaped!

I saw Jim the next day and asked what happened to him. "I went to get the bouncers" he said, "where from? Stringfellows?" I answered! Anyway we are still mates today so all is forgiven.

Danny Crainie was a good mate during that period and was loved by Wolves fans for scoring a great goal in a win against the arch enemy West Brom. He was a skilful player who suffered by having to play in the more physical lower leagues and ultimately couldn't adapt to it. Danny was the first player I ever saw use a hairdryer in the changing room and he was always playing with his hair. I also had a fantastic mullett but wasn't ever going to be using a hairdryer – chance would be a fine thing for both of us now!

I had a very good pre-season scoring a few goals and securing my position as the first choice centre forward, not that Sammy had a great deal of choice! I made my debut against Brentford away, playing against a tank of a man called Terry Hurlock who had a fearsome reputation and was quite an intimidating figure. I played quite well and hit the post from around the halfway line having seen the keeper off his line. I also played Neil Edwards through to round the keeper and score our consolation goal in a 2-1 defeat.

Neil was a good foil for me, very quick and strong and he could finish too, but unfortunately he never got much chance to show what he could do due to a horrific knee injury which he never recovered from. I still see him now when we both play for Wolves All Stars for charity.

Unfortunately we weren't the strongest team and defensively we were pretty awful – it seemed we conceded every time anyone got near our goal. The dressing room had a constant turnover of players coming and going on trial and short term deals. God knows how many hours Sammy must have been working on the phone and attending matches, but one thing is for sure he was trying everything in his power without money to improve the squad.

Later in my first season when I had been playing quite well and had received a few newspaper headlines, I received a call from a Daily Mail reporter and was told there was a lot of talk about me moving to a big club and asked me my opinion of the manager and certain players at Wolves. I was answering all these questions honestly and talking to this chap for about 30 minutes when he started giggling and then about 3 other lads started howling with laughter – it was Danny the whole time putting on an accent! I walked into the dressing room a little sheepish the next day – they got me good and proper!

I have been attributed to a story involving Tommy Docherty but, although a good story, it wasn't me because I wasn't at Wolves with him! Apparently "the Doc" called through to the tea room asking an apprentice to bring him a cup of tea to the manager's office and the young lad told him to get his own effing tea. The Doc said "do you know who you're talking to son?" The lad answered, "yes – do you?" The Doc admitted that he didn't, so the lad said "I didn't think so" and told him to eff off again before slamming the phone down and running off!

During this first season the apprentices were having a problem with someone stealing their sandwiches and this was known as the 'phantom sandwich nicker', anyway after a few weeks my apprentice Carl Dwyer organised all the young lads to bring in double the amount of sandwiches one day. He then proceeded to hide one lot for them to have for lunch and then smeared the second lot with deep heat and left them out where they were normally kept. It wasn't too long before the culprit could be heard screaming in pain and desperately drinking water to put the fire out! Peter Zelem was the Phantom sandwich nicker'

During half time in one game Zelem came in moaning under his breath and was asked what the problem was, he replied that some players aren't good enough and weren't pulling their weight! Campbell Chapman asked him to name names and Zelem said "you're one of them for a start" at which point Campbell got up and marched across the dressing room to square up to him, but before he could blink Zelem landed a right hook which Mike Tyson would have been proud of! It all got calmed down and we went out for the second half but it showed we were in trouble as a team and we duly got relegated.

Wolves team
photo

Alistair Robertson (Wolves)

Jon wasn't just a good player, although he was certainly that. Almost as importantly, and perhaps even more so, I soon found out that he was also a great bloke – a man who you could both turn to and rely upon, and those traits were invaluable to me in 1986 as I arrived as his captain and sought about turning around a sinking ship. Some 35 years later I am still proud to call Purds a mate.

I noticed his footballing ability on my very first morning. Straight away I could tell he could play. He'd like to get it down and pass, he had a lovely touch, a change of pace and an eye for goal. In terms of ability he was a step above most of the group.

I remember the good days as if they were yesterday with him at the fulcrum of what we were doing in a good dressing room which is paramount for success. We had it at the Albion under Johnny Giles and Ron Atkinson, and I'm happy to look back now and say that we had it at Wolves.

I was proud to be Jon's skipper and I'm fiercely proud of what we did during those days in the mid-to-late 1980s.

I'm also delighted to pen these few short words.

Enjoy the book. And remember that without the likes of Jon, Wolves would never have got to where they are today.

* * *

———————————

CHAPTER EIGHT

Partners In Crime At Molineux

One of the lads who turned up was Micky Holmes, he was put in the same digs as me and we hit it off straight away. Mick liked a beer and a night out and was naturally very funny, sometimes without meaning to be!

After training one winter's day Mick was in a real hurry to get home to spend some time with his mum in Bradford. He had told everyone before training not to keep us any longer than necessary because he needed to shoot off. Mick had brought an overnight bag with spare clothes in it which in reality was a Sainsbury's carrier bag, no designer man bags for us! Dave 'Digger' Barnes overheard his plans and, as he was injured and not training, decided to have some fun – he cut the bottom out of the carrier bag and placed it back where Mick had left it. Mick came in from training like the Tazmanian devil, had a quick shower, threw his tracksuit on and picked up his carrier bag to leave. All his good clothes fell straight into a muddy puddle in the changing room! Everyone fell about laughing but Mick wasn't best pleased and gave us all a departing mouthful!

After a few beers Mick thought he could sing like Whitney Houston or George Michael. He also had a habit of pinching a girl's bum and looking away so I was the one who got accused and left pleading my innocence! On one occasion he picked on the wrong girl who picked up a pint of Guinness and poured it all over me! Cheers mate!

After a few first team games and some appearance money Mick wanted to buy a new suit – this was a relief as he was normally dressed in a bright yellow tracksuit, so we went to Beatties store together and he bought a lovely new designer suit. Mick was so proud of his new purchase he was determined to go out in it on the next Saturday night. As we were getting ready to go out he was about to pull the labels off the sleeve when I convinced him it was fashionable to keep them on so everyone could see the designer label and he believed me! After a couple of hours of him getting funny looks I had to tell him as I couldn't see him suffer anymore.

Mullet in full flow for Wolves.

After one midweek game we had a couple of beers in the players' lounge and decided to go for a meal with my mum and dad and Alan Wortley – my mate from Corby. There weren't many restaurants open in Wolverhampton then and we managed to get a table at Pickwicks. During the meal Alan needed to go to the toilet and as he was longer than expected Mick went to see if he was ok or more likely to give him some stick. It turned out that he was on the toilet so after throwing a few things at him over the cubicle – Mick decided to stand on the urinal to see him for reasons unbeknown to me! Unfortunately for Mick, the urinal couldn't handle his weight and fell crashing down off the wall with Mick left hanging off the cubicle. He came running out saying we had to leave quickly – fortunately we had all finished eating so paid up and made a hasty retreat. It was only when we were well on our way that he explained what all the rush was about!

Mick and I were the founder members of the 'Tuesday Club' which basically meant that after training on a Tuesday if we didn't have a game we would go straight out for an all-day drinking session. The tradition was for the players to get Wednesdays off whether we had a game on a Tuesday night or not. If there was no game we would generally have a tough training session involving lots of running, lapping the pitch and doing sprints up the old South Bank which certainly worked up a thirst! There were usually quite a few of us to start with and the numbers would dwindle as the married lads had to go home.

Although most of us don't get together too often anymore, we are occasionally invited to Wolves to appear as part of the modern day hospitality. Mick was asked to take part before one game and was paraded around the different areas where people are usually having meals and get to ask questions to the ex-pros. One chap put his hand up and asked Mick who the worst player he'd ever played with at Wolves, Mick had one or two players in mind but being a thoughtful fella he was concerned that they may hear about it. So instead he thought he would choose the person who lived the furthest away and wouldn't be affected. So he picked Ricky Herbert and continued to say how bad a player he was lightheartedly. Ricky was a wholehearted player though perhaps not the most technically gifted, but he was the New Zealand captain (not as impressive as being their Rugby skipper!) and has gone on to be a very successful coach in their national set up. As it happens, Ricky was on a coaching trip to England and was standing in the back of the room! You couldn't make it up!

Mick and I became very close and we started going out with our girlfriends, Julie and Bernadette, and we all got on like a house on fire, so much so that while they were waiting for their house purchase to complete they moved into my flat with us for a few weeks. One afternoon I came home from training and Bernie was sat on the sofa reading the paper and I asked her if she was ok and she said, "no not really Jon, I thought I had found a job that looks perfect for me but there's just one problem!" "What's the problem?" I asked. "At the end it says that you have to be self-motivated and I can't drive!" I nearly fell over but she really meant it. Needless to say once I had explained she had a good laugh and she actually got the job! I couldn't help myself and managed to get the story in the Wolves programme for the next home game!

Mick was part of Wolves' double winning team that won the old Fourth Division title and Sherpa Van Trophy at Wembley in 1987-88. He was skilful, hardworking, and had an eye for goal, but more importantly to me he was a great lad and remains a good friend to this day. But just to show there's no sentiment in football, a week after getting injured in the final at Wembley, Mick received a letter through the post from the manager Graham Turner informing him he was being given a free transfer. There was no face-to-face meeting, not even a phone call. That gives you a taste of life as a lower league footballer and in my opinion was disgraceful treatment.

In action for Wolves against Bolton Wanderers.

At the end of that first season I went on a lads' holiday to the capital of Ibiza, San Antonio with Micky, Dean Edwards, another team-mate Nicky Clarke plus a couple of Dean's lifelong pals. On the first night we went out for a few beers and ended up in a club. We were messing about on the dancefloor when I suddenly got the feeling we weren't welcome. Glancing around, it seemed everyone apart from us was Spanish and we were definitely getting dirty looks from everywhere. The other lads were blissfully unaware of this but I told them all, adding we needed to leg it sharpish. We started to drift towards the exit but all hell broke loose and we got chased out with bottles being thrown at us. We managed to escape but I was hit by a flying bottle as I made it out on the street – I just kept running until I couldn't breathe! I had never been so scared and I dread to think what would have happened if we had stayed five minutes longer. None of us really had any money so it was far from the glamorous holidays that footballers enjoy these days – we were on a tight budget and took advantage of any happy hour offers.

Although we had a few nights out we generally started drinking at lunchtime so weren't really in any fit state for posing in nightclubs. One of Dean's pals hit the sauce a bit hard one afternoon and was trying to chat up a couple of girls sunning themselves by the pool. Watching on with interest, it came to our attention that his speedos were a bit baggy and we noticed one of his testicles was hanging out of his trunks! Obviously we never told him and watched him continue his efforts while howling with laughter!

Dean had been released by Graham Turner at Shrewsbury prior to being signed by Wolves, and when Graham was having a tough time in charge at Aston Villa, Dean saw him after a game and cheekily said "Alright Graham, are you feeling the pressure?"

Looking determined for Wolves with Floyd Streete looking on.

Graham just gave him his 'death stare'! Two weeks later Graham was sacked and within three weeks he got the Wolves job. Dean knew the writing was on the wall as soon as he heard of the appointment, and he was right as he was released again by Turner pretty quickly. It wasn't long before I realised I wasn't going to be his cup of tea either.

Regardless of whatever lay ahead, it didn't stop us all enjoying ourselves. In the early days of the Tuesday Club, we would go into town to Kipps wine bar where we got to know the owner Bob Stokes through Deano. Although Bob was slow in getting rid of us he was still very aware of the 3pm shutting time. Deano was a Wolverhampton boy and knew lots of people and places so our next stop was generally the Phoenix snooker club which was hidden out of the way and would give us a drink if we played pool or snooker. We would then move on to the normal haunts of Rockies, The Mermaid and the Castlecroft Hotel with Eves Nightclub being the final destination if we still had it in us. This formative time of the Tuesday Club was reasonably low key and just allowed the lads to have a drink and a laugh together, but the arrival of Ally Robertson took us to another level.

Ally arrived after a great career at West Brom and after he'd hit a low period under Ron Saunders, when he was very much out of favour and was given the normal treatment of training with the kids to try to get him to leave. He turned up in his Black Porsche with a private number plate and parked next to my old Volkswagen Polo, Mick's Ford Escort, Bully's orange Cortina, etc. and we all thought 'who's this flash old git?' He had first arrived to help Brian Little with the coaching and obviously we were all a little wary of him, I do think Ally wanted to get involved in the management side of things and if Brian had kept his job things may have been different. When Graham Turner arrived Ally was quickly told that he was just a player and there was nothing for him on the coaching side.

Having spoken to Ally and still being mates now, he was desperate to get away from Albion but didn't realise what state Molineux and the Wolves set up was in at the time and I think he was having doubts about his decision especially when Brian was sacked. Ally was one of the best captains and hardest centre halves I played with but he was also very clever with it – his favourite trick was to rake the standing leg of a centre forward when the ball was played up to him but he always put his arms out in a signal of innocence and was never penalised! Quite often in training Ally would mark me and we had a 'gentlemans' agreement that I wouldn't turn and run at him if he didn't kick me – a win-win situation.

Anyway he soon settled in to being 'one of the lads' and once he realised we were a decent group he became one of the leaders of the 'Tuesday Club'. After a few sessions in and around Wolverhampton, Ally suggested we go further afield and he said he knew of a decent place that stayed open all day and had live music on called 'The Oddspot'. We were all up for a change of scenery, though in hindsight Ally lived in Great Barr so it was probably more convenient for him! So after training one day we had a convoy to Birmingham and I was with Mick in his Escort XR3i following Ally in his very nice Porsche. We arrived and walked into heaven! This place was full of footballers from Albion, Villa and Blues and consequently there were quite a lot of girls around who obviously thought we were all loaded – who were we to spoil their dreams! To say we had some great times would be an understatement and we would either hang around Brum or get ourselves back to Wolves to carry on the session. Although I knew a few Albion lads such as Derek Statham and Cyrille Regis, it wasn't long before I was mixing with some famous Midlands players such as Gary Shaw who also loved a night out.

Derek Statham is from Wolverhampton and lived there when playing for Albion so we used to drink together quite regularly in the Mermaid, Rocky's and Eves. Despite being one of the best players in the country he was a very down to earth chap who was a pleasure to be around. I met him one night in Eves when he had just failed a medical at Liverpool, understandably he was devastated and we certainly drank his sorrows away that night. Although he got a move to Glasgow Rangers soon after, I imagine that move to Liverpool would have been a dream for him.

As success started coming on the pitch for us, so did the win bonuses and the lads started upgrading their cars to try and keep up with Ally I guess. On one Tuesday we were following one of the lads in a lovely sports car – remember this was before we had Sat Navs – and Mick and I hadn't got a clue how to find the Oddspot, when suddenly this team mate started speeding up on the Hagley Road and then suddenly took a sharp left. We had no idea what was going on but fortunately I saw which turning he took so we managed to follow him, when we eventually caught up he had parked his car outside some plush apartments and had left his car running so we thought he wouldn't be long and sat in the car waiting. After 5 minutes there was no sign of him so for a laugh I decided to move his car and find a place to hide and watch his reaction when he discovered his car had gone! Another 5 minutes went by and still no sign of him. Mick was getting hungry and we decided to go for a bite to eat, while we were eating we thought it best to go back and put his car back where it was but not before getting some directions to the Oddspot from someone working in McDonald's – so after finishing our burgers I duly moved his car back and we carried on with our day out.

This player came into training on the Thursday very confused and a little angry and started questioning me and Mick (we generally got the blame for most things) but we just denied knowing anything. It transpires that he had parked up to visit a young lady to try and arrange a get together later in the afternoon but she was more accommodating than he thought and he got side tracked into forgetting about his lovely car! When he bid the young lady goodbye he went outside to find his car missing and went back upstairs to use her phone and called the police to report it stolen. After a while he went back downstairs to miraculously find his car where he had left it and drove off. On his way home he was pulled over by the police and had to convince them he hadn't stolen his own car!

On the subject of cars I was driving to Molineux one evening to play a game for the reserves having just recovered from an injury in my first season at Wolves and my old VW Polo conked out on the main ring road. I couldn't get it started so locked it up and walked the rest of the way to the ground. Once there I searched for Greg Fellows and asked him to get the mini bus and tow it to the ground which he agreed to do. At half time he was waiting for me and I thought he was going to say he'd sorted it but he said "Purds – I went to get your car but there were two fire engines around it and it was in flames!" I told my dad about it the next day and he asked, "when did you last put oil and water in it? I told him I didn't know I had to!

My knowledge of cars wasn't great and on another occasion when I was on loan at Cambridge United and I stayed in digs with Gary Poole who I knew from my Arsenal days when he was there for a while. On the way home from training the oil light came on in the car so I stopped and bought some from a garage. Unfortunately, we were both clueless about motors and we couldn't find where the oil went. It was starting to get dark so I ended up rolling up a magazine and attempted to pour it into the dipstick hole! Needless to say most of it ended up on the floor.

Wolves Players

Andy King

Kingy was probably most famous for his tremendous volleyed goal for Everton against Liverpool and then subsequently being shoved off the pitch by a policeman whilst getting interviewed by match of the day!

He certainly was an interesting character as well as being a very good player, we used to sit opposite each other on the dressing room floor keeping a ball up between us and passing it back and forward to each other, he was better sat down than most players were standing up! He had a great goalscoring record as an attacking midfield player in his short time at Wolves and although he quickly moved on (quite rightly as he should have been playing at a higher level), he left an impression with a few incidents.

On one occasion we were having a drink at the mermaid pub when Campbell and Cavan Chapman turned up in their Mum's Citroen C5 (which was like a little bubble on wheels), as soon as they parked up Kingy ran at the car and ran straight up and over it! Campbell said 'oi Kingy you're denting it' at which point Kingy pulled some loose change out of his pocket and shouted 'here, go and get another one' a bit brutal but funny nonetheless!

Kingy could be a bit volatile and he wasn't the most patient of older pro's. We were training at Castlecroft one morning and during a training match Kingy had a go at Nicky Clarke who was an 18 year old centre half with a lot of potential at the time but had a tendency to get dragged out of position by more experienced strikers. I think Kingy was trying to help Nicky but perhaps didn't put it across very well and Nicky told him to F*** Off! Well, the red mist descended and before anyone could get between them, Kingy had pulled Nicky's shirt over his head and was kicking him repeatedly! After the initial shock of what was happening the lads split them up and I think Nicky was relieved to see the back of him when he left!

It was sad to hear of his premature death recently and the world certainly lost a real character.

Floyd Streete

Floydy was a lovely big bloke who I first encountered playing for Wolves against Derby at the old Baseball ground. He was built like a fit heavyweight boxer and was good in the air and very quick with it. The Wolves fans soon took a shine to him and you would often hear 'Bruno Bruno' being chanted around Molineux, after Frank Bruno who was Britains great boxing hope at the time.

Floyd was very laid back so Micky Holmes and I used to try and wind him up to see if we could get any reaction, but he just used to smile and shake his head at us.

The usual focus on our antics was the fact that Floyd was particularly well blessed in the trouser department, in fact like Alex Ferguson said about Dion Dublin – it was magnificent!

We would poke a bit of fun at Floydy saying he'd pass out if he got an erection and at least we can use ours etc! After a match on a Saturday I would ask him if I could borrow half of it for the weekend as he surely didn't need it all and Holmesy used to try and slap it in the showers!

Well after a few months of this I think we finally got to him after training one day when we were in the communal baths, which were so unhygienic looking back but good for banter and talking with your pals. He said 'I'll show you pair' he proceeded to bring life into the monster and bent his head down and kissed it ' saying 'my beauty'

Well you've never seen two blokes get out of the bath so quickly feeling very inadequate with our tails between our legs literally!

I haven't seen Floyd for a long time unfortunately and the last I heard he was working in the community with disadvantaged kids.

David 'Digger' Barnes

Digger was a very talented left back, who was an England youth international, he had a lovely left foot and was aggressive with a bit of pace and probably was frustrated to find himself in the lower reaches of league football. He was brought up as an orphan in Dr Barnados prior to being adopted and he was a very intelligent if complex character.

One morning Peter Eastoe turned up for his first day at Wolves and unwittingly got changed into his training kit and put his clothes on Digger's peg, Digger just came into the dressing room, walked over to his peg and picked up the offending clothes and threw them on the dressing room floor! The next morning Digger made a beeline for Peter Eastoe and sat next to him and apologised about the previous day and welcomed him to the club, he then proceeded to get changed and took his jeans and jumper off revealing him wearing a basque, stockings and suspenders! How to make a new signing feel welcome!

After a short injury Digger was asked to play in the reserves away somewhere, which he didn't feel necessary as had been back in training and to be fair he was very naturally fit. Anyway he was made to play and a disgruntled Digger travelled on the mini bus with a lot of young players. By the time the game kicked off he had worked himself up into a fury and proceeded to snap the opposition winger in half after two minutes with a horrendous tackle, the referee gave him a straight red and asked him for his name? Digger replied Billy Bandu for some reason only known to Digger and the ref asked him to spell it? 'B-A-N-D-U' Digger shouted into his face snarling at him and then he turned and stormed off the pitch ! About a week later Sammy Chapman came bounding into the dressing room waving a disciplinary form from the FA shouting in his strong Northern Irish accent 'Who the F..k is Billy Bandu' It was hilarious at the time!

Doctor Tweddle was the eccentric Club doctor and he always reminded me of Basil Fawlty, he would say something and then say ' What What?' before anyone had chance to say anything! Digger was never slow to pick up on something and before long he did a regular impression of the doc skipping around the dressing room with a tubigrip on the top of his head and nothing else on shouting 'What What?' at the top of his voice. It's difficult to describe but it's a wonder we could manage to train after witnessing it!

Digger regularly picked me up on the way to Molineux as it was on his way but on quite a few occasions he would have to get out of his car and come up to the second floor of the apartment block to knock the door to get me up after I'd slept in, he used to call me all sorts of names and he made sure he got his revenge in other ways! When Graham Turner arrived at Molineux he was a very serious individual and you did well to ever see a hint of a smile. He used to call regular team meetings to get a point across about something and Digger took these opportunities to have some fun at my expense. During one of these meetings as Graham looked to the other side of the dressing room Digger grabbed the inside of my leg and pinched me really hard, pulling all the hairs out of my leg and I squealed loudly! Obviously I got the death stare from Turner and was told to stop messing about and Digger got away scot free! When the next meeting was called I waited until the last second and made sure I was sat away from Digger on the opposite side of the dressing room in an attempt to stay out of trouble. Turner then started his talk and he was facing me and I have a quick glance at Digger and he's grinning at me with his front teeth blacked out with Liquorice!, it was so difficult not to giggle and I think Graham spotted me breaking into a smirk and swivelled around to have a look at Digger but of course he had shut his mouth and looked deadly serious! He kept this up throughout the meeting – it was so funny and painful at the same time!

Digger didn't see eye to eye with Turner, I guess they were polar opposites as personalities and Digger made it clear he wanted a move. To make his point Digger failed to report until two weeks after we were due back for pre-season training. When he finally arrived he walked into the dressing room as Turner was holding another meeting and Digger just said 'sorry I'm late, I slept in!'

He proceeded to train at the racecourse winning all the races no matter what the distance comfortably! The following day he ran at the back with me and the keepers just to be awkward!

Mark Kendall was a great lad with a good sense of humour and he was also a great keeper, however one day Digger spotted that Kendo was sporting massive y fronts and started taking the mickey. Once the spotlight had gone Kendo got changed and thought the heat had gone. Unfortunately for Kendo, Digger had been waiting for this and decided to pick his Y fronts off his peg with an upside down broom and paraded them around the dressing room up in the air! This became a daily broom held inspection of Kendo's pants until Digger left much to Kendo's relief I'm sure!

I attended Mark's funeral with quite a few of the lads from that era, it was very sad to prematurely lose such a lovely chap and one of our old pals at the age of just 49.

Digger was sold to Aldershot at a knock down price, I was sad to see him go at the time but I don't think Turner could or would manage him and Digger wanted to leave anyway. I still think of Digger very fondly and he was certainly the funniest player I ever played with. Unfortunately I have lost all contact with him but I hope he's doing ok.

Greg Fellows

Greg was a funny bloke who started his career at Man Utd but by this point was looking after the youth team and sometimes the reserves at Wolves. He still had a great touch and would take on all comers at volleys from 5 yards apart – however Greg had expanded a bit from his playing days and couldn't really run around much anymore. Greg used to have regular banter with Bill Pilbeam who was the groundsman at Molineux and was stereotypical in as much as he tried to stop anyone going on the pitch and Greg would wind him up by walking across it. Bill would react by telling Greg he was a disgrace and how can he coach football when so overweight (or words to that effect!). This would go on until one day Bill challenged Greg to race the length of Molineux's pitch!

Now Bill was also a big man and I would guess that both were around the 20 stone mark so this turned out to be THE funniest thing I have ever witnessed. Greg in his shorts, t-shirt and trainers and Bill in his holey jumper, work trousers and hob nail boots. The lads started taking bets and it was built up to take place on a Friday lunchtime after training. They both desperately wanted to win and when the race began they both gave it their all but we were all creased up laughing at the sight of two very overweight men trying to run as fast as they could. I can't even remember who won but just recall both being flat out in a heap at the end! We should really have had the paramedics at the ready!

During that first season at Wolves I was playing well in a poor team and there was paper talk of other clubs being interested in me, Sammy Chapman even valued me at a million pounds to scare them away! Greg was a good bloke and he told me to get in for a pay rise as there were lots of players on more money than me, I should have listened but naively thought the club would look after me if they valued me. They didn't and soon afterward the manager's office was fitted with a revolving door.

Andy Mutch

When Andy Mutch first came to the club from Southport he ruffled a few feathers as he was a very confident young man and to say he could talk would be an understatement! He was a hard working player who went on to form a great partnership with Steve Bull, but when he first arrived his first touch wasn't great and during training if anyone miscontrolled the ball I would say '"How's your Andy Mutch" (rhyming slang for 'touch'). To be fair to Andy he worked hard at his game and improved immeasurably with a lot of this down to self-belief I believe.

Anyway one day Bill Pilbeam had heard enough of Mutchy gobbing off so he told him he was crap and challenged him into a hit the crossbar competition from the 18 yard line. Again this was great sport and similarly to the race we built this up for all to witness on a Friday after training. Bill let Mutchy go first and his first side footed effort floated into the back of the net, Bill stepped up with his hob nailed boots and toe ended the ball like a missile which crashed onto the crossbar which shook ferociously! Bill just walked off saying "I told ya yum crap". We ripped Mutchy for weeks after but he took it in his stride.

Steve Bull

Steve Bull arrived with Andy Thompson in a bright orange Cortina and the tightest jeans you've ever seen a few weeks after we had played a friendly against Albion at Molineux. I remember this wiry lad up front for them scoring a couple of goals. It was probably arranged for Graham Turner to have a look at some of them and he subsequently signed Robbie Dennison as well. During Bully's first couple of days we went for a drink in the Goal Post pub by the ground. We had a few beers and played some pool, after a couple of hours my wife-to-be Julie joined us and Bully proceeded to talk to her for about an hour while I was playing pool. After a while she excused herself to go to the toilet and came to me and said "who's that bloke?" I told her his name was Steve Bull and that he'd just signed for us. She replied "well he's been talking to me for an hour and I haven't understood a word he's said!" I couldn't really help her as Bully had the broadest Black Country accent you could imagine, which is normal in his home town of Tipton just up the road from Wolverhampton.

Bully became a regular in the Tuesday club with Thommo and boy he could drink without ever looking affected – I believe he has replaced the lager with white wine these days!

Bully was the hungriest striker I ever played with and he certainly made the most of his ability. Once we realised to play to his strengths - which was basically to put the ball into space behind the opposing defence he made it his business to get on the end of it and he had an appetite for goals which couldn't be satisfied. I had been brought up to play the ball into a strikers feet and build the play but this wasn't Bully or Mutchy's style, and nor was it what Graham Turner wanted. His game plan was built on percentage football, which turned out to be very effective in getting Wolves out of the old 4th and 3rd divisions, which I guess was Graham Turner's objective, but then levelled out in the Championship.

Graham Turner

Graham arrived replacing Brian Little and on his first day came into the dressing room with intent, flanked by Paul Darby (physio) and Garry Pendrey (coach) who resembled the chuckle brothers with their matching moustaches, but there weren't many laughs when Graham was about. He had a very serious, dour demeanour and sometimes if he passed you in the corridor he would say good morning and other times he would ignore you. He laid the law down – it was his way or the highway, which was quite right, but his way didn't suit me unfortunately. I struggled to adjust to his long ball approach and ended up with neck ache as the ball constantly bypassed my feet but I still played in the team quite a lot. The results were good but I wasn't enjoy my football and didn't really think I was contributing much so it was no real surprise when I started finding myself on the bench and playing in the reserves.

Graham later actually went on record as saying I had the most ability at the club so it is disappointing that he never tried to get the best out of me or talk to me about what I could do to improve. I had been playing first team football regularly for over a year when he arrived, I was still only 19 and felt I had a lot to offer. I guess he didn't have the time or the inclination to try and 'manage' me. When I was initially dropped I thought 'I'll show you' but no matter how well I played in the reserves or how many goals I scored I made no impact on him. After about 6 weeks of playing out of my skin and getting nowhere I went to see him to ask what I had to do to get back in the team only to be told I couldn't do anything. He proceeded to draw a line halfway across a blackboard in his office and he said he wanted players who guarantee him a 6 or 7 every week, and I was either a 9 or 10, or a 5 which he didn't want or like. I was a little inconsistent but I was only 19 and still learning but I guess I was at the right club at the wrong time. Indeed I left when Wolves were promoted to the 3rd division and Graham said he would have kept me if they were going into the 2nd division but couldn't afford to carry me for a year in the hope of getting another promotion. Presumably he knew he would have to play more passing football at a higher level but that was no good to me at the time.

Graham ruled by fear and knew that the players weren't in a very strong position as we were all young and trying to make our way in the game so would basically do as we were told to keep our jobs, and if we didn't do what he wanted there were plenty of others around who would.

I played against Man City at Maine Road in the League cup on the right wing directly against Andy Hinchcliffe and had a really good game. We won 1-0 with the second leg at Molineux a week later- they had a good side with a veteran, Peter Barnes, who I watched play for England when I was a lad on one wing, and a young Paul Simpson who I later became teammates with at Oxford on the other. We had a great trip back and we were buzzing to have beaten a team from the 1st division. However it was a case of 'after the Lord Mayor's show' and the following Saturday we played poorly and lost at Bolton. However we had the second leg against City on the Tuesday and I was looking forward to showing what I could do in this big game with my family and friends coming to watch. I arrived at the ground as normal before the game and sat in the dressing room with all the lads waiting for the manager to arrive and name the team. Well he did name the team and the subs and I wasn't amongst any of them – I had to get up and walk out of the dressing room with my tail between my legs. He didn't even have the decency to talk to me beforehand and save my embarrassment. I went straight back to my flat and cried my eyes out, I didn't want to play football anymore – I hated the game that I used to love. I knew I had to get away and I had no respect for the manager of the club I loved.

My final memory of being at Wolves was an incident at Lilleshall in the days leading up to the Sherpa Van Trophy final at Wembley. There was a full scale game organised with the 1st team playing against the reserves. I knew I wasn't going to be in the 1st team as I had got myself cup tied playing for Cambridge earlier in the season. But lo and behold I was named as sub for the first team which initially I didn't understand but Ally later told me that Graham Turner didn't want me playing against the first team in case I damaged their confidence. So I basically watched the game from the side lines without getting a kick. I was having a moan on the side of the pitch and Barry Powell, who had been a teammate previously and had recently got on the coaching staff, commented "I thought you wanted to be in the first team" – a nasty comment which hasn't been forgotten.

I always thought Barry was a decent bloke. That comment changed my opinion at the time, though he probably thought he was being funny. All is forgiven now!

* * *

Micky Holmes (Wolves)

I first met Jon when I signed for Wolves, I didn't know anyone at first and straight away he made me feel at home. He's one of the nicest, most genuine people I've ever met as he would do anything for anyone and he has a great, very dry sense of humour. As for football he was one of the most talented players I've ever seen and believe me I've played with some great players. It's a pleasure knowing Jon and his mum and dad, they should be proud of a great, funny guy and I'm proud to say that he's one of my closest friends, top man Jon.

Player profile picture with Wolves.

CHAPTER NINE

The Cambridge Diet

Af005fter the Man City experience it soon became obvious that I wasn't going to be in Graham Turner's plans as a first eleven player. I was finding myself with splinters off the bench more often than not and sometimes getting the weekend off without splinters at all. I found this quite difficult to accept after two seasons of playing regularly but there was nothing I could do. I soon got fed up of playing in the reserves and as luck had it Cambridge United came to Molineux for a game and Roy Johnson was their physio who was at Arsenal with me. We had a chat and he asked if I'd be interested in going there on loan, to be honest I just wanted to play so said yes without realising quite how far away it was! I had recently turned down a loan move to Stockport County which I regret now because I would have had the opportunity to play with Frank Worthington and, even better, maybe had a few nights out with him! I saw Frank one night in Eves with his wife at the time, the ex-model Carol Dwyer, who was from Wolverhampton. Frank was ageing but he still had a swagger about him and I was in complete awe! It's very sad that Frank has recently passed away after a battle with dementia.

Anyway, I set off for Cambridge in my VW Polo and about 5 hours later I finally got there! I met Chris Turner the manager for a chat and he put me up for the night and he seemed ok with a dry sense of humour – sadly he's no longer with us. The next morning we went off to training and I met up with the lads including Gary Poole who I knew from my Arsenal days, Ian Benjamin who became a travelling companion, Peter Butler who went on to play for Albion, and a surly character called John Beck. Becky had been a good player but was coming to the end of his playing days and was now player coach, this wasn't a problem until one rainy, cold winter's day…

After being at Cambridge for a few weeks, the travelling backwards and forwards to see Julie was starting to get me down and I knew being at the club wasn't going to be for the long term so was beginning to loathe going back there. This particular morning we were training on a crap school pitch and one of the goalmouths had a massive puddle from the six yard box to the penalty spot. Becky was standing at the side of the goal throwing balls insisting that the lads dive full length to head the ball and then land head first in the puddle! I couldn't believe my eyes when all the lads were doing it! I kept hiding at the back of the group until he clocked me and said I had to do it, but when my turn came I just stepped back and volleyed the ball into the net – this happened about three times and I knew he was getting more and more annoyed with me! I couldn't see the point in this drill and wasn't going to do it – full stop. He finally said if you don't do it the next time you can f*** off! The next time he threw the ball I stepped back and volleyed it about 60 yards over his head and said "I'm going to f*** off now!" I went back to the ground, had a shower, went back to my digs to pack my bag and never went back!

As luck would have it, the next time I saw John Beck I was playing for Kidderminster and he was manager of Preston when we met in the 4th round of the FA Cup. Our manager Graham Allner had been to watch them and made us very aware of his liking for a very direct style of football. I thought Graham Turner's liking for percentage football was bad enough but Preston were on another level, their players, including David Moyes, were complete robots, playing to order and trying to get the ball into our box as quickly and directly as possible. Allner had let them see our pitch the day before which was a bit dry and cut up and would suit there style, however as soon as they left he had the pitch saturated and made it more to our liking of playing football on the grass! Anyway I had a good game and set up the winner for Delwyn Humphries to put us into the 5th round – quite a feat for a non-league team. I know a lot of players would have milked it by celebrating in front of John Beck but that's not my style and I just carried on as normal, quietly satisfied.

This meant I was back at Molineux, not really wanted and very much a squad player who was also cup tied for the Sherpa Van Trophy! I knew my days were numbered and there's not a lot you can say when the team are top of the league led by the free-scoring Steve Bull.

CHAPTER TEN
_____

Deadline Day (March '87)

Having accepted my fate of leaving Wolves at the end of the season I wanted to try and get a move before the deadline and went into see Graham Turner to ask for a transfer. He wasn't going to stand in my way but also wasn't going to go out of his way to help me as I think he found me a useful squad member who could play a bit if needed. I spoke to my old manager Sammy Chapman and we came to a financial agreement if he managed to secure me a move! Sammy called a few people and after a couple of days he told me that Harry Redknapp at Bournemouth was keen on me. I'd played well a couple of times against Bournemouth the previous season when Sammy was manager. After a few days I got told to stay by the phone as a fee had been agreed! I waited all day, speaking to Sammy throughout who was acting as a middle man, but it all led to nothing. Apparently Redknapp was trying to get a player out to free the budget to bring me in and whoever that player was decided against the move. Who knows what may have happened if I'd got a new lease of life on the south coast under Harry Redknapp!

Once this opportunity passed and I knew I was at Wolves until the end of the season I decided to just enjoy the last few months of my time there. I tried to stay cheerful and be there if needed, which I was a few times. At the time the background staff had been thinned out, with their hours cut back etc, so there was no one to run the players' bar and we were told it was being closed. So I asked the secretary Keith Pearson if I could try and run the bar for the lads and he had no objections.

Training on a Friday was generally a short session of 10 a side on the north bank car park which has become legendary but started off because we had nowhere to train! We regularly had to bounce cars out of the way so we could set up a pitch and often shoppers would come back confused as their cars had been moved somehow! This helped with the strong bond that was running through the squad and obviously confidence grows when you're winning games and it just kept growing for a couple of years. I'm not sure how much this has helped all our knees and ankles though!

After the lads had gone home after training I would go to Blakemore's cash and carry and buy cans of Kestrel lager and Banks's bitter, with a few bottles of wine and pop, to make sure both teams and their families were able to enjoy an hour or two after the match, this also helped with the team spirit I believe. I would serve behind the bar helped by the likes of John 'Foz' Hendley who was Mr Wolves (he has since sadly passed away) and a few of the lads would also help occasionally. The small profit made would pay for a behind closed doors Christmas do at Rockies which paid for the beer and a couple of strippers into the bargain! I also had the odd drink out of it too which I think was well deserved.

For the rest of the season, it was at least a pleasure to watch Bully in full flow – knocking anything in his way over to get his shots at goal! The celebrations when we finally won the league were memorable and although I had made a small contribution I was well aware that I hadn't played enough to warrant a medal. Even worse was that the squad for the Sherpa Van final went away to Spain for a week of relaxation which I understand was good fun but I was left behind with all the rest of the dead wood! When the final came around a few of us that weren't involved in the squad for the game travelled down on a bus with all the lads' wives and girlfriends, and although I was with Julie – I took it upon myself to make sure everyone had a great day and there was lots of fizz enjoyed on the way to Wembley! The lads did the business and won the trophy and a big night was had at the hotel afterwards – even Mr Turner let his hair down so he was human after all!

At this point I had no idea where my next penny was coming from but Ally Rob reassured me that I would be ok, he had been sounded out by somebody but I didn't know who and he felt obliged not to say at that point…

Player profile pic for Oxford United.

CHAPTER ELEVEN

The Oxford Blues

So during the summer of 1988 I found myself without a club again and my contract at Wolves expired at the end of June, I had a mortgage and bills like everyone else and had no idea if I was going to get a club, and where I may have to relocate to! You can't help but get down and I was struggling to cope with this insecurity and felt like a complete failure. I loved being at Wolves and was very happy living there but I knew it was very unlikely that I wouldn't have to relocate to seek employment. This side of the game is overlooked by most who view the game as a glamorous profession, don't get me wrong, I know it's not grafting for 12 hours a day for a living – I'm just making the point that it's not all a bed of roses.

This situation also put a strain on my relationship with Julie and we ended up splitting up for a period, probably because I was a miserable git and really unsure of my future.

I did speak to Ally Rob a couple of times and he reassured me that I would be ok but still wouldn't commit to how! I since know he spoke to Ron Atkinson at Aston Villa telling him to have a look at me but unfortunately nothing came of that, normally in that situation the manager will speak to other managers that are their friends – and generally they take their word as gospel – so someone probably scared him off me! I have to admit – in the last few months at Wolves when I knew I wasn't going to play I was going out more and more as I couldn't see the point in living like a monk for the occasional reserve game and this probably didn't help any reference I was going to get!

At this time there were no mobile phones so I had an answerphone installed to ensure if any club called they could leave a message. After a few weeks of silence I came home one afternoon and noticed the answerphone flashing and I had received two messages! The first one was from Steve Coppell at Crystal Palace asking me to call him back – and the second was from Mark Lawrenson at Oxford United, both of these clubs were in the old second division, which was a league higher than Wolves had just been promoted to.

Now Steve Coppell was one of my heroes as a boy when I supported Man Utd, I remember crying my eyes out when Bobby Stokes scored the winner against them in the 1976 FA Cup final and then being on top of the world the following year when Utd beat Liverpool to lift the trophy. So to say I was nervous calling him back was an understatement and when I got through to him he was an absolute gentleman. He told me he wanted me to go to Palace because he thought I was a good player and that he could get me back on track. I was offered a 1 year deal on £250 a week plus appearance and bonuses, which was £50 more than I was on at Wolves, although I would have to pay London prices and live back in the smoke. Wow – Steve Coppell thought I was a good player! I thanked him and told him I would come back to him quickly but that I had a couple of other clubs to talk to, although there was only one!

I called Oxford back too and got put through to Brian Horton who was Mark Lawrenson's assistant. He was keen on me having watched me play a few times when he was manager of Hull City. I'm pretty sure he made an enquiry at the time which led to Sammy putting the 1 million pound fee on my head – even though I was only earning £150 basic wage at the time! He said he knew me and wanted me to sign for three months on £250 a week and we'd see how it goes. I told him I had already been offered a twelve month deal at Palace so wouldn't be taking a three month offer! He said he would see what he could do and called me back the next day, as promised, and offered a twelve month deal. That's how it worked in football then, they would try and get you for as little as possible and you had to try and get the best deal you could – this was before agents so you were on your own to look after yourself.

To be honest I was still gutted about leaving Wolves and didn't really want to sign for either club. However, needs must and I chose Oxford because it was nearer to Wolverhampton where I could get back to see Julie whenever possible, although I wasn't sure she wanted to see me! In hindsight, I should have made the decision for football reasons but I didn't want to live in London, it's just not for me, and the cost of living also played a factor.

I travelled to Oxford the day before pre-season and was taken to a lovely house owned by Robert Maxwell, complete with a housekeeper to cook meals and do all the cleaning. I was joined by the other new signings that summer Paul Simpson from Man City, Phillip Heath from Stoke, Jimmy Phillips from Bolton and Mickey Lewis from West Brom. As you can imagine we all hit it off pretty quickly. We were all in the same boat and we had some good laughs together as lads and also together with our girlfriends.

Having started to make amends, I persuaded Julie to come and stay with me for the weekend in this fabulous house. Unbeknownst to her, she left that weekend with a car boot full of top quality towels and bedding from the linen cupboard which served us well for a long number of years afterwards!

I eventually moved in with Mickey Lewis at his house in Banbury for a short period and discovered I'd found another drinking partner! I was really sad to hear the recent news that Mickey had passed away from Lung Cancer at the age of 56 after a very short illness.

Although I had a 12 month contract I did feel very much on trial and was below Paul Simpson and Phil Heath in the pecking order as they had been bought from Man City and Stoke City for transfer fees. The reality in football is that if a manager buys a player he's always going to try and justify the investment by playing them. It's understandable but not always fair if, like I was, you're signed on a free transfer. I was generally a sub but started getting a few starts on either wing and remember Dean Saunders saying to me in the bath after a victory in a local derby against Swindon, "you can play a bit can't you Purds?" A backhanded compliment if ever there was one.

Dean was a chirpy, confident lad and there were lots of rumours about him getting a big move somewhere and I think he knew he would be moving on. He was quick and skilful, with an eye for goal and went on to have a great career as a player, not so much as a manager with Wolves when he was disastrous!

I was still in and out of the team but had a good little run playing well against Portsmouth away – their supporters were fantastic and never stopped singing, and then against Chelsea at a dilapidated Stamford Bridge where I had a blinder against Steve Clarke who had a long and successful career and is currently the Scotland manager – also playing that day was Graham Roberts and Gordon Durie. Things were looking good, and then disaster struck – Dean Saunders was transferred to Derby County without any money changing hands by Robert Maxwell who was also the Derby Chairman. Unsurprisingly this led to Mark Lawrenson resigning as the deal was done without his knowledge. Not only had he lost his best striker but he had no money in return to buy a replacement! His assistant – Brian 'Nobby' Horton was given the job!

I think I had begun to get on Lawrenson's good side. He had started selecting me to start and I was never out of the squad, he liked to play good football, as you would imagine from his background at Liverpool, and I felt happy working for him. I'm not sure what age he was then but he could also still play a bit! During one training session we played a full scale practice match. He played right back and I was in front of him on the right wing, all was going well and we were linking up swimmingly until he received the ball across the pitch from our centre half. The opposition left winger was blocking the direct pass to me so I thought he could only play it up to our centre forward. I turned and set off to support the front man when, to my surprise, Lawrenson bent a pass with the outside of his right foot to where I had been stood just a second before and the ball went out for a throw! He looked at me as if I'd never played the game before and I could only say "sorry, no one's ever done that before!" He had played at a different level to all the full-backs I'd played with before or would play with ever again!

So Lawro had gone and we were left with the raving lunatic that was Nobby Horton! He fitted all the stereotypical, eye-bulging, teacup-kicking managers that were standard practice in those days. From wanting me to sign as a skilful, touch player, he now wanted me to change into a grafting, aggressive player, which just wasn't me. I lost count of the amount of times he told me to be more like Steve Bull and that wasn't ever going to happen! I just used to say "I'm not Bully Nobby, why don't you sign him!?"

Bully was great but we were complete opposites. I couldn't do what he did and equally he couldn't manipulate the ball like I could. As much as I would have liked to have had that aggression and desire, I just didn't. I accept that's probably one of the reasons I didn't do as well as I should have in my career.

So I found myself yet again playing in the reserves and training with the kids – boy did I hate this game! I played well in the reserves forming a good strike partnership with Dave Leworthy who had signed from Spurs but he didn't see eye to eye with Nobby either. Dave was a great lad originally from Portsmouth and he wasn't slow to give an opinion, which I liked but most managers don't want to hear a contrary opinion to their own.

During that period we were drawn against Man Utd away in the fourth round of the FA cup, which I didn't get over excited about as I wasn't really involved in Nobby's plans. We played a full scale first team versus reserves on the Thursday before this cup game and, as was normal, the reserve team including me were winning (I think motivation is the key factor for this). Nobby was getting increasingly agitated at his underperforming team. I was playing well and the first team back four were struggling to cope with me dropping into the hole and Dave Leworthy getting in behind their back four. He kept halting the game to coach them to attempt to stop us, but they couldn't and we were loving it – and Dave was taking the mickey a bit! Then fate struck. Martin Foyle who was the first choice striker had to go off with a cricked neck. Nobby put Dave into the first team line up and Dave reluctantly put their colour bib on. It wasn't long before Nobby had a go at Dave for not trying as hard as he was in the reserve team and Dave exploded telling him he didn't want to play for him and to stick his first team up his arse! Dave proceeded to storm off back to the club which promptly ended the training session! It was only when we were all having a bite to eat back at the ground that the lads started telling me I could be playing on the Saturday at Old Trafford. I didn't take this seriously to start with but it slowly dawned on me that he hadn't really got anyone else to play up front if Martin Foyle wasn't fit. They gave Foyley as much time as possible to recover but by lunchtime on the Saturday he had ruled himself out and I was in. Crikey! The nerves started kicking in and before I knew it I was walking out in front of a packed Old Trafford nervous as a kitten!

The Manchester United team that day included Bryan Robson, Gordon Strachan, Mark Hughes, Brian Mclair, Remi Moses, Steve Bruce and Paul McGrath, and I was playing up front on my own against the last two! They were a joy to watch and that's about all I did because very rarely did we get the ball, and when we did they swiftly took it back off us! The first time the ball was played into my feet I controlled it and looked up for some support which wasn't too quick in coming and before I could blink Bryan Robson had cut me in half whilst taking the ball cleanly off me – "you'll have to be quicker than that son". The next time I had a ball played down the channel between Lee Martin and Paul McGrath and I was one on one with McGrath, I feinted to cross it and tried to nutmeg him but he clearly read my intentions and took it off me like a sweet from a baby!

The rest of my afternoon was spent watching Bruce and McGrath take the ball down on their chest and play majestically out from the back while I chased between them hopelessly. We lost 4-0, I was subbed and I think that was the last game of my Oxford career! I always vowed if I got another big game like that I wouldn't freeze again but I guess I was just overawed. After this game I was put back in the deep freeze with the reserves and was training back with the kids. I hated every second of being there.

The only real highlight of my time at Oxford was the fancy dress Christmas do which started at a hotel at lunchtime and ended up in the early hours around the streets of Oxford. I was a fluffy pink elephant which was fine until I was in a nightclub sweating profusely. Mickey Lewis was a fairy, which was hilarious as Mickey was about 5 feet 4 inches and 13 stone! Everyone took part and we all went out together for the day and night. At some point though a few of the lads went over the top and decided to run along the top of a row of parked cars for some reason, the headline in the paper the next day was 'The Police are looking for a Red Indian, a Cowboy and a Fairy to help with their enquiries'!

During that season a very large scary bloke turned up for training by the name of Billy Whitehurst who was training with us for a few days while sorting out the sale of his house having recently left the club. If you've ever seen the film Kes you will get the picture, nobody would go near him during 5 a side. He scored about 10 and believed it was genuine, but we were all just scared to death to tackle him! Another intimidating figure at Oxford was Gary Briggs who was an old school centre half that would head and kick anything that moved near him and occasionally the ball would be involved! If a ball was played up to a centre forward and Gary couldn't head the ball he just used to head the back of the centre forward's head so the ball would get cleared!

Eventually I got called into Nobby's office and he said that Steve Perryman at Brentford wanted to take me on loan and asked if I wanted to go. To be honest I would have gone to the Outer Hebrides to get away from Nobby!

CHAPTER TWELVE

Not the Bees Knees

I travelled to South London to speak to Steve Perryman and I was impressed with his manner and enthusiasm for the game. This was confirmed when he took the first training session – everything we did involved a football but he made it interesting as well as hard work.

I think a good football coach should be able to make a training session enjoyable as well as getting tactical messages across. Too many coaches hammer home one message for two hours believing it will sink in when in reality most players switch off with tedium after about 30 minutes. In my view, the best way is to alternate between the message you're trying to impose with some ball work, fitness work or whatever, but don't bore players to death!

Steve was in the team when I went to watch Glenn Hoddle at Spurs so he commanded immediate respect from me and he deserved it anyway with his humility and professionalism. John Gorman was on the coaching staff at the time and he was also a good, bubbly football coach.

I had first met John when I was with Arsenal and he was youth coach at Spurs. We, along with the Chelsea and West Ham, apprentices went on an outward bounds weekend in the Brecon Beacons for team bonding. I viewed this as a welcome release from the ultra-competitive life as a young footballer but John was using it to judge our characters. I've never been the quickest walker and regularly get overtaken by grannies doing their shopping so I was always at the back during any hikes or mountaineering exercises. John pulled me for a chat questioning my motivation, which was fair comment, but once he realised how easy going I am we formed a mutual respect and got on well. He went on to become assistant manager for England with Glenn Hoddle so I guess he had more drive than me!

As impressive as Steve Perryman was for Brentford, it was a different story off the pitch at the club. I was told that I would be staying in an apartment which was part of the club and was adjacent to the ground. This sounded ok until I got there and walked into an apartment which could have been nice but was full of Chinese takeaway cartons and about three weeks' worth of washing up! I hadn't been told I would be sharing with a rare individual called Andy Feeley or 'Chisel' as he was affectionately known – I don't know the reason for his nickname but I could take a good guess! Chisel had played for Leicester previously and was the wildest person I had ever come across. He had tattoos on his arms and legs before they were trendy and was built like an ox.

I knew I was running out of time to progress my football career and had signed with Brentford to try and get back on track and make a good impression to secure a contract for the following season. However, Chisel was having none of this and as soon as I walked in the door he told me we were going out to get to know each other. He took me around all the pubs introducing me to all the local pub dwellers, many of whom were Brentford fans but he couldn't have cared less. We ended up back in the apartment when the pub closed adding to the washing up and Chinese takeaway rubbish!

Chisel took a shine to me and I would definitely rather have him on my side than against me, but to be honest I was scared to death of him! On one occasion he wanted to borrow my car (a Vauxhall Nova Saloon no less) to go back to Leicester to sort something out and I agreed as I couldn't work the courage up to say no! I knew he wasn't insured and I doubt he had a licence either so I was a little concerned about my Nobby the Nova! I explained this to one of the lads in the pub and he showed me a way to disconnect a lead in the engine which would stop the car from starting, so when Chisel was fast asleep the night before he was going I crept out and did my mechanic impression to foil his plans. Unfortunately I'm a big softie and felt guilty about doing it, so after a couple of sleepless hours I went back to the car and fixed it! He left early the next morning and thankfully came back a couple of days later with the car in one piece.

A few of us went out one night including Tony Parks, the ex-Tottenham keeper, and John Buttigige, the Malta captain. Parksy was another loose cannon and after a couple of shandies he would get a bit lairy, gobbing off and offering all and sundry out for a fight. Just what you want on a night out – not! I never saw him actually have a fight so think it was probably all macho bravado, but Chisel was a different story. I remember one night we had just walked into a club and ordered our first drink when Chisel ordered me to follow him and just said "watch my back". Oh god, what have I got myself into here? He followed this man-mountain of a skinhead into the toilets, got right behind him and tapped him on the shoulder. This lad was about to say something when Chisel nutted him and then kept hitting him until he collapsed to the floor – Chisel just winked at me and said 'let's go!' He walked straight out the club and I went and rounded the lads up to get out quick! John Buttigige tried to complain that we'd just arrived but I explained what had happened and you've never seen anyone move so fast to escape in your life! I don't think John was used to this behaviour in sunny Malta!

Other lads who were at the club at the time were Andy Ansah, who was a lively, sharp striker and has gone on to do well working on the other side of the camera on Dream Team among countless other projects; Keith Millen, a classy centre-half who has gone on to carve a long career at Crystal Palace; and Keith Jones, who was an ex-Chelsea midfield player who I'd come across countless times in youth and reserve football at Arsenal. Unfortunately on the pitch I suffered a foot injury kicking the underside of someone's boot and looking back I think I broke a metatarsal before we knew they existed! It was murder and Steve Perryman let me go back to Wolverhampton to recover as there wasn't really any treatment that could help my foot. I did manage to get back for the end of the season but I'd lost my fitness through lack of activity. I played against Wolves at the Molineux but my heart wasn't in it and I felt like I had the wrong coloured shirt on!

I met Steve Perryman at the end of the season and we had a chat from the stand overlooking the Griffin Park pitch and it was the nicest release I ever experienced. He knew I didn't want to live in London and I hadn't done enough for him to try and convince me otherwise. He said that I had been born 20 years too late as the game had changed from an attacking, skilful style of football to hard-working, functional play. We shook hands and parted very amicably. It was a nice way of parting company but the reality was that I was back on the scrapheap!

CHAPTER THIRTEEN

Taming of the Shrew, Not!

So here I was again, at another crossroads waiting to see if I was going to be offered any work. I had a call from Ian Evans who was the manager of Swansea City and was a former Crystal Palace and Wales player. I agreed to meet him halfway at Gordano services on the M5 where he offered me a one year deal on £250 a week plus the usual appearance and bonuses. The problem was it took me two hours to get to Gordano and if that was halfway I didn't really fancy it!

Fortunately I had played well for Oxford against Shrewsbury in a 5-1 win and their manager Ian McNeill, the old Chelsea manager, had remembered me and soon got in touch to offer me the same deal as Swansea. This was attractive to me as I could commute from Wolverhampton within half an hour and not spend hours on the motorway. When I was at Brentford I would often leave Julie at 4 in the morning to get to London at 6 to then try and grab another couple of hour's kip, which was hardly ideal preparation for training as a professional footballer. Another Wolverhampton lad, Richard Green, was also at Shrewsbury and we shared the driving which was ideal. Rich was a good player and we became drinking partners as well as travelling companions for a while. He also liked to try and nutmeg people in training and was quick to take the mickey when successful, but when I megged him on one occasion he didn't like it and forearm smashed me in the face to stop me going around him. I kicked him square in the balls and we were quickly split up. After an awkward half hour we went for a beer and had a laugh about it!

Another Wolverhampton-based lad joined us a bit later in the season called Kim Wassell who had carved a life for himself in Finland but came back during their mid-season break. I first met Kim when he came on trial at Wolves while I was there and he seemed a decent lad. He was at WBA as a young player and knew lads like Derek Statham and Cyrille Regis. When he got released from Albion he went on trial somewhere down south and after that mysteriously spoke with a cockney accent! We kept in touch and when he came back from Finland he would always visit for a catch up and a drink. Eventually this petered out and it came as a real shock when I picked up the local paper some years later to see him on a murder charge. I haven't seen or heard from him for many years now.

I was doing quite well during pre-season for Shrewsbury, but the club had a few wide players already and I could see they were struggling for central midfield players so I thought I would offer to play there. Soon enough I cemented my place in the team alongside Dougie Bell which worked out quite well. I actually received the biggest football compliment of my life during that period when Ian McNeill said I reminded him of Bobby Charlton! Perhaps Mr McNeill was partial to a tipple like his players!

Mr McNeill obviously had strong contacts in Scotland as there were quite a few Scottish lads at the club – maybe too many to be honest as they were wild! On my first day at Shrewsbury, there was a lad strutting about called Victor Kasule. He was the first black man I'd ever heard with a strong Glaswegian accent and from all accounts he was a bit of a hell raiser around town. Mr Mcneill had got fed up with his antics and I soon found out was trying to transfer him out. Other lads there were John McGinley and Steve Pitmen who were like the Kray Twins, taking the mickey out of everyone to try and get a reaction – they were both drinkers and often turned up for training worse for wear. John obviously knew were the net was and went on to do well for Bolton. Steve eventually disappeared back to Scotland after one too many episodes like Kasule.

Another Scottish player at the club was David Moyes who was part of the same Celtic batch that produced Charlie Nicholas and Danny Crainie. He was different from the other Scottish lads and took his career very seriously often doing extra training and doing sit ups etc. He was a nice enough lad but was obviously very driven and seemed to have a settled family life unlike most of us. If he wasn't happy his eyes would bulge and he was quick to let you know. He could train all day and all night but he was never going to be the best kicker of a ball and was just a reasonably effective stopper as a centre half. Moyes is another classic example of attitude winning out over ability and I'm sure this attitude is why he has gone on to have a successful career as a manager – and good luck to him. I came up against him a few years later in the FA cup when he was at Preston and I was with Kidderminster. We beat them 1-0 and he was very courteous in defeat.

Probably the best player I ever played with technically was Dougie Bell who had played for Aberdeen and Glasgow Rangers. He literally seemed like the ball was glued to his feet and in training he was unbelievable – his only problem was he wanted a ball to himself and was reluctant to let it go unless he had no choice. He was definitely better suited to small sided games than 11 a side but I have to say he was brilliant at times.

During that season I played against Brentford which featured many of the lads I had played with during the previous season, including Keith Jones who, at the time, I thought of as a pal. Anyway, during that game, we were getting the better of them in midfield and as I skipped past Keith he grabbed me giving away a free kick around the halfway line. I went to put my hand on the ball to take it quickly when Keith spat in my face. I have always thought that spitting is the lowest of the low and reacted by doing something quite out of character, punching him in the face! Straight red for me for the first time in my career! I remember sitting in the dressing room fuming, wishing that I'd hit him harder when I heard a rumpus and then saw him coming down the tunnel – he'd got himself sent off perhaps through guilt of spitting!

I received a three match ban and although Mr McNeill wasn't happy, I think he kind of understood why I did it. I was a bit annoyed because I had been playing well and was now a regular in the team. I vowed to keep fit and be ready for when my ban was over. However, as part of this effort to keep match fit I agreed to play in a friendly game with some pals but this turned out to be an error of judgement as an over enthusiastic opponent caught me late and I hurt my ankle ligaments, which put me out for another month. I had to tell Ian McNeill that I went for a run and went over on my ankle, he didn't believe me and suggested I had done it playing on a Sunday morning, which obviously wasn't true but he said I'd be in real trouble if he found out that I had!

Unfortunately, the physio at Shrewsbury was an ex-boxer and my recovery involved five weeks spent in the gym. By the time my ankle had recovered, I looked more like Mike Tyson than a footballer. I felt muscle-bound and uncomfortable in my own body and I truly believe this over-conditioning affected my performances detrimentally after that and then Mr McNeill left as well, so it was downhill from there.

Asa Hartford was the player coach then and was still very fit even though he was about 39, he was obviously trying to keep playing as long as he could which meant he very often took us for runs alongside the river after training. He played at left back then as he could still play but his legs had gone a little. He would get changed with us in the dressing room but obviously had a bit of distance as he was the coach, not that anyone worried too much as he wasn't the manager. The morning after the Christmas do that year, one of the lads stripped off to get changed into his training kit to reveal a pair of French knickers from the previous evening's conquest, judging by the knickers she must have been quite a large lady to say the least. Everyone thought it was hilarious but Asa wasn't amused and proceeded to run us all into the ground despite us all feeling worse for wear. He obviously formed his own opinions about us, and shortly after Christmas Ian McNeill was sacked. Lo and behold Asa was given the job. I'm not certain but I have a feeling he had taken it personally when I didn't sign for him on loan at Stockport from Wolves and it soon became apparent I was surplus to requirements yet again!

After a few weeks of suffering I was told that Cheltenham wanted to sign me and I went to meet their manager Jim Barron who I'd met when he did some coaching at Wolves. The slippery slope continued.

CHAPTER FOURTEEN

Non League Cheltenham Festival

So I set off on the journey to Cheltenham to sign for them having agreed to take a £25 per week drop in wages to play semi-professionally and start looking for another "proper job". I was due to get married in the summer of '91 and had to prove to my future wife that I could make a success of life without football being my main income.

At this time, I honestly didn't want to play football any more as I had become so disillusioned with the whole business, but I had a mortgage to pay so agreed to travel the 180 minute round trip to Cheltenham three times a week. I arrived to meet Jim Barron on a Friday morning where I quickly signed the contract and passed a medical which amounted to touching my toes! Shortly after I concluded the necessary paperwork, a loud Scottish voice could be heard coming towards the office and in came Andy Gray – the ex-Aston Villa, Wolves and Scotland international. Jim introduced us and when he found out that I played wide, he said "well let's go see if you can cross a ball". So we went out onto the Whaddon Road pitch and I crossed balls for him for over an hour with both feet from different angles for him to practise his finishing and in particular his heading, which everyone who knows football acknowledges was exceptional. I did feel a little pressure when we first started but soon realised he was happy with the standard of my crossing.

At the end, he gave me a pat on the back and said "great quality kid". Unfortunately Andy didn't hang around long as he got an offer to become the main football pundit on the newly-launched Sky Sports TV channel, which I think he excelled at until he and Richard Keys were fired for alleged sexist remarks, so I only played a couple of games with him.

The Cheltenham team were full of lads in their 30s who had been around at conference level for a while and knew each other quite well. It's always a test for a new player to gel at a new club, but at 21 I had already experienced it a few times and being a bit of a joker I was quickly accepted with the lads. We were an average team at that level and a few of the lads were coming to the end of their days but had enough know-how and quality to survive in the league.

Personally I was trying to get match fit and needed a run of games to get there after a spell on the side-lines at Shrewsbury. Unfortunately Jim Barron didn't see this and kept substituting me with 20, 15 or 10 minutes to go. After a few weeks I had to do a player profile for the match programme, I didn't take it too seriously and decided to vent my discontent through this public vehicle. In hindsight, this wasn't too clever but I wasn't looking to stay there long term anyway. One of the questions was 'What's your biggest ambition in football?' I replied, 'to complete 90 minutes for Cheltenham Town'. This was one of about twenty questions which were answered this way, the lads all thought it was hilarious but I don't think Mr Barron saw the funny side. Jim Barron was a proper old school football manager, which included spending more time in front of the mirror than anyone I've ever known. The saying 'if he was made of chocolate he would eat himself' was made for him. I don't really like people who are that image conscious and I'm not very good at hiding it.

My short period at Cheltenham was concluded with a very long bus journey. We had played Darlington away who were winning the league and needed to beat us to secure the title, which they duly did. This was one of the last games of the season and as I wasn't named in the team or as sub I knew the writing was on the wall. The group of older lads decided that we were going to have a good drink on the way back, playing cards and having a laugh and a sing song. This kind of thing is generally accepted if you win, but normally frowned upon when the team loses but the boys knew it was probably going to be one of their last trips together and wanted to enjoy each other's company on the 5 hour bus trip home. I was glad to join them and we enjoyed the trip immensely. We had stocked up well but it was becoming apparent around the Manchester area that we were going to run out of booze in the next hour, so I came to the rescue! I called Julie, and asked her to pick up a few bottles of quality wine – these lads were quite refined drinking good wine – as well as a few beers for them as I was getting off earlier near Wolverhampton. So I nipped off the bus and brought the new supplies on for the lads to be met with daggers by Jim Barron! He said "see you on Monday for the reserve game at Bishops Cleeve" I replied "I don't think so! All the best gaffer!" and off I went thinking that would be the end of my playing days at Cheltenham Town.

CHAPTER FIFTEEN

Worcester Sorcery

So that's it, I thought, no more football for me. Eight years after playing for England Schoolboys at Wembley I'd had enough. Enough rejection, enough character testing, enough being treated like a piece of meat. I just wanted a normal life, to be able to earn a living and settle down.

Julie and I got married on June 8, 1991 and it was a perfect day. Julie was beautiful and we were ready to spend our lives together. The wedding was a very plush affair at Patshull Park Hotel despite there were being many people I didn't know, unfortunately invited by my father-in-law. To give you an idea, I was visiting the toilet and the chap next to me asked if I was on the bride or groom's side! I just said "the groom's" and went back to the party! The highlight of the wedding (apart from getting married!) – was when my two musical uncles, Donald Gracie (who sadly passed away in 2018) and Bill Clark, sent the classical pianist off to the bar with a few quid and started playing and singing together. It was brilliant, and took me back to my early days in Corby when the family would watch Big Don and wee Billy Clark entertaining everyone in the working men's clubs around Corby. Needless to say the party continued into the early hours, although the aforementioned father-in-law thought it was a good idea to book Julie and me into a separate hotel so we had to leave early! I have never been one for leaving a party early and a lot of people had made an effort to come and see us, so to say I was unhappy is an understatement.

Within a couple of days we flew off to St. Lucia on a perfect honeymoon and I started to think seriously about how I was going to make a living. Upon my return I had a few calls from clubs, but I wasn't interested. I had really lost the love of the game and didn't want to go through it again. I started applying for sales jobs as I thought I could make a decent living and business people I knew thought I could be successful. However, I hadn't banked on it being so difficult to get a position – generally because I had no experience, but I also got the feeling that people believed I would go back into football, despite me insisting I wasn't going to. Then I got a call from my old pal Ally Robertson. As is the way in football, when you leave a club very few people keep in touch as everyone just gets on with their own lives despite being best pals for whatever length of time. So I hadn't heard from him for a couple of years and I was wondering what he was calling for. After a few minutes of small talk he said "right laddie", in his gentle Scottish accent, "I've just got the manager's job at Worcester City and you're going to come and help me". "I'm not!" I insisted and told him I didn't want to play anymore. I was adamant and eventually he went away, but asked me to think about it and he'd call back in a week. I spoke to Julie in the evening over a bottle of wine and she said that Ally would look after me if anyone would and also mentioned that the money would be useful too as I still hadn't got any work. So I went to bed in a confused state. I knew Ally well, he knew my strengths and weaknesses (such as defending!) and I liked him as a person. So I gave him a call and said I would go to pre-season and see how things went, and he was happy enough with that.

Within a few days I also got offered two jobs on the same day. Why is life like that? Nothing for ages, and then a decision to make. One was as a photocopier salesman for a local company run by someone I knew socially but he was a bit of a wide boy to say the least. The other was from a telecommunications company based near Burton-upon-Trent. Although Burton was 45 minutes away, I just had a feeling that it was right for me and I plumped for that. So within a week I had gone from no income to having a good sales job and a new start with an old pal at Worcester City.

Having been out running every day for a couple of weeks beforehand, I duly reported for pre-season training. Around the same time I began my new career as a telephone system salesman. This meant that for two evenings a week I would leave the house at 7.30am to get to work, get home from work at 6pm for a quick sandwich before driving to Worcester for training at 7pm, and then finally arrive home after 10pm. These were long, tiring days for me as I had been very spoilt – generally training from 10am and being finished at 1pm – but both new jobs were going well.

Ally had pulled together some good players with a mix of youth and experience, including Martyn Bennett whose back injury had forced him to retire from full-time football with West Brom; Andy Dornan who was at Walsall and Motherwell; Mark Gayle who went on to play for Walsall, Crewe and had a spell with Liverpool; and Des Little who bounced back from rejection at Wolves to make a good career for himself at Forest and West Brom. In addition to this we also had some very good non-league players like Steve Fergusson, Paul Joinson, Jock McGrath, Ian Cotterill, Brendan Hackett and Joe Jackson.

I used to share the driving and the costs of travelling with Joe as he was also from Wolverhampton. Our relationship started with total wariness of one another to becoming good friends with a mutual respect (I hope). Joe was released from Wolves as a young professional and I think it hurt him badly and he became well known on the streets of Wolverhampton. I don't think he will mind me saying that he started mixing with the wrong crowd. I'm really happy that he turned his life around though, and now he helps kids become involved in community football and I know he is well respected around the town.

When I first met him he had a Rastafarian flag on the front of his car and when I got in the passenger seat I smiled and said pleased to meet you. I was greeted with a grunt and a death stare. Gulp, he was a little scary to be honest! Anyway, later in the season we went out into the town centre after a match with Worcester and he asked if I wanted to go to a party with him. How could I possibly refuse? So we strutted into a bar in the centre of Wolverhampton and it took about 30 seconds for me to realise I was the only white person in there. It was quite intimidating at first but being with Joe I felt comfortable enough and after a couple of beers I became a little braver. I had noticed how all the black guys fist punched each other and I thought I would give it a try. Wrong move apparently as I got an evil look from a big guy built like Mike Tyson! Thankfully Joe wasn't far away and he told the nice chap I wasn't being disrespectful but just trying to be friendly.

CHAPTER SIXTEEN

Ally's Ally

So things were going well on the pitch and due to the mixture of ex-pro's and top non-league players we were romping the league – until the wheels came off! As is often the way, we were being bankrolled by a businessman who must have been stroking his own ego as I can't think of any other reason why you would give money to a non-league football club. Apparently his business started to struggle and he basically pulled the plug on the budget. Before long Joe Jackson, Marcus Gayle and Des Lyttle had been sold, and Andy Dornan and Martyn Bennett left.

Ally started to play again occasionally as we were a little short of numbers and he wasn't having a problem until one night-game where he got caught by a stray elbow. It split his eye and made a bit of a mess of the old fox's face, he was stretchered off and taken to hospital. As a pal I went to visit him and although he was ok in himself, he didn't look too good to me and I think he knew it was time to hang his boots up. For 20 years it had been him dishing it out and generally coming out on top. The season fizzled out much to our disappointment, however our earlier good form had caught the attention of another club not so far away and Ally got offered the manager's job at… Cheltenham Town!

Cheltenham were in the Conference, which was a step up for Ally as a manager, and he asked me to join him as one of his allies. I actually wasn't too keen as my previous experience hadn't been great and Cheltenham hadn't moved any closer to

Leeds United
Association Football Club Limited
INCORPORATED 1920

GROUND AND REGISTERED OFFICE
ELLAND ROAD • LEEDS LS11 0ES
TELEPHONE: (0532) 716037, FAX: (0532) 706560
TICKET OFFICE DIRECT LINE (0532) 710710

Your Ref:

Our Ref:

Friday 5th July '91.

Dear John,

I would like to confirm that we shall expect to see you Monday 5th Aug '91 around mid day.

I would suggest a 12 day stay to 16th Aug '91 — no doubt you will be in good shape by then, our pre season games will give you the opportunity to show us what you can do. Wishing you all the best

Yours sincerely

Ian MacFarlane
Chief Scout.

President: THE RIGHT HONOURABLE THE EARL OF HAREWOOD LL.D.
Directors: LESLIE SILVER, O.B.E. (CHAIRMAN), PETER J. GILMAN (VICE-CHAIRMAN), JACK W. G. MARJASON (DEPUTY CHAIRMAN), WILLIAM J. FOTHERBY (MANAGING DIRECTOR), RAYNER BARKER M.C.I.T., M.B.I.M., MALCOLM J. BEDFORD, ERIC CARLILE, RONALD D. FELDMAN, ALEC HUDSON, G. MAXWELL HOLMES B.Sc (Econ), PETER RIDSDALE
Company Secretary: NIGEL PLEASANTS   Team Manager HOWARD WILKINSON
REGD. No. 170600 LONDON   V.A.T. No. 170 8492 50

Invitation to trial at Leeds United.

Wolverhampton! Worcester also asked me to stay and I went to a couple of pre-season training sessions with the new manager, but ultimately my loyalty and friendship with Ally made the decision obvious.

Ally attempted to overhaul the playing side by bringing a lot of young players into the squad in pre-season and also ruffled a few feathers amongst the veterans. Ally admits it now but at the time he was expecting too much commitment from semi-pro players whose main source of income was not their football so work always came first. Ally had always been a professional player and he expected professional standards of commitment, which just wasn't realistic especially from the older lads.

I had worked hard in pre-season and was in good form in some games against some league clubs and was spotted by the Leeds chief scout Ian Macfarlane, he got in touch with Ally and subsequently I was asked to go to Elland Road for a week for them to have a look at me. I thought long and hard and discussed it with Julie and together we decided this was probably my last chance to get back into professional football at the top level. I asked Ally to ensure that I was going to train and play with the first team to test myself and find out if I was good enough. At 24 I didn't want to be signed just to play in the reserves. I gave up drinking and got myself super fit, ready for this last opportunity and determined to give it my best shot.

So I packed my bags to leave for the journey to Yorkshire, leaving my family and comfortable surroundings behind for a week, or so I thought. Upon arrival I was taken to my new home for the week, which was basically a hostel for any lads from outside of town, and I got shown the top bunk bed in the barracks! This wasn't giving me a great feeling of being wanted and I started to regret the decision to try again before I'd kicked a ball. The next morning I was up bright and early looking forward to training and giving it a good go to see how it went with nothing to lose. I always remember training with Tony Adams at Arsenal, he was always in the middle in any possession sessions, demanding the ball and exuding confidence – even if he wasn't technically the best player on show he wanted to be the main man at all times. I was going to do the same as I knew I could play and was determined to show what I could do. However, when training started there was no sign of the first team and I took part in an average light-hearted session with the reserve and youth players! This wasn't what I'd bought into at all and just thought 'here we go again'. I spoke to the chap taking training and explained that I'd been promised to train with the first team and he just said that he didn't know anything but they were in training the next day! Great – another day I won't get back!

True enough, the next day the first team were in training and we all started with a warm up together with the traditional long run and static stretches that was the norm in those days. During these stretches I got chatting to Chris Whyte who I knew from Arsenal and was a lovely lad. He was asking what I was doing there and I explained that I thought I was there to train with the first team but I was beginning to doubt it. Gordon Strachan was next to Huggy Bear and he just gave me a look which told me that I was wasting my time. I had played against Strachan a couple of years earlier at Old Trafford but he didn't remember me unsurprisingly as I was pretty anonymous in that game with Oxford. We went into a couple of mixed groups of possession games and Howard Wilkinson was watching over us so I was in the thick of things showing my ability as much as possible and thought I had done well. Then it was game time and I was ready to play and try to impress but when the two teams were picked I wasn't selected and just watched the game from the side-lines. It was pretty obvious that I wasn't going to get the opportunity I was promised and as soon as the game was over I made my way back to the dressing room to get changed and go home. I spoke to John Lukic on the way back and although he was sympathetic he wasn't sure what to say. Let's be honest, he was like any other footballer and had to look after himself.

Lee Chapman was also there and he kind of acknowledged me from a distance. I once shared the tube with him on the journey home from Highbury after training and he was quite a low-key quiet character or perhaps he was having trouble adjusting to life in London like me. He was never 'one of the lads' and I never saw him out socially like all the other first team boys. Perhaps he was taking his career seriously, which paid off in the end for him. He was never the best technically or the quickest but he made the best of his ability and certainly knew where the back of the net was, which I found out to my cost not long after my Leeds trip. He struck me as quite an intelligent guy and probably could have done well in the media after his playing days but perhaps the domestic scandal with Leslie Ash put paid to that avenue.

I thought that I may as well clarify the situation and waited by the changing rooms for Howard Wilkinson with his clipboard, looking very much like the ex-school teacher I believe he was. I asked him if he knew anything about me being there and his furrowed brow gave me the answer without him trying to wriggle his way out of it. He told me that the first team squad were going abroad the next day for a pre-season tournament and he would have a look at me when they returned. I just said not to worry as I wouldn't be there. I had a shower and drove back home to lovely Wolverhampton totally disillusioned with the shambles that could be professional football. I had lost a week's wages for nothing!

So, back to the turmoil at Cheltenham! I do believe that players try their best when they cross the white line but if you don't like the manager it's human nature not to go the extra mile and I guess this resulted in a non-harmonious squad. Ultimately we ended up in a relegation battle and I think it's fair to say not many sleeves were being rolled up.

Towards the end of the season with Ally in charge we played Colchester away who were romping the Conference and we got humiliated 5-1 with Red Card Roy McDonough bullying our back four and helping himself to a couple of goals. Roy is a friend on Facebook these days and he's had some complimentary things to say about me in recent football conversations which is always nice to hear! Ultimately Ally was sacked. I think some of the older players were asked their opinion and I don't think many came down in Ally's favour. So here I go again, sign for a manager and then have another one inherit me!

At the end of the first season with Cheltenham I started really struggling with my left knee, the same one I had Osgood Schlatter's in when I was 13 and I'd also had a couple of cortisone injections in when I was at Wolves. The pain was so intense I just couldn't put my weight on it and once it was obvious that I was no good to the relegation cause, which to be honest wasn't my forte anyway, I went to see a specialist for a consultation. The consultant was Mr El Safty who lived just around the corner from Ally Rob. After visiting his palatial home in Great Barr with his private waiting room and office as part of the downstairs, I was welcomed by his very nice, professional wife and shortly went through to see Mr El Safty. After a quick look and a few tests on my knee I was sent off for a scan and after the results I was quickly booked in for an operation to clean out my knee. Unfortunately this was to be the first of nine knee operations over the next ten years, with Mr El Safty doing all of them. He said to me after about 5 "you do realise Jon, that football is not a sport it's a disease of the knee!" At the time I had complete faith in him and never doubted his ability, how could I? However after I had finished there was a big scandal when Michael Appleton sued him albeit unsuccessfully for making a mess of his knee! Makes you think, eh?

I fully expected to be fit for the following pre-season to prove my worth to Lindsay Parsons, the new manager of Cheltenham. I was fortunate in that I had acquaintances in NJB Physiotherapy in Wolverhampton and they kindly helped with my rehabilitation as best they could. However my knee just wasn't getting better and what I thought was going to take six weeks eventually took six months to recover and I wasn't ready to play until October which wasn't ideal at all. I did my work alone putting in the miles and working with weights until eventually my limp disappeared and I felt strong enough to play. I'm pretty sure the new regime had doubts about the truth of my injury due to my allegiance to Ally, but I can assure anyone I wanted to be fit to play – it just took longer than anticipated.

Anyway, I soon got an opportunity to play and when I did I was delighted when Lindsay told me "You can play Purds, can't you?" I liked Lindsay, he was honest and had a good sense of humour too. He had been a good professional player and was a coach at Bristol Rovers so had a lot of contacts with young players in the Bristol area. He was a nice guy but as is usually the case he wanted to bring in his own players. Fortunately I had the security of a 2 year contract and decent money including a good signing on fee spread over the two seasons, but ultimately this was more of a noose around my neck than a blessing and I started to get restless. Initially everything was going well and we had some good FA cup runs and I played my part in a decent team. Before a game against Gateshead away Lindsay held a team meeting and announced that he wanted to break the game into four halves – meaning four periods of play. I put my hand up and he asked what I wanted, I said "you can't four halves – it's two halves or four quarters!" He just laughed and said that I was too clever to play football!

Charlie, my first born son was born in the October of 1992, and this changed my outlook. I really hated the journey to Cheltenham and the time I was away from home. On a Saturday I often left at breakfast time and wouldn't be back until Charlie was long tucked up in bed, which wasn't fair on Julie and not the type of father I wanted to be so I became restless. Before long, one of the lads that I had got on well with told me that Graham Allner was interested in me at Kidderminster Harriers if I could get out of my contract but didn't have the money to buy me outright. So I had a meeting with the manager and the Chairman and told them I wanted to be released from my contract as I wanted to play local football near my home in Wolverhampton. I didn't mention the fact that I was moving back up to the Conference with Kiddy as there's always been a bit of rivalry between the clubs as they have competed for players over the years. Eventually they agreed to release me and the very next day I signed for Kidderminster. This resulted in a text message from the Cheltenham Chairman advising that I should avoid any future trips to Cheltenham as I may find my knees blown off. Charming!

CHAPTER SEVENTEEN

Kidderminster (Magic) Carpets

I had a couple of incognito conversations with Graham Allner – the Kidderminster Harriers manager – to ensure that financially things were going to be ok. I dropped my weekly wage but Graham agreed to take over my outstanding signing on fee. As I was moving much closer to home and joining a club with a reputation for being one of the best non-league clubs in the country I was very happy with the move.

I had spoken to a couple of lads at Cheltenham who had played for Graham – Mark Buckland who also played at Wolves just before my time and Kevin Willetts who had been around the Conference scene for a good period. Both had spoken so highly about how well run the club was in comparison to most semi-professional clubs and I soon found out that they weren't wrong. I think the key was consistency and stability, Graham had been there for a long time with the Chairman Dave Reynolds and they had a very solid relationship with mutual trust and respect in their roles and they are still friends to this day.

Off the pitch everything was laid on, training kit, tracksuits, money paid on time and regardless of results (which is rare in non-league), and there was always food on the coach at 6pm after an away game so we always had an hour in the bar before boarding the coach.

The club secretary Ray Mercer who was a lovely eccentric little chap would come to the back of the coach to take our orders on the way to the game and ensure it was all sorted for on the way home.

Before one away game he came to get the order and went around each of us asking in his nasal tone 'fish, chicken or pie?' to go with the chips from the chippy. We all had a bit of fun with him and although we knew what he was going to ask we would make him ask each of us individually, which was funny to us at the time! When he got to Kim Casey (a prolific non-league striker), Kim did an impression of a chicken by clucking and flapping his arms with elbows bent, so Ray said "ok chicken then", and Kim said "no pie please, but I can't do a pie". Hilarious!

On the pitch I certainly wasn't an instant success, I struggled to adapt to Graham's preferred formation of 4-3-3 having been used to the less flexible 4-4 2 throughout my struggling adult football life and I was dropped after a couple of particularly unconvincing performances. My initial thoughts were 'here we go again', but Graham had a chat with me and made it very clear that he hadn't signed me to do what I'd had to try to do before. On the contrary, he wanted me to save my energy and do my stuff in the attacking half only! This was like music to my ears and I was put back in the team shortly afterwards. All of a sudden we just clicked and went on an unbeaten run of around 14 games until the end of the season and played fantastic attacking football which no one could cope with at that level.

A couple of these games stand out in my memory in particular, the first one being at Woking who were also one of the top teams around at the time and this is where I somehow managed to score a hat trick which was very rare for me. The moment that particularly stood out happened just in front of our bench when I chased a ball out to the touchline and got there a yard before their full back who proceeded to try and wipe me out as I turned towards the play, fortunately I anticipated his thoughts and poked the ball between his legs as he jumped in and I hurdled over him and carried on playing while he slid off the pitch into the hoardings. There were a few young lads on the bench that day who had travelled for the experience and to help with the kit etc, and on the way home they loved telling me about the full back's face when the realisation set in that he was being made to look like a fool! I loved nutmegging players, it was and still is one of the best and cheekiest things you can do on a football pitch.

Towards the end of that season we played Kettering Town away which is ten minutes away from my home town of Corby, so a few of my old pals and my parents made the short trip to watch and to say hello afterwards. Again we played very well as a team and I remember having a good game, I was buzzing with pride afterwards and we were feeling on top of the world as a team. I took the opportunity to introduce my dad to Graham Allner and after spending a few minutes I left them to have a chat. It was only on the bus home that I found out that their conversation included Graham complimenting me to my dad, to which my dad replied "aye I thought I'd won the pools with how he can play". Graham saw the funny side of the comment but was clever enough to know there was a serious side to it.

Although there's not much I can do about it now I do feel a sense of guilt that I didn't do better with my football ability and I do wish I could have set my parents up for life which I guess very successful players can do. I'm just grateful that they have both done well and live a very nice life anyway, nowadays spending most of winter in the warmer climate of Lanzarote.

Graham Allner was not only the best manager but also the best coach I ever played under, his training was always hard work but with a purpose – normally based on pressing the opposition as early as possible in their half. This is now called 'a high press' but Graham had been preaching this for a long time before I arrived at Aggborough. He coached us to encourage the opposition to pass and then press aggressively to win the ball back as high up the pitch as possible with the whole team following the first one. Once everyone listened it worked nine times out of ten with the only concern being the occasional long ball exposing the space behind the back four. Once we were getting success from this it just became normal, we all knew what to do and it became second nature although Graham continued to keep us practising in training. He also used to insist on changing rules in training games to keep us alive mentally and test our ability, so from as many touches as you like to 3 touch, 2 touch and 1 touch games. These games make you think about where you're going to pass before you receive the ball and is really enjoyable if you have a sharp brain!

Playing for Kidderminster under Graham took me back to before I joined the professional ranks at Arsenal, he encouraged me to use my ability in the right places and gave me a certain amount of freedom within the team framework. I built a bit of a reputation and I felt great when the fans used to sing 'Purdie is a wizard' – I just loved playing the game again finally!

Many years later Graham Allner was asked to do one of those questionnaires that often fill football programmes, and one of the question asked was ' Who's the best player you have managed?' I'm very proud to say he named me and said that I could play 1 touch, 2 touch, dribble and that I should have been playing at the top and not under him at Kidderminster. Well, perhaps I would have been if he was in his rightful place at the top too, he was definitely better than the majority of managers I came across in the league game.

My defensive responsibility was basically to stop the opposing full back going forwards. Once our reputation grew I just refused to go back and they then had to make a decision between leaving me unmarked or staying and marking me. This was a bit of a psychological battle but I stuck to my guns and very rarely did a full back take the risk and leave me. This obviously put pressure on the defence but Graham's philosophy was that if they weren't good enough to defend as a back four he would get players in that could, similarly he also expected us forwards to deliver or he would replace us, and the midfield had to support both! How simple is that. Everyone knew their jobs and what was expected of us and boy did we click as a team.

Graham wasn't like most managers and seemed to relish in having to deal with strong characters. He treated us like adults and we could discuss football and anything else with him. The whole team at the time was full of characters but I don't remember any of us falling out at all, possibly due to the fact that we very rarely lost. The whole club had a family feel about it, including the directors, players, staff and supporters. We all used to have a drink in the bar after training or games and got to know the regulars well. We ended that season on a real high and none of us wanted it to end because we were murdering everyone.

So, all of a sudden, I was enjoying playing the beautiful game again and was really optimistic about the following season…

CHAPTER EIGHTEEN

Back in the High Life Again – Finally!

At this stage in my life everything was going well, I had a pretty good sales job in the field of telecomms and Julie was also doing well in the same business. We had just moved to a lovely cottage on the outskirts of Wolverhampton and Charlie was a very amiable, happy bouncing baby boy.

I had a few weeks off at the end of the season but was training hard by running around West Park near the Molineux every day for a month before returning to Kidderminster for the new season in good shape. It had been a long time since I had looked forward to the start of a new football season with such optimism and just couldn't wait to get back to pre-season training, even though it was traditionally every footballer's dread due to the arduous running element. However, although we did do a fair bit of running we were always rewarded with a good amount of ball work which I think Graham recognised was important to maintain our enthusiasm, especially as part time players who had been working during the day.

There were a couple of surprises awaiting us however, the first one being that our left back John 'Jock' McGrath had left to return to his adopted home town club down the road, Worcester City. I was really disappointed with this as Jock was not only a great lad off the pitch but also probably the best left back, for me personally, that I played in front of throughout my career. He was happy to give me the ball under any circumstance – marked closely or not, which gave me great confidence and showed his trust in me which I really appreciated. If I was ever in a situation where I couldn't wriggle a way forward Jock would always be available for me to lay the ball off to his left foot for him to play forward for us. He very rarely overlapped and left me to do the attacking part and I think he knew he was pretty much on his own defensively! Perhaps that was why he left! Graham had already replaced Jock with a very good non-league left sided player in Paul Bancroft who had previously been at Burton Albion as a midfield player.

The other surprise for us was that Graham had brought in Colin Gordon as player coach to replace his long standing and loyal servant Paul 'Ocker' Davies. Ocker had been with Kiddy for a long time and was a legend there having had a great goal scoring record over the years. Ocker could score all sorts of goals and I'm pretty sure he scored more miskicks than I scored at all in my whole career. He was a non-league international forward, and although he was coming to the end of his career he was still an important member of the team that had such a good balance at the end of the previous season.

Colin wasn't a very popular addition and he didn't help himself by being quite aloof and condescending in his manner. Colin was local from just up the road in Stourbridge and had been a professional with Birmingham City along with a few other clubs. Not that it really matters, but quite a few of us had also played league football and we didn't take too kindly to his superior attitude. He was now taking the place of one of our mates and also changing the way we were training, this seemed crazy to me as we had been doing so well previously! Why try and fix something that wasn't broken? During one of his early training sessions he did some work with our defence who were certainly no mugs anyway. During this quite long boring session he was coaching Simeon Hodson, who was our captain and previously played for West Bromwich Albion, to show me inside (this took me back to the session when I was at Arsenal), and this ended with the same result – me bending a shot into the top far corner of Kevin Rose's goal. This didn't go down very well, especially when quite a few of the lads started laughing out loud and I got the dead eye from Colin, I just shrugged my shoulders and carried on training regardless!

Colin has gone on to seemingly be a successful businessman, football agent and until recently was Chairman at my beloved club Kidderminster Harriers. From what I understand he has proved as popular this time around as he was in our dressing room! Colin was also struggling on the pitch which coincided with the team struggling to score any goals. We had basically gone from a free scoring team playing attractive attacking football to a team looking like we had never played together before. I'm pretty sure Graham could see that it wasn't working but he was very stubborn and equally could be patient enough to give players a bit of time to adjust. However this lack of form continued into the first month of the season and we were showing no signs of returning to being the team we had been the previous season. I remember having a conversation with Graham on the team coach on the way home from another disappointing result and he felt that the results would come if the performances were good. Personally I didn't think we were anywhere near the level of the previous season or showing any signs of getting there and I expressed my concerns.

I honestly don't know what happened over the weekend but when we came into training on the following Monday evening, Colin was nowhere to be seen and Graham was taking training again with Ocker back in the fold. You could literally feel the relief in the dressing room and the atmosphere changed immediately. We didn't play particularly well on the Saturday but we won and we were off and running again thankfully! I don't know the statistics but we started firing on all cylinders again and we just kept on winning game after game.

I think it's worth giving you some background on the squad – which amounted to about 15 or 16 for most of the season.

Goalkeepers

Kevin Rose – The quiet man of the dressing room, he was a fantastic shot stopper and very unassuming. He showered in five seconds flat and was first in the bar for a couple of ciders before making his way back to Hereford.

Darren Steadman – An able deputy when called upon, he was definitely one of the lads and the Del Trotter of the squad – always ducking and diving and getting into a few scrapes but a good lad around the club. A local boy that came through the ranks and I think Graham knew how to keep him reigned in.

Defenders

Simeon Hodson – Right back and captain. Simeon was picked up from West Brom after being released and given a new lease of life with Kidderminster. Very dependable and consistent and a good lad off the pitch.

Paul Bancroft – Left Back – Banky was an experienced player from Derbyshire, very dry off the pitch and quietly efficient on it with a lovely left foot. Always had the feeling he would have liked more defensive help from me (not allowed – I was under orders!).

Martin Weir – Centre Back – Weirdo was a quality player, strong in the air and a very good footballer on the floor. His positional sense made up for his lack of pace and he always looked to play out from the back. He had no fear in passing the ball into midfield when possible but would clear his lines when needed. Mr consistent and reliable and I'm sure he was a manager's dream. A quiet gentleman off the pitch.

Chris Brindley – Centre Half – Brinners was unbeatable in the air on his day and a big game player too. He was pretty consistent but came into his own in the important games. A no nonsense centre half but was also tidy on the floor and very rarely got done for pace due to his long rangy stride. A strong character off the pitch and not afraid to voice his opinion but very amiable too. He was at Wolves for a short period during my time there.

Midfield 3 (out of 4)

Paul Grainger – Centre Midfield – Grainge was a snarling, energetic, aggressive ball winner who was tidy on the ball. He kept it simple and never let the opposition rest. Generally a happy bloke off the pitch with an infectious laugh. Played against Grainge for Arsenal youth v Aston Villa youth at Villa Park and he was also at Wolves with me for a short time. Graham Turner released him at Villa and then he signed for him at Wolves and released him again!

Richard Forsyth – Centre Left Midfield – Fozzie was technically very good and composed on the ball, he had a great range of passing and our relationship on the pitch became almost telepathic - he knew what run I would be making and had the ability to put it where I wanted. He was great to play in front of and he worked very hard for the team. Off the pitch he was a strong character and voiced his opinion.

During the title winning season we had a long chat after training one night over a couple of pints and a pork pie with mustard! He asked me if I thought he was good enough to be a pro and the answer was without doubt he had the ability. However I explained that ability wasn't enough as I had proved and that the modern game demanded consistency and hard work as a basic requirement. There was no doubt in my mind that Fozzie was a much better player than quite a few of the midfield players I had played with and against at Wolves and I played with Peter Butler at Cambridge who was doing well for West Brom at the time and he was a tenacious, hard-working player but didn't have fozzie's touch, skill, vision or passing range. To be fair to fozzie he definitely added the graft to his game – possibly because he was playing behind me! I am delighted he went on to do well for Blues, Stoke, etc. I have seen him a few times over the years and I understand he is now back involved with Kiddy to try and get them back to where they belong at the top of the non-league pyramid.

Neil Cartwright – Right Midfield – Carty was strong and skilful and not afraid to get stuck in. Nothing seemed to worry him on or off the pitch. Great lad to have around, he was a little unfortunate with injuries throughout his career.

John Deakin – Right Midfield – Deaks had lovely feet and balance and was a very tidy passer of the ball who worked hard for the team. He never let the team down when selected. Easy going lad and was on the edge of the banter.

Carty and Deaks shared the Right Midfield position throughout the season. Graham called this position the dog leg as he wanted them to play right midfield and right wing depending where the ball was and whether we were in possession or not.

Front Three

Delwyn Humphries – Forward Right – Delboy was lightning quick, direct, cocky and a real handful for any defence to handle – he just never stopped running. Del was a cheeky chappy and a larger than life character. I played against him for Cheltenham against Kiddy and resorted to booting him up in the air because he was giving our back four such a hard time! He didn't bat an eyelid and just carried on murdering us. Another strong character who definitely wasn't afraid of giving his opinion.

Paul Davies – Centre Forward – Ocker was Mr Kidderminster Harriers and was part of the legendary team that won the FA Trophy previously. He was as strong as an ox and one of the most dedicated players I've ever known. He would play with injuries when most people wouldn't think about it, I'm sure his back was fused at this time but he was such a determined character he took no notice. I think Graham had tried to ship him out a few times during their time at Kiddy but he always found a way back into the team. He had lost his pace by now but changed his game to be a target man and he let his goals do the talking. Off the pitch he was a decent lad and became player coach!

Me – Forward Left – Purds – I loved playing in this team!

Les Palmer – Forward – Les was a young lad who had been a bright hope at West Brom but unfortunately didn't get too many opportunities during this time as the three above played most games. A lovely lad who just wanted to play.

Emergency Players

Mark Dearlove – A Centre half who had a bright career ahead of him curtailed by injury, he was a Graham disciple and would run through brick walls for the cause and play anywhere asked. He was actually the Goalkeeper sub at Wembley in the FA Trophy final the following year. A good character to have around.

Martin Woodhall – Midfield – Woody signed towards the end of the season to help as we were low on numbers. He was back from emigrating to Australia for family reasons and had played for Graham at some point previously. Guaranteed to get booked every game and had a bit of a wild reputation off the pitch although I never witnessed that.

So, this is the small group that Graham had put together at a fantastic non-league football club overlooking the Severn Railway Line, and I don't think any of us expected the season to unfold as it did. Our form was back and we started winning game after game, it began to feel like the end of the previous season again. Only Graham Carr's Kettering Town were putting up a challenge.

I had experienced playing against Graham Carr's teams before when he was at Northampton Town against Wolves, if any two managers could be polar opposites it was the two Graham's (Allner and Carr). Graham Allner would sit quietly observing the game with the occasional instruction whilst Graham Carr was a barking, vessel popping barrel of rage on the sidelines who believed in the percentage long ball game taking the offside trap to the maximum, literally squeezing up to the halfway line as soon as possible in unison to try and catch the opposition offside. This was a lower league endemic at the time and he wasn't the only one with this belief, I do understand it but it gave very little freedom or trust in a player's ability. I think it was basically saying to players 'you aren't good enough to play good football so we will get results by being direct and playing the percentage game'. I'm sure he was a different person in his private life but it's still quite amazing that he's the father of funny man Alan Carr!

The truth is that players at that level had to do what they are told or lose their jobs and income as I found out at Wolves where I couldn't fit into the style under yet another Graham – Turner! I have to say it was a relief and a pleasure to be playing for Kiddy under Allner.

* * *

Delwyn Humphries (Kidderminster Harriers)

What can I say about Jon... my career was going ok until Jon came into the team, then all of a sudden it went up another level – playing with someone that could do what he did with the ball at his feet. He knew exactly where to put the ball for me and other forwards to score. Jon was capable of changing any game and I'm privileged to have played with him and I'm pleased that we are still good mates now.

* * *

CHAPTER NINETEEN

The Magic of the FA Cup

Penalty Notice

Amongst the fixtures that we were taking in our stride was the FA Cup, I don't think this was regarded as any different to the league matches and we just approached each game as another that we were confident in winning.

The 1st round proper gave us a draw against our old rivals Woking – always a good game with probably the best footballing team in the league alongside ourselves. Woking had a few outstanding players with Clive Walker (ex-Chelsea, Sunderland, Fulham) and Scott Steele being their stand out attacking players. Walker was late 30s then and still fit and quick, and I think he played into his early 40s which is remarkable. Steeley was a throwback to the Scottish ball players of the past with great skill and definitely should have played at a higher level.

The atmosphere on the day was a little bit special and it was a bigger crowd than normal, I guess it was probably the biggest game in the FA cup first round. As normal it was a very closely fought game with very little between us, although we were playing well we couldn't find a way to break the deadlock and it looked like it was heading for a replay. I was having a good game as I always enjoyed playing against Woking and their right back Andy Clement, who was previously with Wimbledon during the Crazy Gang days.

Towards the end of the game, Paul Grainger played a ball inside Andy and I was onto it with a yard on him, my first touch took me into the box and across him and he took me down – penalty for us! I had done my bit and was just relieved I wasn't taking it, fortunately Fozzie was very confident in himself and struck a great penalty against their non-league England International goalkeeper Laurence Batty. The game finished 1-0 and we were through to the next round.

There was usually a few weeks gap between the FA Cup games and we just carried on as normal, playing and winning league games home or away. There was no change in tactics for us regardless – Graham was happy to try and score more goals than the opposition with no fear of losing the odd game. This was very refreshing and unusual for any manager at any standard and I loved it!

Some of our trips could be long, including playing at places like Gateshead and Dover! A lot of time was killed by playing cards for most of us, with a game called 'Nominations' being a favourite at the time as it took about an hour per game if there were about 8 of us on both of the card playing tables. Even though the coaches were always of a good standard I avoid coach journeys whenever possible now – twenty years of travelling on them was enough!

Sometimes on a Saturday I would take my laptop with me to do some quotations for work, I would get some stick but didn't care to be honest – it passed some time and meant I was up to date for the start of the following week's work schedule. Occasionally we would have one of these long away trips which meant we would get back to Kidderminster in the early hours of the morning, midweek. This was bad enough for me but I could plan the following day accordingly. A lot of the boys weren't so lucky and had to be up at 6 to start their working day and big Chris Brindley was a hod carrier at the time and had a physical day ahead of him. If you have played football at any level, you'll know there is always a level of soreness with bruises and general fatigue after matches, so I have nothing but admiration for big Chris and the like. This side of non-league football is often overlooked and it's a testament to a lot of the lads who did and I'm sure still do it.

Seeing Red

Anyway back to the FA Cup – we drew Chesham United in the next round, I don't think that most of us had heard of it never mind knew where it was! I think we probably went into this game a bit over-confident and obviously they were right up for it and it became obvious we needed to up our game. They had a gobby little fella in midfield who never stopped baiting us, basically saying we were crap etc. Well, he got told to shut up a few times but his ears weren't working so an opportunity came to let him know that we knew what we were doing – a long, high clearance came towards me and after one bounce I controlled the ball on my chest and as the 'mouth' came towards me from the side I caught him full in the nose with my elbow! I thought I'd been clever enough not to make it look intentional but the referee had other ideas and as soon as the whistle went a fear of dread ran through me and I got a straight red card for the second time in my career! Everyone was shocked and a lot of the lads were pleading my innocence as it was completely out of character and I did think it looked quite accidental but the referee was quite rightly convinced that I elbowed him and I got my marching orders.

Fortunately for me the lads raised their game and we came out winners by a 4-1 margin! After the game Graham asked me what happened and if it was worth questioning the referee to see if anything could be done – I had no idea that there was video footage as it was quite unusual in those days! Once Graham had seen it he said he was surprised and didn't know I had it in me. I'm not sure if he was disappointed or pleased!

I then had to serve a 3 game suspension and Les Palmer came into the side and did well in my absence so I was concerned about losing my place. Les had great feet and knew where the back of the net was – he was at West Bromwich Albion prior to joining us and I know there were big hopes for him at one time. He was physically quite slight and I think he may be another one who struggled to adjust to lower level football and was probably just a little unlucky.

Getting The Blues

At this time we knew that the league teams came into the cup draw but I don't think we expected such a plum draw to happen – Birmingham City away!

This was literally just up the road for us and we had a lot of connections with the Blues – Martin Weir and John Deakin were both previously on their books and Graham Allner was a lifelong Blues fan from the area originally. They were managed by the larger than life character Barry Fry who had tried to sign me for Barnet when I left Arsenal about 9 years previously, he hadn't been in charge that long and he was signing players left, right and centre! I think they had over 50 professionals on their books which was unheard of and there's no doubt that the club was in turmoil. Although we were still very much underdogs, there was no better time to play them. Also with the Blues was Chris Whyte who had been with me at Arsenal and I met him at Leeds a couple of years previously. In hindsight, the club must have been delighted from a financial point of view as they received money from the Football Association and also from the TV companies too. At the time, I was totally oblivious to this aspect and just excited about playing in a big game again.

The press had started to show some interest in us at this point although Graham was quite protective and playing it down, he dealt with it all himself and I think he just wanted us to concentrate on the game. He did pull off a masterstroke though, if it was intended – with a visit to St. Andrews on one of the nights during the week leading up to the match. This allowed us to have a look around and familiarise ourselves with the surroundings a little bit. This was going to be the biggest game of our lives for most of us and I think Graham was trying to help ease the tension. Either that or he just wanted a look around himself! Of course this couldn't replicate match day but it may have helped us all a little bit. Some of the lads had played on big occasions before, including FA Trophy Wembley appearances for Chris Brindley and Paul Grainger and some league appearances for most of us.

The game was treated pretty much the same as a normal away match albeit if any other game was this local we would have probably made our own way to the ground. On this occasion we had a pre-match meal and team meeting at the Moat House Hotel in West Bromwich and then went on our way to the ground. We were all pretty focused and there was definitely some nervous tension around. On a personal level I was determined to do myself justice performance-wise and not freeze as I had done a few years back at Old Trafford. However I was approaching this game in a completely different mindset and physical condition – I was confident, fit and happy in my life all round.

In addition to that I knew that I was an important part of a good team and I didn't want to let Graham, the lads or my family down.

Before the game Graham told us that he had confidence in us and he thought we could win, whether this was just psychology or he actually believed it I don't know. We did have one problem before the game which was Ocker (Paul Davies) was struggling with injury. It must have been serious as he couldn't pass a fitness test. Graham pushed Neil Cartwright forward and John Deakin came into right midfield. In hindsight I'm sure Les Palmer was devastated but Graham made a brave decision as Neil hadn't played in our front three at all before. I remember warming up before the game and being surprised about the poor condition of the pitch, it was really heavy and was already cut up before kick-off. Normally that would have been in the non-league team's favour but we really needed a good surface to play our game on.

We started quite slowly and were under severe pressure for the first 25 minutes, with Ted Mcminn (the 'Tin Man') giving us a torrid time and they deservedly took the lead at around the 25 minute mark. I hadn't been involved much in the game and was pretty much a bystander waiting and hoping for the game to change in our favour. I'm not sure if it was Graham or sorted by the lads on the pitch, but Richard Forsyth swapped with John Deakin to stop the supply and offer a more physical support to stop Mcminn. This worked and we started coming into the game and from our first attack Paul Bancroft made a rare run down the left wing and put a great cross to the far post over me, Neil Cartwright rose and planted a header into the net! It was 1-1 and all of a sudden we started to believe we could get a result. Just before half-time is always a great time to score and the mood in the dressing room was suddenly positive. We had ridden the storm and were still in the game. I think we knew we could only get better and we went out for the second half with optimism.

The pitch had become even heavier by this stage and there was no doubt that the wings were probably the best part of the pitch to be on. The game restarted and it was all very even for the first 15 – 20 minutes and I was starting to get more involved, I went for a bit of a wander onto the right hand side as I felt I could have more of an influence on the game. By this stage my nervousness had gone and I was feeling confident. I had a good turn and a left foot shot from outside the box which I hit well but Ian Bennett was equal to it, I also felt I should have had a penalty when I was brought down after a good run, it was a definite penalty in my mind but for some reason it wasn't given – I then had another effort cutting in from the right and drilling a low shot which again Ian Bennett got down well to pull off a good save.

However, the moment came that I still remember very clearly and ironically it was the result of direct football – not our normal style! Kevin Rose took a goal kick, Delwyn headed on and Carty flicked the ball towards me with the outside of his foot, I was just inside their half and started carrying the ball forwards and cutting inside towards the middle of the pitch and Scott Hiley kept backing off – I was about to let fly when the ball hit a divot so I took another touch and it sat up perfectly. I hit it sweetly towards the top corner of the goal with all the Kiddy fans watching from behind and although Ian Bennett got a hand to the ball he couldn't prevent it from flying into the back of the net. I have no idea why but I just stood and raised my right hand and before I knew it I was being mobbed by my team mates and the Kiddy fans were going crazy! When the lads finally made their way back to their positions I just waved at Julie and my mum and dad with a clenched fist – I had finally given them something to be proud of after all the hard times they had been through with me.

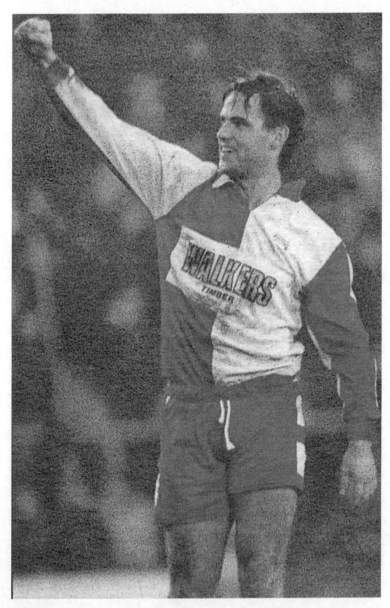

Signalling to Julie and my parents after the goal against Blues.

The game wasn't over though and the last 25 minutes must have felt like an hour to anyone who wanted us to win, let alone all the boys on the pitch. The lads were tremendous, every one of us worked our socks off (yes even me!) and we defended heroically – Chris Brindley and Martin Weir put their bodies on the line to protect our penalty area. We also had a little bit of lady luck on our side – with Andy Saville missing a dubious penalty and also having a goal disallowed for offside which I think VAR would have given today! The whistle finally went and the adrenalin rush gave us some energy which had been hard to find a minute earlier – we all ran towards the Kiddy fans behind the goal we scored the winner in and it was just an unbelievable feeling to have beaten the Blues after a fantastic FA Cup giant killing!

Celebrating Neil Cartwright's equaliser against Blues.

The FA Cup winning goal for Kidderminster against Blues.

We did a lap of the pitch and the Blues fans were tremendous towards us and it was a nice touch from them although it was all a bit of a blur of celebrating and photos. Once we finally got back to the dressing room we were ecstatic and the beer started flowing pretty quickly and we all ended up in the communal bath together!

I really wanted to see Julie, my parents and friends but a few of us had to do a few interviews for the press in any quiet corner by the dressing rooms – I ended up on some stairs doing a few interviews for different papers.

Purdie's precocious talents could grace the Premiership

Football nomad who is enjoying his resurrection at Conference side Kidderminster.

Those who saw Jon Purdie shatter Birmingham City's defence with a 25-yard strike fit to join January's Goal of the Month contenders will recognise what a rare and precious talent it was that Kidderminster Harriers recovered from football's large scrapheap of broken dreams.

Furthermore, those who remember his fitful and wasted career at Wolverhampton Wanderers will be right to conclude that the Harriers winger, a former England youth international who in many ways had it all too early, is currently producing the most inspired and effective football of his life.

The same could be said of Purdie's old Wolves team-mate Chris Brindley, another who lost his sense of purpose as a Molineux teenager but found fulfilment years later when Graham Allner succeeded in maximising his defensive talents at Aggborough.

It is hard to believe that Wolves have changed divisions half a dozen times since they left the club, and yet Purdie is only 26 and Brindley not yet in his prime at 24.

Allner hopes it never happens but the Harriers manager is prepared for the day when the telephone rings to summon one or both to a Premiership club.

"My assistant Jimmy Conway assumed that Purdie was at least 30," Allner said. "When he found out he was only 26 he told him straight it was a disgrace that he wasn't playing with a top club.

"Let's be honest, he's far too good to be playing at non-League level — especially at his age. But he won't leave Kidderminster for any Football League club. If a Premiership club came along and offered him £5,000 a week, then he might be interested."

On the ball: Jon Purdie in relaxed mood after another training session at the Aggborough Stadium, Kidderminster.

Getting some attention from the national press.

I think this all took so long we just got straight on the coach back to the Moat House to have a drink together with friends and family, although Martin Weir got the bus home! After the initial euphoria of seeing our loved ones it all became quite low key, we were too spread out and the lads dispersed at different times. There was nothing really laid on and I guess no one really expected us to win – in hindsight it would have been great to have gone back to 'The Harriers Arms' at the club for us all to celebrate together but the reality is we all had families – Julie was 6 months pregnant with my youngest, Jack, and Charlie was being looked after by my mother in law so we also had to get home. My celebrations ended up being a Chinese takeaway and a bottle of wine or two while watching Match of the Day – much like any other Saturday night!

The next morning started much the same as normal, waking up early to look after Charlie who was 15 months old and doing my dad duties as usual. However, about 10am I had a call from Graham Allner and after talking about the game for a while he asked if I was willing to be interviewed by The Sun newspaper. I thought this would be on the telephone so agreed straight away, only to find out they wanted to come to the house and get a bit more of a back story.

I went to the local paper shop and bought most of the newspapers. We had made headlines in nearly all of them which I must admit felt great, though Julie wasn't so delighted with the headline of 'When I scored I was worried my Mrs was going to pop' – I don't remember saying those words in the interviews after the game but it was all such a blur I really don't know!

The reporter came in the afternoon and stayed for an hour or so and then life went on as normal and it was back to work on the Monday as usual. Some of the people at work were interested and some had no idea or indeed any interest in football at all, which was fine – I just wanted to get on with my work and try to make some money as usual.

At the time I was oblivious to how important the goal and the result was to so many people involved with Kidderminster, and indeed to Blues fans. Due to the rivalry between the two Birmingham clubs the Villa fans now loved me too! I'm not one to live in the past at all and prefer to just get on with life but this goal still comes up every year when the FA Cup starts and I am proud to have done something memorable to some people.

There is a documentary about Birmingham City and in particular their new Chairman Karren Brady that was filmed during the period of that cup tie and it is obvious that they never

THE GIANT KILLERS!

BEAMING Jon Purdie (left) and Neil Cartwright are the giant killers who booted Birmingham City out of the FA Cup yesterday.

They were the goal-scoring heroes of non-league Kidderminster Harriers who sensationally defeated First Division Blues.

The part-timers pulled off an astonishing 2-1 victory in front of a stunned St Andrew's crowd of nearly 20,000 and shot into the Fourth Round of the cup for the

Harriers strike duo give City the Blues

first time. The win sparked celebrations in the town last night. Mayor of Kidderminster, Coun Wilfrid Clarke, originally from Birmingham, said: "What a wonderful day to be Mayor!

"I'm on top of the world. I just

can't get over it. It's great for the team but also great for the town.

"We've had a hard time recently with a spate of redund-

With fellow goalscorer Neil Cartwright after victory against Blues in the FA Cup.

contemplated that they could lose the game to us. It's quite an interesting behind the scenes film – well worth a watch, as is the game itself for those that are interested in looking back to when the FA Cup meant something.

Mine's a Beck's

It's fair to say we were on the crest of a wave and our form continued into the league, which we were well clear at the top of at this time too. Unfortunately the week before the next FA Cup game we had an FA Trophy game at home to Dagenham and Redbridge who were the big spenders from London at the time.

We simply didn't perform on the day and deservedly got knocked out 2 – 0. It was probably too much for our small squad to cope with among the League and FA Cup efforts.

During the week after the Blues game, the FA Cup draw was made. I think most of us were hoping for a plum draw against one of the big boys to help the club financially and for us

THE TIMES MONDAY JANUARY 31 1994

Kidderminster spring Cup surprise

Harriers rise to challenge of Beck's bombers

Kidderminster Harriers... 1
Preston North End 0

By WALTER GAMMIE

FA CUP

REPLAY DATES: February 9: Black-
burn Rovers v Charlton Athletic, Luton
Town v Newcastle United. February 9:
Sheffield Wednesday v Chelsea, West
Ham United v Notts County, Stoke City
v Oldham Athletic. Leeds United v
Oxford United. Barnsley v Plymouth
Argyle.

THE two players who stand at the heart of the Kidderminster Harriers defence knew exactly what was in store for them at Aggborough on Saturday: bombardment from the muck-or-nettles brigade of John Beck's latest team of warriors, Preston North End.

Throughout the season, Graham Allner, Kidderminster's eminently sensible manager, when pressed to single out the outstanding performers in his team, has answered: "Chris Brindley and Martin Weir they have been magnificent."

The central defenders proved every bit as good as Allner promised, as they ensured Preston's witlessly predictable assault came to nothing on a day when Harriers, leaders of the GM Vauxhall Conference, became the first non-League side since Telford United in 1985 to reach the fifth round of the FA Cup. Brindley and Weir headed away or chased, retrieved and hacked clear every ball sent soaring their way.

When seated behind a table on a raised dais at a presidential-style press conference that would not have disgraced an FA Carling Premiership club – although the holes in the roof and dust in the corners of the hall betrayed a part-time club stylishly staging a special day – Kidderminster's central defenders admitted that Preston had generously played to their strength.

By contrast, Kidderminster's prime attacking weapon lurked with intent on the left touchline. Jon Purdie proved his creative skills far exceeded anything offered by opponents from the third division of the Endsleigh Insurance League.

The first time the ball was played to him, two defenders charged in to tackle and Purdie stepped deftly out of the way, ball still securely under control. As the second half started, Preston had seen enough to have become exceedingly wary of him.

So when Purdie evaded a challenge near halfway, Fensome held off as the winger moved serenely towards the byline. Before the half-hearted tackle finally went in, Purdie had slipped the ball towards Delwyn Humphreys at the near post, who swept it home with aplomb.

Humphreys careered away towards the stand and performed two huge somersaults that would have brought 9.3 or 9.4 for Vitaly Scherbo on the floor at the Olympic Games. A party piece, first practised in emulation of Peter Beagrie, of Everton, it suitably excited the Harriers supporters, who cheered and stamped their feet on the wooden planking that has brought the disapproval of the Hereford and Worcester Fire Brigade, who have told Harriers the stand will be closed in April. The need to replace it, at £425,000, remains the biggest obstacle to further advancement.

That they have nothing to fear in playing terms was swiftly made clear again when Purdie nodded back Deakin's cross to Humphreys, who headed against the bar. Humphreys held his head, and did so again when, in trying to help out his back-four, he delayed his pass and tried to flick the ball on to Purdie. It cannoned off Nebbeling's toe through the startled Kidderminster defence but Norbury, the Preston substitute, blazed the chance over the bar.

Norbury had just replaced Ellis, scorer of 23 goals this season. Ineffectiveness, not injury, was Ellis's demise. As he angrily loosened his shin pads and sat on the grass next to the Preston dugout, his view of Messrs Brindley and Weir at work cannot have been improved. Rarely can a shut-out have looked more certain.

"I really don't know how good this team is," Allner said. "We've beaten Birmingham City in front of 20,000 on their own ground. Now, we've beaten the team that most in the lower two divisions would say they'd least like to face."

KIDDERMINSTER HARRIERS (4-3-3): K
Rose — S Hodson, M Weir, C Brindley, P
Barnett — N Cartwright, R Forsyth (sub: J
Deakin, 81min), P Davies — D Humphreys, P Davies (sub: M Wooder, 88), J
Purdie.
PRESTON NORTH END (4-4-2): S Woods
— A Fensome, D Moyes, G Nebbeling, R
Kidd — D Ainsworth, R Lucas, L Cartwright,
R Raynor — M Conroy, A Ellis (sub: M
Norbury, 65).
Referee: R Alcock.

Purdie, left, the Kidderminster winger, eyes an opportunity against Preston

On the ball against Preston North End.

to have the experience of playing against top opposition from the Premier League. I was watching the draw at home and when our number came out as a home draw the excitement was building about who would come out next. It turned out to be one of the country's most famous clubs but unfortunately they were not at the peak of their powers and had found themselves in the lower leagues for some time – Preston North End! I think still most famous for Tom Finney, and that Bobby Charlton had an attempt at management there. My first thought was 'we can win that'! I had no doubt that our team could beat any team in the 3rd or 4th division at that time.

At this point the media, both locally and nationally, were showing a lot of interest in us as a team and it was becoming quite normal for the press and TV cameras to be at training and I appeared on Football Focus alongside Ocker. I think the interest in our two stories was because our backgrounds were completely opposite. Ocker having played for Kidderminster for such a long time and my journey starting with Arsenal and 7 clubs later ending up at the same club somehow.

Before one training session Graham came storming into the dressing room and started laying down the law about the bonus involved in the upcoming game. I'm not sure who had upset him but someone must have riled him. He basically said if anyone wasn't happy with what was on offer then he would play the kids and we'd get nothing and he didn't want to hear another word about money – so I couldn't resist putting my hand up and asking "how much is the bonus as a matter of interest?" Fortunately he knew I was only joking and all the lads had a giggle, I think it diffused the situation and we carried on and went training as normal. I'm not really sure what the bonus was to be honest as money wasn't really the motivating factor for me.

In the build up to the game it became apparent that John Beck was now the manager at Preston which I was totally unaware of at the time, and following my previous experience of him when he was coach at Cambridge I was looking forward to proving a point alongside trying to win the game as normal for our club. Graham went to see them play and held a players meeting to let us know what we were in for against them. As I remember I don't think he could quite believe how regimented and direct Beck had made his players, there was no room for individuality or freedom of expression. This was taking direct football to the next level and although I knew from first-hand experience of how belligerent he was, it was still quite shocking to hear how rigid they were.

The Preston team came to look at the pitch on the Friday lunchtime and it was pretty dry and bumpy which suited them as the ball was rarely on the floor anyway. However as soon as they left Graham had arranged for the pitch to be saturated by the local fire brigade to make it more suited to our 'on the floor' style of football.

The first half was quite cagey and even with not many chances being created by either side and they were doubling up on me whenever I got the ball which wasn't too often in the opening exchanges, not uncommonly in those days. The first 20 minutes were always a bit hectic with the battle for supremacy being normal. However I did have a couple of runs and I felt confident that I had the beating of their right back Andy Fensome – who honestly looked frightened to death.

David Moyes was playing for them and I remember during the second half, while they were taking yet another long throw into the box when there was a player to throw it to close by, I asked Moyes why they didn't throw it to the winger and have it back to cross it. He just said "he's not allowed – the gaffer would go mental". Paul Raynor was their captain and I had first come across him when at Nottingham Forest as a kid. He was a decent player but it was obvious he had become a Beck disciple and was constantly shouting and reminding everyone to stick to the plan. I believe he is now the assistant to another manager – Steve Evans that I don't think I would enjoy being around but I guess he's happy making a living in the game.

The second half was also nip and tuck with nothing between the two teams albeit we were trying to win with contrasting styles. As the game slowed down a bit I was beginning to see more of the ball. I picked it up just inside their half and started advancing down the left with Fensome retreating and backing off me until I was in the box which is where I wanted to be, I dummied to go inside on my right foot and dragged it on the outside and pulled the ball back to the edge of the six yard box where Delwyn had made a run to the near post. He struck it with his left foot into the back of the net and he did his trademark celebration with a cartwheel and a flick flack which would have put me in hospital had I ever attempted it!

We continued to cope pretty well with their attempts to get back into the game, with our two towers – Brindley and Weir dealing with their aerial attack admirably. They did have a couple of chances and Micky Norbury (who became a teammate a couple of years later) blazed a one on one over the bar to everyone's relief. My job for the rest of the game was to retain possession for as long as possible and win free kicks to take the pressure off our defence. We had a chance for Delwyn to double our lead when he hit the bar – a header after a long cross to the far post found me and I nodded the ball back to him. He probably should have scored. I felt at the time that the angle was too tight to score myself but having looked at it again on video I probably could have scored if I had that selfish streak that goalscorers need.

When the final whistle blew the pitch was invaded with ecstatic Kidderminster fans and we made our way back to the changing rooms to celebrate in the traditional communal bath in the old changing rooms. Delwyn quite rightly got the attention this time which I think he thoroughly enjoyed, but I was delighted to have played my part in a memorable victory. Again after a few beers with the lads and friends and family I made my way home for a normal Saturday night in with a takeaway, some wine and Match of the Day. Graham called again mid-morning on the Sunday to invite everyone to come to the club as the cup draw was going to be on the Sunday afternoon after a live televised game. We had a great afternoon with everyone together – there really was a great spirit in the camp which success usually brings. All the talk was about who we could get in the draw with dreams of Man Utd, Liverpool, etc. As the time for the draw got closer there was a great feeling of anticipation and excitement and this ultimately led to some mixed feelings as we drew a Premiership club but not the dream tie we hoped for – West Ham United at home.

Bursting our Bubble

There was talk of switching the tie to play at Upton Park to cash in as much as possible but Graham wanted to give us the best chance of progressing to the quarter finals and he felt playing at home would give us the best opportunity, which is difficult to argue against. I wasn't really concerned either way and was just looking forward to proving myself against premiership opposition. They had a few lads playing for them that I had known in the past: Steve Potts and Martin Allen were roughly my age and I had played against them in the youth team at Arsenal against the Hammers and QPR; Trevor Morley was at Northampton when I was at Wolves; and Lee Chapman was a teammate at Arsenal.

The town of Kidderminster had now got cup fever and there was a lot of media attention on the club with training being disrupted due to a cold snap and it was difficult for us to find anywhere to train. Graham arranged a visit to a local community centre to meet the local kids from the area which was a nice thing although I think we were all a little embarrassed about the attention as we were just a bunch of normal working class lads enjoying playing football together. We also had an evening at the Droitwich brine baths to keep us together during the build up to the big game.

Behind the scenes the club were working like Trojans to host this historic game and try to make a good impression to our visitors and the national media. They even built a temporary stand to try and accommodate the extra thousands that wanted to come to the game. I think they had managed to get the capacity up to the 8000 mark.

I drove to the match as normal and was a little nervous but in a good way, looking forward to the game ahead. I honestly can't remember what was said in the dressing room in the build up to the game, I was just focused on doing myself justice. Before the game there was a bit of a panic as Chris Brindley broke down on the way – he arrived very late and it was touch and go if he was going to get on the team sheet in time but thankfully he just made it. There was an electric atmosphere coming onto the pitch with one end packed with the claret and blue singing 'I'm forever blowing bubbles' and letting off balloons in their colours and the rest of the ground was full of excited Kiddy fans.

The game started and there was really nothing between the teams. They seemed very reluctant to open up and have a real go at us, possibly fearing an embarrassment in the making. Not long into the game I made a run through the middle of the pitch and Fozzie found me with a perfect pass. I got to the ball in front of their captain and former England centre half, Alvin Martin, who brought me down as I was bearing down on Ludo Miklosko! There was lots of chanting of "off! off!' to try and influence the ref to give him a red card but to no avail. He got a yellow and we had to settle for a free kick just outside of the penalty area, which I took and whistled a shot just over the bar. I have a print of a painting of this moment as a reminder of that fantastic cup run.

At half-time our belief was growing and our only concerns were the passing ability of Ian Bishop in their midfield who always seemed to have time on the ball, and the finishing threat of Clive Allen who had scored goals throughout his career. The second half got underway with very little incident until a long hopeful, looping cross was put in from their left by Matty Holmes. Kevin Rose probably made his only mistake that season by coming out for the cross and not quite getting there, and Lee Chapman managed to get his head to it and I watched agonisingly as the ball dropped over the line just out of the reach of Martin Weir.

There was about 20 minutes left for us to get back into the game and I had a couple of opportunities. First a deep cross from Simeon found me on the edge of the box which I cushioned on my left foot and hit a half volley well but it flew too high over the bar which I was disappointed with and felt I should have done better. Late on in the game I had a stonewall penalty not given when I beat a couple of players in the box and was brought down but the ball rolled to John Deakin who had a chance to shoot. Unfortunately he delayed and the chance was gone – I think the ref played advantage but I do believe to this day it was a penalty and I have no doubt that Fozzie would have scored and took us to Upton Park for a well-deserved replay.

● *SO CLOSE ... Harriers' Jon Purdie turns away in anguish after shooting over.*

Disappointed not to hit the target against West Ham.

There was a real feeling of disappointment and frustration afterwards as we had gone out of the cup to a disappointing goal and a team that weren't really better than us on the day. I think Delwyn summed it up in his Match of the Day interview when he said it would be easier to take if we'd been played off the park and lost 5-0. It was that feeling of so close but yet so far. I just remember feeling empty and everyone was trying to comfort us after but I think we all just felt robbed.

I'm pretty sure that Graham said he was proud of us and that we now had to make sure that we secured the league title.

Towards the end of the season on April 3rd my second son, Jack, was born.

The day before we played Yeovil away and I drove there to play and get back as soon as possible. We played well and won.

I just showered and jumped in the car and was back in time to take Julie to hospital later that evening and Jack was born in the early hours of the morning.

The rest of the season was all a bit of an anti-climax and we did just enough to win the title although we did run out of steam towards the end and at one stage it looked like Kettering were going to catch up. Personally I was struggling with my ankles and my left knee was also playing up and I was looking forward to a rest to be totally honest. We won the league on the last day of the season at home to Altrincham although we weren't great and lost the game. We were awarded the trophy after the game in the old wooden stand which was soon to be demolished in an effort for us to meet the required standards to get into the league the following season.

I was personally relieved that we had both won the league and that the season was over, although I didn't know at the time that that was the end of the best season of my football career...

At the end of the season Ocker had a testimonial against Aston Villa at Aggborough. I guess this was as good a time as it was going to ever be to get a big crowd and he got the turn out he deserved. I wasn't really fit to play and watched from the stand only half interested to be honest. I thought about saying hello to Paul Merson who was now the star at Villa but whenever I saw him he was surrounded with autograph hunters and I didn't want to bother him. I wasn't even sure he would remember me as we weren't that close at Arsenal and I also didn't want the embarrassment of being snubbed, so I left him alone. After the previous season I was rewarded with a new 2 year contract on improved money and a signing on fee which was a nice way of being rewarded and appreciated. I was never one to drive too hard a bargain, as long as I felt I was being treated fairly I was happy.

* * *

Richard Forsyth (Kidderminster Harriers)

Jon is a great fella and a very intelligent footballer and one of the most skilful players I had the pleasure of playing with, he knew when to dribble, pass and shoot and had two great feet. He always produced a moment of magic in a tight or big game when it was needed. The FA cup run in 93/4 was him at his best, he created and scored goals and we should have had a penalty against West Ham in the 5th round when he was brought down. It's great to still be in touch after all this time.

* * *

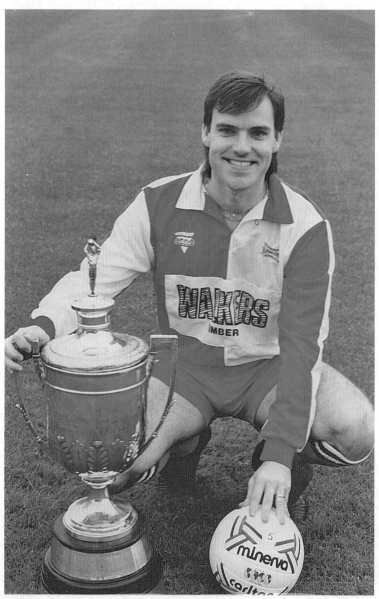

With the Conference Winners Trophy for Kidderminster.

CHAPTER TWENTY

After the Lord Mayor's Show

During the summer we had our annual holiday and went to Lanzarote for a couple of weeks with my parents to help us look after the boys, especially as Jack was only a couple of months old. Towards the end of the holiday we had a day at the beach, and Charlie started playing football with another little boy who turned out to be the son of Glenn Hoddle, who was one of my boyhood heroes. Because of the boys playing together we ended up having a chat and obviously we had a few things to talk about. He actually asked if I played football and I told him I was with Kidderminster and he knew about the cup run. I had played against his brother Carl when he was at Spurs as a youth and reserve player – Carl has subsequently sadly died at a very young age due to a brain tumour.

I know Glenn Hoddle divides opinion as a manager and as a football commentator but whatever your views are about him it was nice to have met him and had a casual chat as a fellow dad on the beach with his son.

When I returned from holiday it was time to start training to get fit for the new season, fortunately there were some fields behind my house on Yew Tree Lane in Tettenhall Wood and I could go running every day (not for too long as I hate running without a ball involved).

Graham Allner had arranged a pre-season trip to Guernsey as a bonding exercise but also to get a couple of games in for fitness reasons. These trips are always good with a great group of lads and I was really looking forward to it. However a few days before the trip I strained my calf muscle when out running and knew I wasn't going to be fit for the trip, I rang Graham to tell him and he said I couldn't go as he was only taking a small squad. I understood his point of view but was disappointed nonetheless.

During the summer the old wooden stand had been knocked down and replaced with a very impressive new stand with corporate facilities and new dressing rooms etc, this was in an effort to meet the requirements for us to take our place in the Football League. As it turned out, we were denied our place as the stand wasn't ready for a ridiculous deadline which couldn't be met as they couldn't start work until the season was over and we didn't know if we would win the league until the end anyway.

Obviously it's difficult to know how we would have fared in the Football League but I personally think we would have held our own, perhaps with the help of a bigger squad. There's no doubt that there was more ability in that team than in a lot of players I played with and against for both Wolves and Shrewsbury in the lower leagues and our spirit was as good as it gets. The only issue may have been if the lads really wanted to step up as quite a few were content with their jobs and playing at the top non-league level. There was talk of us training an extra night and I presume we would have got paid more, but if the intention was to go full time I'm not sure there would be too many that would have sacrificed the stability of their jobs for perhaps a one or two year professional career. The reality is that the majority of us had mortgages, a family and the future to consider and it would be unrealistic and short-sighted to think otherwise in my opinion.

I certainly wouldn't have gone back in the league just to say 'I'm a professional footballer', but I know it's easy for me to say as I had a few years as a professional. There were a few rumours that Martin O'Neill was interested in taking me to Wycombe Wanderers with him but Graham never mentioned it and I wasn't really interested anyway. The only intrigue for me was to have been able to get to know John Robertson who was one of my boyhood heroes. I have heard since that 'Robbo' was a good lad as I have a couple of mates who played with him at my home town club Corby when he was finishing his career.

Kidderminster eventually got into the league in 2000 when they won the conference under Jan Molby, albeit under different owners and a very different financial budget (which the club has never really recovered from) and sadly the club has now slipped down the leagues.

I think we all knew that living up to the previous season was going to be pretty impossible, and I remember having a conversation with Chris Brindley saying it would be a good time to move on as the only way was down from the heights of the '93/4 campaign. However we all loved the place and there would be only one reason to move elsewhere and money wasn't really why we were playing football – there was no better non-league club to be with at the time.

I was fit to play when they returned from Guernsey to take part in the pre-season games including against Blues ironically and their team was pretty unrecognisable from the FA Cup game. We also had a game against West Bromwich Albion with Ossie Ardiles in charge. At this time of year the fitness difference between full time pros and non-league players is quite noticeable, as life as a pro is basically a few weeks of running twice a day until you're sick and then eat, rest and repeat. In my humble opinion, you have to have something wrong with your mental state if you enjoyed this period – very often it is weeks without even seeing a ball!

Ironically as the season wore on the full time routine came more into line with the non-league player, training hard on Monday, Tuesday and Thursday, with Wednesday off and very little work on a Friday. Certainly during our cup run in the previous season, from January onwards there was no noticeable difference in fitness levels in my mind anyway.

The team had suffered a double blow with the loss of Paul Grainger and Martin Weir, both with long term cruciate knee injuries that certainly ended their respective seasons. Weirdo recovered reasonably quickly and came back to play for quite a few seasons at his normal high standard but Grainge never really got back to being the player he was before, although I believe he still plays cricket at a reasonably high local standard.

Graham brought in Paul Webb from our local rivals Bromsgrove Rovers and Mark Yates from out of the league as replacements. Webby was a great lad and a very good player, he was from Wolverhampton and we travelled together for the rest of the season. He had started off as a goalkeeper in the local Sunday leagues but he was someone who had the ability, consistency and football brain to have played League football throughout his career without doubt. He eventually realised his ambition to become a professional footballer when Kiddy won the Conference in 2000, he gave up his steady job with the Express and Star newspaper and sadly only played a handful of games before going back into non-league. I understand that he is now a policeman and I hope life is good for him.

Yatesy was a different kettle of fish and he arrived with a bit of a swagger and ego about him, he certainly wasn't going to settle in quietly. He was also given the captaincy ahead of Simeon which I think upset Simeon and I wasn't really happy about it either, along with a few of the lads. Simeon had everyone's respect and we all liked him as a bloke and it's hard to see how he could have done any better during the previous season. Obviously I don't know the reason for this change, was it Graham's decision or part of the deal to sign Yatesy? He was a decent player but certainly not our best player by a long way, but he had a lot of self-confidence which seems to help people in most walks of life. Mark went on to become a reasonably successful manager and I guess this self-belief is one of the requirements for the role. I never had any problems with him but just didn't really warm to him due to his superior air at the time.

The beginning of the season didn't start so well and we were struggling to find the form of the previous season. It's not easy to know why but it just wasn't happening for us and I remember really starting to struggle with my left knee as winter started to come. It culminated with me playing against St. Albans in the FA Trophy when I was virtually on one leg. We were down to the bare bones and I was asked to try and get us through this round and then I could have an operation to get back for the end of the season and to continue the attempt to win the FA Trophy at Wembley. We won the game and I scored two good goals somehow and as soon as victory was in sight I came off knowing I was going under the knife as soon as possible.

In the period leading up to the St. Albans game in the FA Trophy I went to visit a specialist who was a large Asian chap called Mr Chandra for a cortisone injection in my left knee to try and solve the problem. This was against my better judgement but I guess I was hoping it might do the trick even though I didn't really believe it would. Mr Chandra basically pinned me down and produced a very large needle which frightened the life out of me and proceeded to insert it deeply into the area under my kneecap which was incredibly painful and created a reflex response of my right leg kicking up – straight into his family jewels! I said to him as I left "I'm not sure who that hurt the most – you or me!" As expected it masked the problem for a few days but the pain soon returned.

I now look back and wonder if the first operation I had when I was at Cheltenham was done correctly as it took me six months to get back playing and I'm sure it should have only been six weeks or so. From then on I needed my knees cleaning out more or less every other season and I'm now left with no cartilage in either knee, although the left one is definitely the worst by far and is the one I suffered Osgood-Schlatters in and had my first operation on at 23.

After a scan on my knee I was booked in quickly for an operation and I was fortunate to be covered by Bupa so the surgery was at the plush Little Aston hospital near Sutton Coldfield.

I was able to play again around six weeks later and had my sights on helping the team get to Wembley and to win the FA Trophy, this would have been some consolation for an otherwise unmemorable season. Unfortunately, after playing for a month or so, the problem with my knee flared up again. Either the initial problem wasn't sorted properly or there was another issue that was overlooked, whichever – it wasn't satisfactory for me. I wanted to keep playing so I didn't say anything and tried to get on with it. I was compensating so much I was getting cramp in my groin when driving home after a match, I knew deep down I would need another operation or maybe just some rest during the close season, but as you can imagine it's not the most pleasant experience going under the knife and then rehabilitating afterwards. So I kept my mouth shut and kept playing, although I was probably at 70% of the previous season. Somehow the adrenalin gets you through the match and after a couple of days rest I could try again. One thing I am sure of is that Graham Allner wouldn't have continued to pick me if I wasn't performing well enough for the team, he definitely had a ruthless streak when required.

The team had beaten Kingstonian after a replay in the second game and I had returned in time to play in the next round against Ilkeston which we managed to get through reasonably comfortably despite a hostile reception from their renowned supporters. Next up was Altrincham at home in the quarter final who had a good history and were traditionally tough opponents, but we murdered them 5 – 0 on the day.

We had progressed through to the semi-final of the Trophy being drawn against Hyde United over two legs who were from the Northern League. We won the home tie 2 – 0 and the following week had to travel for the away leg, this was probably the most hostile atmosphere I have experienced as a player. I'm not sure if this was their normal following or the tie just attracted any hooligan in the Manchester area but they were out in numbers that day and the security was not really up for the task in hand. They played on what seemed like a community centre with an old artificial surface which really didn't help my dodgy knee at all. We lost the game 1 – 0 but scraped through the tie on aggregate as our lead from the home tie got us through. We just wanted to get on the team coach with our lives intact and escape the intimidation. Once we got on the way home we could start celebrating the fact that we were going to Wembley in the biggest cup competition in non-League football!

The previous time I played there for England Schoolboys I was obviously nervous but thought it was going to become a regular experience with the world at my feet, and here I was with another opportunity to play at the home of English football thirteen years later under entirely different circumstances. I realised that this was probably going to be my last opportunity to play there and win a trophy.

The only other highlights of that season were the traditional festive fixtures against our local rivals Bromsgrove Rovers, normally played on Boxing Day and New Year's Day. Although we generally had the upper hand, Bromsgrove were a very good team, managed by one of the best players ever to play for West Bromwich Albion – Bobby Hope. He came across as a very genial Scot and was always pretty quiet and polite. Even though the weather could be pretty bad at this time of year I don't think a game was ever called off as it was always the biggest gates of the season and a money spinner for both clubs. There's no doubt it was a special atmosphere and the games were always pretty tasty too as you would expect for a local derby.

In one of these games I had a particularly good first half on a very icy pitch at Bromsgrove and when I came out for the second half Paul Webb had been moved to mark me and the normal right back Jimmy Skelding had been taken off. I asked Webby "what's happened to Jimmy?" Webby replied "he's been taken off with twisted blood!" Funny and a compliment at the same time.

In another one of these games I was taken off at half time myself having been replaced by a young emerging Lee Hughes. I remember being angry and humiliated, but that's football – full of ups and downs throughout any player's career I'm sure.

Les Palmer got married at the end of the previous amazing season and he invited us all to the reception. We were all having a few drinks and Lee was leading the way and getting drunk quickly with as much gold on him as Mr T from *The A Team*.

I tried to talk to him about him not wasting his chance in football and to just concentrate on his game and forget about being 'Jack the Lad' but I'm pretty sure he listened as much as I would have at 18. We all think we are men and know it all at that age, it's not until it's all over that we look back and wish we'd done things differently. On another occasion after Lee had just broken into the first team squad he came into the bar at Kiddy and told me he'd just been offered his first professional contract and had agreed to it and I asked him if he wanted any help. He then told me what he'd been offered and it wasn't very good but I asked him if he was happy- he said he was and I replied that I was pleased for him but perhaps he should ask for appearance money when selected for the first team. I don't know if he did or not but in any case he went on to make a lot more money from football than I ever did and scored goals everywhere he went. I know Lee made a huge mistake and was sentenced to do time in prison but knowing him I'm sure it wasn't anything premeditated but more likely something daft done without any thought of the consequences. I'm not condoning what he did but just don't think he would have realised what he was doing. I've seen Lee a few times at charity games and he is still the same lad really with no edge to him. I believe he is back helping his dad's scaffolding business again now after just hanging his boots up in his early forties.

The rest of the season was really about making sure I was playing well enough to be selected for the final at Wembley. Our league position was 11th in the end which was really disappointing and we certainly weren't the fluid force from the season and a half before, obviously my performance level and availability were a lot lower than before and I was still really struggling with my knee and the cramps were getting worse in my groin because of it. The honest truth is that I wanted to win at Wembley, put the season behind me and hope my knee was ok for the next season.

We travelled down to London on the Friday night as we were playing our game on the Sunday and stayed in one of the hotels that the FA Cup finalists traditionally stayed in which was top quality. After having some dinner most of us had a couple of pints and had an early night. To help pass some time we went to watch the FA Vase on the Saturday lunchtime which gave us a flavour of the special old stadium. I don't really remember much about the game as I was already thinking about our match the following afternoon.

Once we got back to the hotel I had a power-nap and then went down for dinner. After dinner we had a team meeting where the team was picked without any real surprises and Graham said to make sure we prepared properly but said he trusted us if we wanted a couple of pints to help us sleep. Graham always treated us like men and expected us to behave responsibly which I liked but it can be taken advantage of sometimes.

On this particular night a few of us met in the bar and one by one we all drifted off to bed at different times. Martin Weir, Paul Grainger and some of the reserve players were having a few beers with Ian Britton the reserve team manager who was a good lad and one of the boys really. Grainge and Weirdo were obviously gutted about not being able to play in the final due to their injuries. One of the lads got a bit lively after a few beers and unfortunately this attracted a local Londoner who was staying in the hotel that night. This chap tried to join in the banter with the lads and as is usual he was getting slaughtered, he was trying his best to fit in which he was never going to do as, simply put, he just wasn't one of us. He pulled a chair over and sat with us,

On the Wembley trail for Kiddy.

which was a sign to go to bed for me, but before I got up one of the lads came back from the bar and grabbed this chap by the neck from behind and although I think this was supposed to be a joke he took offence and stood up and head-butted our player straight on the nose, which instantly started pouring with blood! We all got in between them and I told Britt to get the lad out of the way and I took our player to the toilets to clean him up and try to calm him down. Once a few minutes passed and the blood had stopped running our player was ready to go looking for him, "where is he – I'll kill him!" Well that ship had sailed and the other fella was nowhere to be seen thankfully, we all pledged a vow of silence before going to bed so the story didn't get out before the game and I think it has been kept under wraps ever since.

It still wasn't very late and I had a decent night's sleep before waking up with the birds with the excitement and tension of going to play at Wembley. I remember wishing the kick off was earlier than 1pm as I was ready to go at 7 in the morning. We met for a walk and a quick meeting before setting off for Wembley Stadium. We had to have a look at the pitch and have a few photos taken but I really just wanted to play the game.

Once kick off finally came it was a reasonably even contest as usual against Woking although they took an early lead with a good goal through Scott Steele. However we didn't take too long to equalise with Ocker turning a cross home from about 10 yards – he had a knack for scoring on big occasions and scored the winner when we won the Trophy before my time in 1987. Although I was really conscious of my left knee which wasn't right I was still getting the better of their right back Lloyd Wye who wasn't venturing very far from me at all. Halfway through the first half I made a run in between him and their centre half and I was in against Laurence Batty, however the linesman had stuck his flag up for offside even though I know I was at least a yard onside when Richard Forsyth played a great through ball – the whistle went and although I carried on and lobbed him I knew it wasn't going to count. I actually hit the post but I know I would have either scored initially or followed up to score if he hadn't blown up. Small margins can decide games like this and the TV coverage confirmed I was well onside.

The rest of the game was pretty even with not too much incident that I can remember and it went into extra time – which I could have done without as my knee was screaming by now. I think we had both settled on a replay when Chris Brindley had to go off with a broken arm with about 5 minutes left after having another immaculate game on the big occasion which he loved – I don't think he lost a header all game. Almost immediately they had a corner which was knocked down and finished from close range – there was literally hardly time to kick off and it was over – we'd lost!

There's no worse feeling than losing a final and especially at Wembley, I just wanted to get off and as soon as I got my medal I gave my family and the Kiddy fans a wave and got back to the dressing room with a mixture of disappointment and relief that I could rest my knee.

We made our way back to a pre-arranged reception at a hotel in Kidderminster and although we all had a drink and a bit of a sing song with our director Colin Youngjohns leading the way it was all a bit subdued and to be honest I just wanted to go home.

Definitely a season to regret but there was worse to come.

CHAPTER TWENTY ONE

Weekend from Hell

The following close season was spent getting on with life as normal hoping that some rest would do the trick with my knee. Looking back, I should have spoken up after the game at Wembley and gone for another operation to sort out whatever the problem was, but at the time I was pretty reluctant to go under the knife yet again.

I started doing some running a few weeks before returning for pre-season and I didn't feel too bad – certainly nothing I couldn't handle. So I reported back in reasonable shape and looking forward to getting back to playing football again. However within a couple of sessions of twisting and turning, which football demands, my knee flared up again and I knew I had a problem but didn't really know how to deal with it. I felt stupid for not just getting on with another operation earlier and to be honest a bit worried about Graham's reaction when I told him. So I then proceeded to make another terrible decision…

Like the previous season there was a weekend in Guernsey arranged to get a couple of games in and obviously bond the group. I'm presuming the previous year's trip was such a success that Graham wanted to repeat the process. I knew if I told Graham I was struggling with my knee he wouldn't have taken me so I decided to tell him when we got there so I could at least enjoy a weekend away. How selfish and stupid of me looking back, I should have explained to him like a man. I was in a position to be able to pay my own way to join the lads anyway which might have been ok – I'll never know.

I realised I had made a mistake and all the way to Guernsey I was trying to work out the best way to tell him but to be honest I was scared of what his reaction would be. Once we settled in to the hotel we were given some free time and most of the boys went for a few beers. I wasn't really in the mood so I went for a meal with Kim Casey, who had just re-joined the club after a previous spell as a prolific goal scorer at Conference level and we had played together at Cheltenham a couple of years previously.

Kim was absolute dynamite in his first spell and was explosively quick over 10 yards and scored a lot of goals which will always attract interest from other clubs. I know that Wolves were interested in him when I was there and I'm sure there would have been a few more too, but Kim was and still is a successful person outside of football. He was earning more money in insurance than Wolves or probably any other lower league club could offer him to give up his career, as well as his happy football life, for the uncertainty and probable short contract offered to be a full time professional footballer. We had a good evening and a chat, and he agreed that I just had to tell Graham about my injury the next morning and see what happens.

The following morning we were due to do some light training and then play the match in the afternoon, it was only at this point that I worked up the courage to talk to Graham and explain I was struggling and couldn't play. He didn't say much but it was obvious he wasn't best pleased so I quickly made myself scarce and tried to stay out of the way so as not to antagonise him and also to let him concentrate on the football match ahead. The weather was fantastic to watch but not so great if you're playing. Although I was some distance away I'm pretty sure that it was noticed that I was sunning myself on the grass while the lads were struggling in the heat, so much so that we played pretty poorly and the result wasn't great which I'm sure didn't lighten Graham's mood.

After we got back to the hotel we had a quick shower and we all went out for a good night on the town with one of the lads noticeably flashing the cash which I didn't think anything of at the time. However In the morning, word soon got around that one of the lads was being questioned by the local police for using counterfeit £20 notes, so the generosity of the previous night was now making some sense!

We still had a game to play early the next afternoon and, in addition to the above, Chris Brindley couldn't play with a bad back picked up the day before, so we were literally down to the bare bones and we got beat handsomely in the boiling early afternoon heat. You could say the weekend wasn't going well but it was about to get a whole lot worse!

The season before, Graham had appointed Ocker as player-coach and as often happens in this situation they became good friends and still are to this day. However there was a feeling around that Ocker didn't balance the role very well as he didn't really spend any time with the lads and had crossed to 'the dark side' completely. Our form had dropped and this new 'situation' was creating a bit of an atmosphere around the camp, but, as normal, most players didn't want to say anything for fear of losing their place at the club.

After the match we had a shower and decided to stay in the hotel, and we started an almighty drinking session, with the normal banter flowing. Graham and Ocker went out for something to eat, but apparently while they were out Graham had heard that there was some kit left in the changing rooms. When he got back he had a go at Geordie, the kit man, who had had a few pints by then and an argument started which ended up with Geordie getting the sack! Understandably, Graham was obviously not in a great mood so went to his room for the evening.

The drinking carried on and I ended up sitting at the bar with Ocker as we always got on well before. After a while I tried to explain the feeling in the camp to him, but he wasn't having it and basically told me to 'f… off' which I reluctantly did telling him that I was just trying to help. I joined Chris Brindley and a couple of the other lads for a beer and told them about my conversation with Ocker, and then I went to bed having had enough to drink and thinking it was probably the best option. However, about an hour later there was a bit of a commotion going on outside the room. Apparently Delwyn Humphries had tried to have the same conversation with Ocker but was probably a bit blunter than me, knowing Del. This developed into a bit of a set to and Ocker stormed off to his room. Delwyn hadn't finished and followed him up the stairs trying to get at him, at which point Graham appeared at his door having heard the noise and Delwyn said "and you can f*** off too with your purple underpants on!" Funny looking back, but not at the time! Everyone quickly went to bed and we all woke up hungover and dreading what lay ahead on the very subdued journey home.

Surprisingly, nothing was said in the morning with most of us expecting a meeting to be called to sort things out. I thought that maybe Graham was going to give it some more thought and possibly deal with it at the ground before our next training session, but when we landed at Birmingham Airport and were waiting for our luggage Graham pulled Delwyn and me to one side and said, "you two are finished here and will never play for the club again!" We were told to stay at home and not to come in again. I think it's fair to say we were both a bit shocked, and I remember saying something stupid like "you will have to post my wages then!" This was definitely bravado masking the fact that I was gutted about my time at Kidderminster Harriers nearing its end.

Solitary Confinement

When I got back home I had the opportunity to reflect on the events of that fateful weekend. I know I should have been honest about my knee problem before going on the trip, but I don't regret having the conversation with Ocker, although admittedly it would have been far better to do it when both of us were sober, but possibly the reaction would not have been any different. Perhaps I should have kept my mouth shut but as one of the senior players I felt it was a situation that needed to be addressed. I guess Graham may have felt Delwyn and I were too big for our boots and it was none of our business and we should have just concentrated on playing, which is a fair point, but I will say that it was only because we cared that we felt something should be said.

Being in the football business can make you quite self-centred and you have to be, to a certain extent, in order to survive. It made me quite belligerent and I just had to get myself back fit and see what lay ahead at that time. My first priority was to have another operation on my left knee, which was quickly sorted out, and I then had to start the rehabilitation process from home. Although I had been treated badly in the past by Graham Turner at Wolves, training with the youth team on occasion, this was a whole new situation – I was basically on my own and it was up to me to get fit and ready to play again.

I endeavoured to get fit as soon as possible to get to a situation where I could either get a move away or possibly get back involved again with the Kiddy squad. Time can heal a lot of things and although the team were doing ok I think I still had a lot to offer at that level. I was running every morning and gradually building up my fitness level, but during one of my runs around the muddy fields at the back of my house I felt a searing pain in the back of my calf which felt like I had been stabbed and it was apparent I had torn my calf quite badly. Yet another setback on the road to recovery. Muscle injuries are in some ways the most difficult injuries to overcome as you're never quite sure when they're healed and it's difficult to judge without risking them going back to square one again. This was a difficult situation and I called the club to inform them and, to be fair, they asked me to go in and see the physio to try and help. Obviously I was no good to them injured and it was in everyone's best interests to get me fit. This took a while and it was a couple of months before I was able to start training with a ball again.

This period of isolation made me realise just how unimportant you actually are as an individual footballer. The team and the club are bigger than any one person and Kidderminster Harriers carried on without me. I was quite bitter and it also hurt that I didn't get one phone call from any of the lads to see how I was, you are soon forgotten in football.

As an aside, I remember having a conversation about this with Robert Kelly at Wolves who I stayed in touch with for a while after we both left. He said at that time that we are all ships in the night and there are no friends in football. He went on to prove this himself some years later when I tried to call him as then manager of Leicester City to try and form a link with a junior set up that my sons were playing in. He got someone else to call me back as he was too busy apparently!

On my first night back training I went onto the pitch and was just getting a feel of the ball by juggling. Chris Brindley came over for a chat and asked how I was and if I was coming back into the fold. I said that I didn't think so and he said he thought it was all wrong. He pointed at the new stand and said "you helped pay for that and you should be treated better." It was a nice touch from a top player and a great lad.

A little time went by and I had a call from Graham asking if I was fit and that there had been an enquiry from Telford but they needed to see me play before they would pursue it so he asked if I wanted to play in the next game, starting as sub. Obviously I wanted to play and Telford wasn't a bad option for me but I was still hoping to get a reprieve from Graham by doing well on the pitch. Before I signed at Kidderminster I had been approached by Telford when Gerry Daly was in charge. He was one of my boyhood heroes having played for Man Utd who I supported for a short time during the Tommy Docherty era. At that time I wanted to sign for Kidderminster due to the stability and reputation of the club. Sure enough Gerry didn't stay too long at Telford so at least I got that decision right! Wayne Clarke was now the Telford manager with Brian Caswell as his assistant. I had first seen Wayne Clarke when I was on trial as a schoolboy at Wolves and he was training with the first team at Castlecroft having not long broken into the first team, he just oozed class with a great first touch and cool finishing. Brian Caswell came on loan at Wolves during my time there and he was a funny, likeable character and a good player too.

Anyway, Graham put me on in the game and I played well making a couple of goals and I felt good. After the match Graham asked to see me and I was hoping he was going to say that he wanted to keep me, but he just said that Telford want to sign you and you can talk to them. I spoke to them briefly and it didn't take long to agree terms. So I collected my boots and left Kidderminster Harriers – for now.

CHAPTER TWENTY TWO

Back to Reality

The following Thursday I turned left out of my drive towards Telford instead of right to Kidderminster and it only took about 20 minutes to get to The Buck's Head. I was used to dealing with a new dressing room and it didn't take me long to settle in with a good set of lads. Wayne had taken over my contract from Kiddy and promised me a new contract if I proved my fitness for the remainder of the season. I was looking forward to playing again and hit the ground running playing well and I know that they were happy with me.

The reality of leaving Kidderminster first hit home on the way to our first long away trip when I realised there was no toilet on the bus. This wasn't so bad on the way as we made a stop at the services, but on the way back after a few beers the lads had to pee into a bucket as the only option to prevent wetting ourselves. Yuck!

There was also no set routine for food after the match – this was treated on an ad hoc basis, as was getting our wages after a match which was dependant on the result and performance on a Saturday, and often we would have to hang around until the powers that be decided to pay us. This was a power game that I didn't like but I only lived 20 minutes away from the ground whereas some of the lads were travelling from as far afield as Mansfield – a good two hours away. Pre-match meals were quite rare and the players were definitely treated as second class citizens – while we had the choice of toast with or without beans, the directors would be enjoying the 'A La Carte' menu.

On one of these occasions the players were left waiting for ages and unfortunately I was sat at the table furthest away from the kitchen which meant I would probably get served last so as soon as the first waitress walked in from the kitchen I put my hand up to catch her attention and said 'beans on toast?' She replied 'yes sir' and I got the first plate! As you can imagine I got dog's abuse from the lads nearest the kitchen expecting their food!

During the remainder of that season we played Macclesfield at home and I scored a pearler from further out than the FA Cup goal having seen their keeper off his line. They were managed by Sammy McIlroy who was another boyhood hero of mine, he was one of the main men for the Man Utd team of the 70s and 80s. I always wanted to impress him and generally played well against Macclesfield as they were always one of the best teams in the league so I was delighted when his assistant Gil Prescott approached me for a chat after the match. He was a lovely fella and after a little while talking football he shook my hand and wished me all the best before whispering that Sammy wanted to sign me for the next season and he slipped a bit of paper into my hand with his number on it.

I was quite happy at Telford and I liked Wayne Clarke although some of the lads thought he was a bit aloof but I never had any problems with him at all, he treated me as a man and he had a dry sense of humour. Brian Caswell was the bubbly one but he could throw the tea cups on the odd occasion. The training was always decent but lacked the focus that Graham had at Kiddy with his high pressing game and belief in the 4-3-3 formation. I guess that most of their contacts were in the League from their playing days and there were quite a few old pros coming and going including Dave Bennett who scored in the FA Cup final win for Coventry against Spurs. Benno was a nice fella but he was still living in his world as a top footballer, although he was coming towards the end of his footballing days. Peter Bodak also had a short spell with us, I had met him when I was at Wolves when he played there too for a short while before moving on – presumably for more money than Wolves could offer at the time. He was another player who lost his way and didn't fulfil his undoubted potential.

It has only been in recent times that people have started to talk about the mental health problems that ex-players suffer, which normally seems to involve drink and depression, and we generally only hear of the high profile players on shows like 'Harry's Heroes' which have highlighted Razor Ruddock's problems along with Paul Merson and Lee Hendrie too. This is only scratching the surface really as I'm aware of a lot of players who have had real problems coming to terms with 'normal' life after football. Indeed my replacement at Wolves, Robbie Dennison, has recently been opening up about his recent depression after struggling to come to terms with life after being a footballer. I'm pleased to see Merse and Robbie both doing okay now.

I guess it's a bit different for the top players now as they are earning enough money to set themselves up for life and it seems that it's treated as more of a business than it ever was before. Not many players before the Premier League were earning enough to retire on and even the top players relied on paying into their footballer's pensions to provide an income after the age of 35. However the lower league players are definitely not earning enough to retire on and have to find a way of finding an income when their very short career as a footballer is over, not easy when the majority of lads have been focused on football from a very early age. So the transition from having a cushy day at work and being given adulation for playing a game we generally love to trying to earn a normal living can be really difficult. There's only so many jobs related to football available. I know the PFA try and help those that come forward but I think the clubs should try and do more to prepare players for life after football as a duty of care. It could be argued that it's not their problem but it would be the decent thing to do.

Anyway at the end of the season I asked to speak to Wayne and told him that Macclesfield had been in touch and as I was out of contract I felt I should talk to them. So after work one day I drove the 90 minutes up the M6 to meet Sammy McIlroy. The journey wasn't much fun and it put me off to be honest. I was met by Gil Prescott and spent a bit of time with him before a brief meeting with Sammy who was in business mode and basically asked what I wanted to sign. I got the impression he had a few irons in the fire and wasn't too interested anyway, so I asked for a £5000 signing on fee and £200 a week cash. He said that he would speak to the board and come back to me, which I took with a pinch of salt.

I had agreed to talk to Wayne Clarke after the meeting and told him a little white lie that they had offered me the terms I asked for and Wayne said he would ask the board. It wasn't long before he came back to me and said they couldn't do the signing on fee but would give me the £200 cash plus bonuses for two years. Happy days! I'd got a decent rise and a two year deal! I never did hear back from Sammy McIlroy and he didn't miss me as Macclesfield won the league the following season just pipping Kiddy to promotion into the football league.

The most memorable game for me the following season was my return visit to Aggborough to play against Kiddy who were flying high at the top of the league. Graham Allner had still got Weir, Brindley, Webb, Yates and Steadman, with Lee Hughes coming through to replace me and was scoring goals for fun prior to his move to West Brom. Graham had recruited Ian Olney (ex-Villa) to lead the line as a replacement for Ocker and Neil Doherty (ex- Blues) to replace Delwyn on the right. He had also added a bit of experience with my old pal Kevin Willetts in midfield and Steve Prindiville at left back who had been a good pro for a long time. The final piece was the attacking full back, Marcus Bignot, who played like a modern day wing back and went on to have a good league career with Crewe, QPR and Blues.

In the week building up to the game Wayne and Cas asked to have a chat for my opinion about how to play against them. We all knew that man-for-man we weren't as good as them by a long way so taking them on in an open game would have been football suicide and I think we would have been hammered. I knew Graham would play 4-3-3 and I felt we had to match them up in midfield and stop their full-backs pushing on. They both agreed and then I suggested that I play as a withdrawn centre-forward to try and find space and keep the ball for us to hit them on the occasional break, I think it's called a false 9 these days. This was because Chris Brindley and Martin Weir liked the physical challenge of marking a centre-forward but weren't too comfortable coming out of the back line. The plan worked well and we were having a pretty even game, albeit a pretty dull one, until Paul Webb scored a scrappy goal from a corner late in the game to seal the points for them. At that time they looked set to win the league, and I left after a few beers wishing them well and believing that they would.

The season was pretty average for us and I think Wayne was having problems getting the players he wanted with the money he had in his budget. After losing a few games on the bounce he decided to resign. He gave me a call and just said that he'd had enough of the hassle dealing with the board, in all honesty I think he probably saw the writing on the wall and decided to jump before he was pushed. There's not much to say in that situation apart from to wish him all the best. As I said before I liked him but perhaps he lacked the obsessive passion that football managers seem to need and I'm sure he was happier living a hassle free life. I've seen him a couple of times over the years and he was doing well working in sales for Coca Cola and then as a postman I believe.

The club already had a replacement lined up it seemed as Jake King took over the team immediately. To be honest I had no idea who he was but soon found out he was a long serving stalwart under the Graham Turner era at Shrewsbury. He came in like a Scottish whirlwind and immediately changed our system to a 5-3-2 which was quite ground breaking at the time and certainly turned our results around quickly. However, I think he wanted to bring his own lads in from his Shrewsbury connections and I'm not sure he was happy with the money I was earning. I was confident I could fit into his system playing behind the front two but more times than not he preferred to play three workers in midfield which was his prerogative. I knew the writing was on the wall long term but kept my mouth shut and just got on with training and being a regular sub. The most memorable part of his reign for me was the Xmas do when we were all out for a few drinks and then went for a curry at the end of the night. I knew I wasn't in his plans so I made the most of a rare night out away from the wife and my two boys in nappies – this led to me getting totally drunk and falling asleep at the table in the curry house before my food had arrived! Not my proudest moment! Fortunately I was staying with Brett Wilcox that night so I didn't have to face Julie in that state. Brett told me at the next training session that I wanted to sleep in the garden for some reason but he managed to get me inside on to the sofa eventually!

Jake King's positive impact on our results obviously alerted our near neighbours Shrewsbury Town and during the close season he was appointed as their new manager, which meant I was waiting for yet another new football boss!

CHAPTER TWENTY THREE

The Daley Express

I was working one afternoon when I received a call from the Shropshire Star journalist Allan Phillips asking for my opinion about the newly appointed manager, which I had no idea about! He told me it was Steve Daley and what did I think?

I just said that it should be good and that I'm looking forward to working with him. I had known Steve for a fair few years, initially as an opponent against Walsall when I was starting at Wolves and he was just coming to the end of his playing days. It was obvious he was a classy player even then with a great passing range with both feet and he was also an amiable person off the pitch – I saw him socially around Wolverhampton's pubs and clubs over the years. He always had a good dry sense of humour and we got on well socially. It was no real surprise that he did very well on the after-dinner scene with his self-deprecating show, which was delivered very well and it's only recently that he has withdrawn from the evening circuit.

It wasn't too long after putting the phone down to the newspaper that I received a call from Steve and he was obviously enthusiastic and excited about getting started which can be very contagious and is a good asset to have. However, eventually he said "Purds, I need your help as I don't know much about the level!" By this time I had been knocking around the Conference level for 5 years and had built up a few contacts and knew a lot of the good players at that level. Steve was naturally confident and had ambitions to do well and move up the football pyramid, he then asked me to become his assistant manager to go with him wherever he moved on to! I was flattered but I was still only 28 and just wanted to play for a while yet, so I said I didn't mind helping him with warm ups etc but didn't want any kind of management responsibility as yet.

The next day I arrived early at training and the headline on the back page of the Shropshire Star was 'Purdie assistant manager to Daley'. He hadn't taken a blind bit of notice of what I had said, so I went to see him in his office, and he said "don't worry it will be fine". I now had a choice of falling out with the new manager or going along with him and hoping for the best, I chose the latter option. I wasn't really comfortable with it but didn't want to rock the boat I guess.

Steve was like a Tasmanian devil with boundless energy and enthusiasm but unfortunately not a lot of money to spend and not too many contacts at Conference level. Therefore we had to recruit lots of young players and hope that they would come through, these included some of the best young players in Wolverhampton, including his son Ryan and a few other 18 year olds such as Tony Collins, Greg Parkes (son of Phil Parkes), Matthew Bytheway, Steve Palmer (son of Geoff, the Wolves stalwart) and Asa Charlton.

It was a lot to ask of these lads to step up to the Conference all at the same time but they were all good lads and I tried to help them as much as possible and we would travel together and often have a few beers after training and enjoy the occasional night out.

If I see any of them these days we still have a bond of sorts. Palmer became a successful non-league player with Telford and Hednesford notably, and Asa has had an outstanding non-league career locally and is still playing at 42!

I recommended a few other players to Dales and we managed to get Steve Taylor from Bromsgrove and Neil Cartwright from Kiddy who had both proved themselves at that level. It was definitely work in progress but unfortunately results are needed immediately, and they weren't easy to come by.

On a personal level I had a slight calf strain in a pre-season game and came off as a precaution so as not to aggravate it and thought no more of it assuming it would be ok in a few days. However, this was to prove to be probably the worst injury in my career – every time I tried to run it felt like I was being stabbed in the calf. After several periods of rest this came to a head at Halifax away when I tried to take the warm up for the lads and I just couldn't jog at all. I knew something serious was up and after witnessing Geoff Horsfield and Jamie Patterson (both excellent players) rip us to bits I travelled home very subdued knowing I had to deal with my calf fearing another operation.

The next morning I booked in to see Mr El Safty yet again and a subsequent scan showed I needed exploratory surgery to find the problem and I was quickly booked in for an operation. The resulting surgery discovered a life-threatening blood clot lodged in my calf but fortunately wasn't able to move up through my body at that time. Mr El Safty said I was very lucky. Julie came to see me with the boys after the surgery and she went a funny colour and needed to lie down after seeing the drain in my calf keeping the blood circulating. I didn't dwell on this as there's not much point and got back to work as soon as possible and then endeavoured to start my rehabilitation to begin playing football again.

I tried to put as much time and effort in as I could to help out Dales and we would be talking for hours at a time most days and I thought we had developed a friendship despite struggling to get results consistently and hovering around the relegation zone throughout. As soon I was able, I took the training most nights which enabled Dales to watch matches to try and strengthen our team. One freezing cold winter's day Dales called me to say he wanted to go and watch Nuneaton as Gez Murphy was scoring goals for fun in the league below and we needed goals desperately. Of course I agreed and took training that night without a hitch. It was only a few weeks later when Dales had a Christmas party for the team and their partners that his wife Lynne was talking to me and inadvertently thanked me for letting him have a night off so they could enjoy dinner together... If he had just said that he wanted a night off it wouldn't have been a problem but I didn't appreciate the deception to be honest.

Anyway, the season continued to falter and even when we played well we couldn't win – conceding late goals or suffering from horrendous defensive mistakes and ultimately the decision was made by the board to sack Dales. I was actually sad to see him go as he was good fun and the place was always a happy one despite the results. Perhaps it was just too relaxed to be successful. We spoke and he was disappointed but had been in football long enough to know how it works. We wished each other well and he thought he might have another job coming up.

I was now in the position that I feared might happen as any new manager would regard me as part of the previous management team when I had been reluctant all along. As is usually the way in football the next appointment was a complete contrast to Dales and the Buck's Head welcomed the strict disciplinarian that was Jimmy Mullen.

CHAPTER TWENTY FOUR

Mullen things over

As often happens in football Jimmy came in to make his mark immediately and laid down the law that things were going to change.

He reckoned that we weren't fit enough and the first few sessions were a combination of running and more running mixed in with the most bizarre session I've ever been involved in. This consisted of the players pairing up with a ball between us and we had to take turns kicking it as far as we could from the six yard line to the other player on the halfway line and deeper. I'm not sure what the purpose of this was but we did it anyway!

Shortly after he arrived he asked to speak to me in private and was quite to the point. He wanted to know how I felt about the situation and I just told him I really just wanted to play but if he wanted any help I would be happy to continue to do the warm ups. He was actually not as scary in private as he liked to portray and lent on me in the first few weeks to get to know about the younger players especially. He wanted to clear them out as Dales had brought them in, but I said he should keep them as our squad was very thin and he might need them. However I did think that the only one that was ready to play was Steve Palmer. I told Jimmy so and he gave him the opportunity which Palms duly took with both hands.

Very soon after Jimmy arrived we were due to play Leek in the FA Trophy – a competition which is important to non-League clubs both financially and for the players to chase the dream of playing at Wembley. He was still in his 'run the balls off them' phase and right at the end of the Thursday session doing box to box sprints I felt my hamstring tighten up and I was out for the game on the Saturday with not enough time to recover. I had never pulled a hamstring before and looking back I reckon it may have only been cramp but fortunately we got a draw and I was available for the replay. I set up a couple of goals for Steve Palmer to enable us to progress.

Jimmy started getting a few players in and results began to improve, but I wasn't sure of my future there and before long Steve Daley called me to tell me he had been offered the Bromsgrove Rovers job and whether I wanted to join him. This presented a dilemma for me. I had never envisaged playing for Bromsgrove as they are Kidderminster's closest rivals and I still had an affinity with Harriers. So I said I was interested but wanted to see how it goes as I didn't really want to drop down from the Conference.

Not long after there were a few incidents involving Jimmy that I wasn't too comfortable with which I don't think it's fair to go into out of respect for him but I felt it best that I moved on and agreed a one and a bit year contract with Steve Daley at Bromsgrove, which I hadn't been offered at Telford. I was in the process of putting my boys through private school and every pound helped even though Julie and I were both doing well workwise. I signed on deadline day and played a few times to see the season out, I think I knew it was a mistake as soon as I played my first game as I just didn't feel comfortable playing in the green of Bromsgrove. I was also having a few problems with my knee again and struggled for form to be honest.

Steve Daley had recruited his big pal Phil 'Lofty' Parkes to join him on the coaching staff, mainly looking after the keepers – who better could a young goalkeeper have to learn from with his outstanding career! He is always full of great stories from his long career at Wolves as well as his time in the MLS playing against Pele, Beckenbauer, Cruyff, etc! Lofty has always been a lovely big, affable fella and always good company with a smile on his face. However when the whistle goes all you could hear was his booming voice shouting from the top of the stand, generally criticising the referee. I've never really understood the logic of this as I would have thought that human nature would turn a referee against a team that's constantly criticising them but it's quite a common opinion that it works the other way. Personally I'm in the Graham Allner camp of treat them well and show respect and you may get a 50/50 decision in your favour. Each to their own I guess and I still enjoy seeing Lofty at Wolves' ex-players 'do's'.

At the end of the season Steve Daley called me by telephone saying that the Chairman had decided that he didn't want me to stay. I simply said "no problem – tell him to get his cheque book out and I'll leave". He was surprisingly taken aback and I just said, "you know how it works Steve – I'll leave it with you". I felt that this sort of conversation should have taken place in person and I may have just left but he got my hackles up by doing it by phone so I dug my heels in.

Fortunately by then I was with Bupa health insurance and decided to get my knee sorted out as soon as possible. I informed Steve by text and turned up for pre-season to rehabilitate as contracted. He wasn't talking to me by then but I wasn't bothered to be honest, I was more concerned with looking after my family. I turned up for every training session and match and made a point of working on my fitness for all to see, doing laps around the pitch before the games so I couldn't be accused of negligence to my contract. As soon as I was fit enough I began playing again in the reserves and then decided to do something I'd never done before and wrote a letter to Graham Allner at Kidderminster to ask for a trial there.

The gist of the letter was that I was now 31 and wanted to finish on a high playing for his team. I added that although I may not be the easiest player to manage, I didn't think I was that difficult either as during my taste of management at Telford we had a certain player who barely spoke to any of us and just got on the back of the bus, put his headphones on, hoody up and went to the toilet to smoke weed! I'm not mentioning names to stay safe!

A few days passed and I then got a call from Mr Allner, I was expecting the thanks but no thanks but we had a long chat and he said that if I got out of my contract with Bromsgrove I was welcome to go training and we would take it from there, but if I was anywhere near the player I was for him before he would have no problem playing me again!

This is all I wanted to hear and I immediately called the Bromsgrove Chairman and asked for a meeting which resulted in me receiving a £2000 pay-off to leave – saving him around £3000 if I had stayed. Thankfully I am on good terms with Steve Daley now and occasionally see him socially at the ex-Wolves players' evenings too.

I then rang Graham and arranged to go training and he agreed to pay me a little until a decision was made. It's fair to say that signing for Bromsgrove was a mistake but in the big scheme of bad decisions it's nowhere near the top of errors in my career decision making!

CHAPTER TWENTY FIVE

Last Chance Saloon

In the days leading up to going back training I was actually feeling like I did when I was trialling for England schoolboys all those years ago, I was nervous but determined to prove my worth. I didn't doubt my ability but this was a step up again to the club I really wanted to play for and where I wanted to finish my playing career so it was important that I hit the ground running.

My first time back was actually to watch the team play against Torquay in the FA Cup and a little winger called Ian Hathaway gave harriers a tough time – Ian was a young kid at Wolves when I played there and wasn't taken on but he looked like a proper player in this game. Some players develop later physically and I think it must be a difficult task in deciding on certain players like this especially if they're on a limited budget like Wolves certainly were when I was there.

I wanted to repay Graham's faith in me and I was working hard on my fitness every day to be able to make the most of this opportunity. Looking back now I realise how important peak fitness is to your form. I found that if I could remain injury free my form remained pretty good, however the difference between rehabilitation then and now has changed unrecognisably. Back then as soon as your injury had healed you were put back in the squad and sometimes even straight into the team and there's no way that you can be match fit for at least 4-6 weeks after a period of inactivity. The squads were much smaller then and it was a case of need more than want from a manager's point of view and some players could adapt better than others. Personally, I needed to be sharp to be able to beat an opponent whereas a good defender or a hard working midfield player doesn't need that. I was also guilty of taking my foot off the gas during the winter months as the usual routine of a professional footballer kicked in – Monday, Tuesday and Thursday were hard days, Wednesday normally off and very little on a Friday to prepare for match day on a Saturday. In hindsight this is very little more than I did as a semi pro, training hard twice a week with a match at the weekend. It was only by the time I arrived at Kidderminster the first time that I actually took my fitness seriously and the rewards and my good form followed. It was all too late and I have to live with the fact that I didn't make the best of my ability and the opportunities offered to me.

So after a couple of weeks of general training sessions Graham did some attack versus defence work and after a while waiting he gave me the chance to play on the left wing against Craig Hinton, who had recently been released by Blues and was very highly thought of, and indeed went on to have a good career after a successful spell with Kiddy. The first few times when the ball was played out to me I generally passed the ball into the strikers and followed my pass to give the option to have it back, after watching this for a while Graham stopped the play and said in front of everyone, "Purds anyone can do what you're doing at the minute – I want to see you test the defence, let's see if you've still got it". So this was it – shit or bust and I had to go for it!

I couldn't go easy on Craig and I had a purple patch for thirty minutes turning him every which way before putting crosses in for the strikers or cutting inside to shoot, it's fair to say that I earned the respect from the players that didn't know me and after the session I looked at Graham and he just smiled. Afterwards he asked how I was feeling fitness wise I told him I was getting there and then he asked how I felt about playing against Woking away on Saturday? I beamed and answered "I'd love to but not sure I'm ready for 90 minutes!"

I was so happy to have got back in his thoughts so quickly and fully expected to be on the bench on Saturday and perhaps get 20 minutes at the end which would have been great. On the Friday before the game he called me and said "prepare properly you're starting tomorrow"!

I couldn't wait and I didn't say anything on the way and still felt a little bit on trial, which I guess I was. It was only when he named the team did everyone know and all the lads wished me all the best which was a nice touch as they all knew my situation. Football is a strange game as, although it is very much a team game, we all have to ensure that we do our best individually within the team framework. That is one of the main reasons I enjoyed playing under Allner, he recognised that it takes different pieces to make a jigsaw and expected different qualities from us in our respective positions. So my main concern was to play well myself and hope everyone else did too. I enjoyed playing at Woking and normally played well there and this was no different. Early in the game I was brought down in their box for a stonewall penalty which wasn't given and then again in the second half which was thankfully awarded and my old pal Kev Willetts hammered it home. I tired towards the end and expected to be taken off but Graham told me afterwards he wanted to build my fitness up as he was impressed with my performance and wanted more.

I remember the bus journey home and began to feel at home again and the respect had grown within the group. I was enjoying my football again and I was back where I wanted to be.

However, the team wasn't as fluent as the old team and the balance wasn't quite right as Graham had lost a few good players in the previous season, including Lee Hughes to Albion, which is probably why I had this opportunity, Marcus Bignot to Crewe, and Ian Olney and Neil Doherty had moved on.

There was also a new board in place and the atmosphere had changed around the place, gone was the family feel club with unquestionable support for the manager, replaced with scrutiny and pressure to succeed. This is normal in general football terms but not at Kidderminster and it would certainly be a new experience for Graham although he hid it well.

Self-preservation was the name of the game and I just concerned myself with keeping my shirt for the next game which I did for the next few games until...

Purdie's Curse Strikes Again

I'm not sure if this was normal in a footballer's career at that time or not but it seemed that more or less every manager that signed me either got the sack or resigned during my period at the club. Obviously I didn't do the decent thing and inform them before signing me as this may have had a bearing on their decision!

The list is long and quite impressive – starting with Terry Neill at Arsenal, followed by Sammy Chapman at Wolves, Mark Lawrenson at Oxford, Ian McNeil at Shrewsbury, Ally Robertson at Cheltenham and Wayne Clarke at Telford! The only one that survived me was Graham Allner at Kidderminster during my first spell there but it turned out he wasn't going to get away with it twice! News filtered through that he had been sacked on the morning of a training night only a few weeks after I had signed again. It's testimony to him that he insisted on coming to training to say goodbye to us before leaving, which was quite a difficult moment as I always saw it as his club. That's football I guess and nothing is forever, however what happened after training that night even shocked me after so long in the game.

It appears that his assistant and physio Jimmy Conway had lined up a replacement immediately with his good friend and business partner Phil Mullen being put in caretaker charge. Jimmy had been Allner's sidekick for a long number of years and so it left a bad taste when he said some derogatory things that night. It was totally uncalled for and unnecessary as we as players will always go into self-protection mode at times like this – basically looking after number one.

Jimmy was a very funny man and always managed to make the lads laugh with his sharp, dry sense of humour. On a trip with Middlesex Wanderers, who are a select British touring team, to Holland and Germany (which included a very young Malky McKay before his move down South) we were having dinner and the team secretary came over to the table looking very forlorn. He said "lads I'm really sorry but I'm going to have to go home early as my mother has passed away". The normal sympathetic responses were forthcoming until he walked away and Jimmy said "he may as well stay for the rest of the trip as she will still be dead when we get back" – brutal and hilarious in equal measure! Jimmy also had a talent for spotting people with unusual or funny ways of walking and at airports he would break the monotony of waiting around by following people literally a couple of feet behind them mimicking and exaggerating their funny walks – it has to be witnessed to be believed – so funny.

After the Woking game Shaun Cunnington said to me that I should go in for a contract straight away but I trusted Graham to look after me – this proved to be yet another mistake as I was on a week to week contract and very vulnerable to be released at a week's notice.

It wasn't long before the captain Mark Yates had manoeuvred a transfer to Cheltenham and one or two of the lads felt he had jumped ship a bit quickly when we needed all the experience and help we could get. My opinion is that he had to do what he felt was best for him and he probably did the right thing for his career. From being in the team consistently, I was now finding myself in and out of favour and I had the feeling that my days were numbered as Phil looked to bring in younger players from the level he knew, which to be honest wasn't really good enough for Kidderminster. The standard of training sessions dropped alarmingly and although I wanted to play for Kidderminster it became quite obvious that this wasn't the same club without the leadership of Allner and the board from my first period there. One of my last games for the club was on New Year's Day against Hereford where I came directly up against my old Wolves teammate Robbie Dennison – we won and I played very well with the extra motivation of playing against Robbie who basically took my shirt at Wolves. Robbie is a great lad and I know he did very well for Wolves and I don't begrudge him that – I just wanted to play well for my own self-worth with the added boost that Graham Turner was the manager of Hereford and it was nice to get one over on him.

Middlesex Wanderers team photo in Holland.

It wasn't very long after leaving Kidderminster that Allner got offered the manager job at Worcester and he called me to ask if I would join him, which I guess was inevitable but I wanted to see how things went at Kiddy first. Unfortunately things didn't improve and after a few weeks I called Allner and asked if he still wanted me – he answered positively and we sorted the money out, which was better than Kiddy were paying me anyway. So I decided that after training I would tell Phil Mullen that I was leaving and give him my one week's notice. However before I went out for training I was asked to go and see him and he told me he was releasing me! I just said ok and left straight away, this meant I could play for Worcester on the Saturday as I didn't have to serve the notice period. Perhaps this gives a little insight into why players aren't very loyal these days and look after themselves as best they can – there's certainly no loyalty in reverse. As soon as you are deemed surplus to requirements or past your sell by date, you are history. It would be some compensation if you were sitting on a big contract but that wasn't the case back in those days even at the top level.

So I joined Allner at Worcester and he promised me a rise in wages in the summer if I did well for him until the end of the season, which I did, I think, albeit with a team being rebuilt under a new manager.

The season actually ended with a 2 legged cup final against Kidderminster with us winning the first leg and I had a stormer – I guess with a point to prove! I think we lost on aggregate in the end which was disappointing, but it was satisfying to play well against them in both games. This certainly made my appetite for the game, and the prospective new season, far greater than it had been for a couple of years and I was looking forward to a good season with Worcester City.

CHAPTER TWENTY SIX

Dad's Army

As is usually the way Graham lent on the players that had served him so well in the past and I guess he knew he could rely on, with good ability and character. We were however, with hindsight, ageing a little and also seemed like an ex-Kidderminster Harriers team, which perhaps didn't go down that well with the Worcester City diehards. Graham signed Martin Weir, John Deakin, Darren Steadman, Kevin Willets, with Jock McGrath and myself already there, and he bolstered the squad with Keith Knight from Gloucester and Andy Ellis and Mark Tucker from Woking who played against Kidderminster at Wembley and won against us which led to some good natured banter as you can imagine. All top class non-league players but all of us the wrong side of 30 with my pal Wilbur (Kevin Willetts) leading the way at 38. The rest of us were in our early to mid-30s and although we all thought we were still good players, the reality is that we were on the decline as is the norm really with the very odd exception. I think there's a few factors to this, the normal ageing process which puts a few pounds on, injuries that take the edge off, a dip in enthusiasm as you have been through the mill a little... Probably all things that you aren't really self-aware of, but just happens naturally as part of the ageing process. A few months later Graham signed another experienced player from Hednesford called Paul Carty who was still very athletic and probably just past 30 at the time and renowned for his pace.

I remember being a young boy watching Liverpool v Newcastle and Kevin Keegan was played through on goal. Before he even got to the ball Mark Lawrenson had put the turbo on and made up about 5 metres to take the ball off him as easy as taking sweets from a baby and casually passed the ball out from the back.

In training one night I had my Kevin Keegan moment. We were doing box to box runs and Paul Carty came past me like I was standing still. Now admittedly I have never been Adama Traore but I was always quick over the first 10 metres, but not anymore and I knew my days were numbered from then on. We did have a couple of young talented strikers in Mark Owen and Sam Bowen who were a good foil together, with Mark being quick, strong and skilful, and Sam being aggressive, quick and a real handful albeit a little undisciplined. There were a lot of clubs looking at Mark and I certainly think he could have played a lot higher but he suffered a broken ankle just at the crucial time of interest which I'm not sure he fully recovered from. Sam is the father of Jarod Bowen who has just broken through at West Ham and looks a very good prospect.

As football fate would have it we were drawn against Telford in the FA Trophy and we quite fancied our chances even though they were from the league above. Jimmy Mullen was still manager of Telford and it was nice when I was sent the content of an interview he did leading up to the game where he said I was his biggest concern as he thought I had the quality to turn the game in an instant. He had been to watch us in a couple of games beforehand and it's always nice to have good things said about you. We drew the first game at home and quite fancied our chances in the replay and we were looking forward to the opportunity to turn them over at the Buck's Head, however

'Mad Dog' Sam Bowen got sent off in the first couple of minutes and that put paid to that, we hung on for a while but once they scored the first there was no coming back. Put the Wembley suits away yet again!

On paper we should have walked that league with the group of players we had but we didn't click immediately and Graham wasn't quite as confident in his beliefs as he was at Kidderminster. At Kidderminster he always played 4-3-3 and he recruited players to fit into that system which served him well time after time, but now we were like square pegs in round holes and he started changing the system and asking us what we thought. Obviously this leads to everyone having their own opinion to suit their own game which probably just led to more confusion. I had a private conversation with Graham and when he asked my opinion I advised him to stick to his beliefs and succeed or fail with them and to be as strong minded as he was at Kiddy. I guess his confidence had taken a knock and his self-belief wasn't as unerring as before. Perhaps he needed a longer break to recover from his departure at Kiddy and it wasn't too long after Christmas before he came to this realisation and resigned. So now I'd seen him off twice sadly!

Probably the most memorable part of this season was the Christmas night out where I took the role as social secretary and managed to get just about everyone out together for a night out. I knew this was probably going to be my last and as there were so many old pals involved I wanted to have a good night with them. I arranged a meal at Shimla Pinks which was a trendy Indian restaurant, block entry to Legs Eleven, the lap dancing club, and then free entry into a nightclub owned by the Llewellyn's that owned Eves back in my Wolves days. It was an excellent night out with no trouble, with Martin Weir refusing to enter Legs

Eleven as he didn't think it was right, so he went off to Cheeky Monkey's for a dance and we caught up with him later – good old Weirdo!

So Allner had left and all his men were left behind waiting to see who was coming next.

* * *

Kevin Willetts (Cheltenham, Kidderminster & Worcester)

I played with Purds at three different clubs. The first was in the early 90s at Cheltenham and it only took ten minutes in the first training session to see that he was a different class with his ability to glide past defenders with what seemed like no pace at all, even though we soon got to know that he wasn't the most enthusiastic trainer.

It became apparent that he was a top lad and was always popular with his peers at every club. Over the next ten years I had the pleasure of his company on and off the pitch. Using today's terminology, Purds was an absolute baller but more importantly he's a top bloke and a good mate to this day.

* * *

CHAPTER TWENTY SEVEN

Special Agent Barton

I'm pretty sure that Graham had arranged for his replacement so as not to leave the club in the lurch and it was one of his previous players from an earlier successful period that was put in place. John 'Barty' Barton was a good player that played for Everton in the league and had a successful non-league career before going into management.

On his first night in charge he held a meeting and made it very clear that he would be playing 4-4-2 and we would be a pretty direct outfit playing predominantly in the oppositions half. I understood this completely but knew immediately that I wouldn't fit into this way of playing and resigned myself that my days were numbered. I thought I may as well have a chat with him to clarify my position as I didn't want to waste either of our time or tie up a chunk of his budget if he wanted to bring someone else in but he assured me he wanted me to hang around until the end of the season to see how it went. He told me I might not start but that he at least wanted to keep me as a squad player.

I did start a game soon afterwards and it was against Burton Albion away and Nigel Clough was in charge for them as player/manager. Before the game this loud, overweight, balding, ageing bloke was making a racket joking around with John Barton outside our dressing room and it took a few minutes for me to realise it was Andy King and they had been teammates together at Everton. I honestly didn't recognise him as the last time I had seen him he was still a young fit footballer. We had a bit of banter and it made me want to show Kingy that I could still play a bit.

In addition to this Brian Clough was also in the stand watching his boy start out in his management career. I must admit that before kick-off I looked over at Brian Clough and wondered how different my career could have been if I had signed for him as a schoolboy nearly 20 years before and whether he even remembered my name? I recently met up with Lee Glover and he said that the way Forest played under Clough would have suited my style – oh well, such is life!

I put in a good performance and the highlight for me was nutmegging Nigel with a nice bit of skill – scant consolation as I would rather have had his career, but it felt good at the time and his face was a picture!

As it turned out I was used generally as an impact substitute to either try to rescue a situation or to just retain possession if we were in a winning position. To be honest I was having problems with both knees at this point and was quite happy on the bench. I helped off the pitch as much as possible – taking warm ups occasionally and generally just encouraging the lads and trying to make myself useful. There were a few comments from the crowd asking why I wasn't starting as I generally did well when I got on but I would just shrug my shoulders and smile. I was relatively happy with the situation and was ready to retire and call it a day at the end of the season. At one point Barty asked if I'd be interested in a player/coach role the following season and I said I could be but nothing materialised. This part of my career was summed up when I was getting over my first career thigh strain and went on as sub thinking I'd recovered and scored with a curling shot from outside the box only for my thigh to go in the process, so I put my hand up and had to be subbed off straight away – that's what you call making an impact!

So that was it for me – the end of a journey from Wembley to Worcester or so I thought.

CHAPTER TWENTY EIGHT

Back to the Steelmen

I finished the previous season really struggling with both knees and arranged to have them both operated on to hopefully put my football career behind me. However I received a call from my old teammate Joe Jackson who was now manager of Bilston Town and he asked what my plans were. I told him I was packing it in and he said would I have a chat with him first so I agreed to meet him.

We met one sunny afternoon at Bilston's football ground which was a proper old fashioned non-league club and he took me up into the stand to sit and have a chat whilst we were overlooking the pitch. They had just narrowly missed out on winning the league the season before and Joe thought my little bit of quality could tip it for him. I wasn't really sure but he said he would play me behind the front two strikers in a 3-5-2 formation which I quite fancied as I knew playing wide in a 4-4-2 was definitely not going to work for either of us. Anyway I explained that I was going in for an operation on my knees and would let him know after some time to think about it.

It's a really difficult thing to do – giving up something that you're reasonably good at and enjoy being a part of, every former player will tell you that it's the dressing room banter that they miss and it's true. It's a unique situation and you are kind of a band of brothers when it's good. However I also knew I would miss playing – it's difficult to explain the feeling when you score an important goal or put one on a plate for a teammate. I guess I didn't want to let go even though the sensible thing was obviously to walk away and look after my knees – but that would be far too sensible for me!

So, as I knew I would, I agreed to go to pre-season training and see how it went – there was less travelling at this level and Bilston was 20 minutes from my house. The last few years had been very successful off the pitch so I was literally playing for the fun of it and getting £100 a week which was beer money for me really.

I didn't realise how difficult it is to have both knees operated on at the same time and I struggled to get about for a while and by the time pre-season came I was still nowhere near ready to join in. I would use my bike to get to training and show my face and bike home again to try and keep some fitness and get some strength into my legs. A lot of the lads at Bilston had been at Wolves as schoolboys, apprentices and young pros and were all decent players and good lads. It was apparent that I was definitely one of the old guard now though along with one or two others. However it was still good crack and the banter was decent and we were doing well on the pitch too although Joe had changed his mind about the formation and reverted to the dreaded 4-4-2! I started playing in late September with us already doing well in the league and after a few weeks I regained some sharpness and hit some good form. The system wasn't so important as we had most of the possession and were good going forward – it's the defending bit I hated.

Before long Joe had an opportunity to sign a player who he obviously thought would be a better long term option for him, which I can understand, and I got 'rested' which meant dropped in my language. This was my last season really and I just wanted to play so training twice a week to sit on the bench really didn't interest me.

In the meantime I had started working for a company in Wolverhampton and the money I was earning became ridiculous for what I was doing – supporting twelve sales people and getting commission from their success, often taking home five figures per month so my money for football became irrelevant but I wanted to play if I was committing myself to it. The sales manager for the company was also running a Sunday team in Bridgnorth and I would occasionally play for them and he gave me £50 a game – which was duly spent directly after the match in the pub linked to the team called 'The Blackboy'. I played as a striker and generally scored a few goals and had a few beers afterwards before going back home for the day or out for lunch with family and friends.

Things came to a head when Bilston were playing away at Cinderford, it was cold and hammered it down with rain and I was named as sub and I was the unhappiest substitute that ever lived. It was time to give up as I couldn't be doing with wasting my Saturdays when I had two young kids at home.

I have no idea how the game was going to be honest but Joe looked at me with 20 minutes to go and asked me to get warmed up as I was going on soon. So I went up the side of the pitch and did some unenthusiastic stretching and when five minutes passed and I hadn't had the call I decided I wasn't going on! Fortunately the clubhouse ran the length of the pitch and I just disappeared around the corner and out of view from Joe, I did peek around the corner a few times and I could see him looking for me but I stayed put until the final whistle blew. When I got in the dressing room he asked where I was and I told him I went for a pee in the bushes and he must have missed me –

but I think he knew really. So, I quickly got changed and went outside and called the Sunday team manager and asked him if he wanted me to play every Sunday and he said he did. I told him I would stop playing for Bilston and just play for him for £80 a game and he said 'it's a deal'. I then went in the bar and asked to have a word with Joe in private and explained that sitting on the bench at my stage of life was no good to me and that I was packing it in – he asked me to reconsider but I was adamant and we shook hands and I wished him well and drove home.

I got a 'Best Wishes' card and popped it into the dressing room before the next training night with individual humorous (I thought) comments about all the lads and wished them all well for the rest of the season.

So that was finally it – football at a decent level was over for me.

* * *

Joe Jackson (Worcester, Bilston Town & Wolves All Stars)

I wasn't at Wolves when Jon arrived as I'd not long left the club and we first met when we played for Worcester together. I later managed him at Bilston and then played together again for Wolves All Stars. Jon was a very cultured player who always seemed to go past players with ease, almost in slow motion but still no-one could get the ball off him. He was such a cool customer and I always thought Jon was an undercover black man due to his laid back nature on and off the pitch.

He's a fantastic guy to know, I'm glad we're still friends and I have a lot of respect for him.

* * *

CHAPTER TWENTY NINE

Sunday Bloody Sunday

The Blackboy

At this point in my life I was concentrating on looking after my boys and making money at work, and I like to think I was doing a good job at both. Julie was very work driven so would leave early in the morning to get to work and I took on the responsibility of waking and getting the boys fed and ready for school. I would then do the school run, go to work, and pick the boys back up from school and feed them before Julie got home. I didn't begrudge these duties, in fact I loved doing it and I miss those days now. However Sunday mornings became a bit of a release from those duties – a bit of 'me' time I guess. I stopped training and literally just turned up on a Sunday, played, showered and had a couple of hours in the pub! I have no idea how many goals I scored that season but it was like being back at school really. Don't get me wrong, I'm not proud of it or bragging but I was too good for that level and I really shouldn't have been playing in it, but to be honest it suited a purpose at the time. The team consisted of a few local lads and then was filled with mercenaries from local non-league who were all getting a few bob to play! Obviously word got around and it ruffled a few feathers amongst other teams in the league who had become accustomed to winning trophies every year.

We won the league at a canter and progressed to the semi-final of the cup against the 'normal' favourites and the manager of their team tried to unsettle us by insisting on seeing our ID to prove that we were registered to play. Apparently this was in his rights and fortunately we had been tipped off that he was going to ask for this so we were prepared but it really annoyed me. He delayed kick off by half an hour and this was eating into my allotted drinking time! This only succeeded in giving me the motivation that I normally lacked and I had a stormer and scored all four goals in a 4-0 win despite their best efforts to man mark me with two players! If only I could have been motivated like that throughout my career!

The final was another story against the roughest, scariest set of blokes I ever played against. It was obvious that my semi-final performance had got back to them as before kick off one of their lads advised me not to score or I would be stabbed. Within a few minutes I had to hurdle a few knee high challenges and was told that my legs would be broken and kneecapped after the game!

Well, not being the bravest man in the world and considering I had a good job and two kids to go home to and look after, I spent the rest of the game doing an excellent job of 'ball avoidance'. No matter how many times my teammates looked for me I was always impossible to pass to – I couldn't wait for the game to be over and I honestly couldn't have cared less if we won or lost. We actually won 1-0 from a penalty that I shied away from and as soon as the final whistle went I got in the shower sharpish and went to the pub. I do remember thinking that if this is what it's about I'm packing in completely and I didn't enjoy the celebrations at all. I went home early, full of self-doubt and shame for not being braver, but I'm just not and I can't change that. I do think my natural sensitivity and gentle nature was a major reason why I didn't fulfil my potential – I didn't deal with setbacks very well as I hadn't really had that many along the way and then I was in a world of constant challenges and didn't know how to deal with them. I guess I have been fortunate that I adjusted to a normal working life relatively well and have always made a good living away from football.

I'm not sure of the reasons why, but the gravy train stopped and that was the end of the Bridgnorth experience.

Diffusion

The previous season my brother in law at the time asked me to sign for his Sunday team which were connected to a chain of trendy clothes shops called Diffusion but I explained I was getting £80 to play in Bridgnorth at the time which he understood. However, that having finished I agreed to go training with them at the beginning of the following season.

Now this was just up my street, these boys were men about town – the two owners, Carl and Gez, were doing very well financially with their clothes shops and other business interests in nightclubs etc and also enjoyed life away from work.

We used The Mitre pub as our base after matches but weren't limited to Wolverhampton, and birthdays and golfing trips would frequently be spent in Marbella and it was always good fun.

The year I signed we were in division 5 I think which was a pretty poor standard but we had a good set of players although we were ageing and really more interested in the pub after the game than the game itself! I was now content to be sub and only actually play if we were in trouble and needed a goal, so I rarely played over 45 minutes and it was normally just for the last twenty minutes which my knees could just about cope with. I was happy to be involved and it helped to make friends that are still pals today, which is a nice benefit of playing with local lads. It's a funny thing playing football at a higher level where you are all from different places, although you have a bond while together it is very rare to remain friends once you go your separate ways – especially prior to the days before social media!

We won the league that year and these lads liked to celebrate in style with a presentation do followed by a party. That year it was held at a lovely hotel just outside Wolverhampton and it was a beautiful sunny day and I arrived in good time with Julie. We were staying there overnight, so we quickly checked in and then got some drinks and went outside where everyone was congregating – it was lovely and there was a feeling it was going to be a good day. The next thing we knew there was a helicopter hovering above us. Before we knew it, it had landed and one of the Diffusion shareholders stepped out followed by six strippers who were coming to the party later on! My wife's face was a picture and I had a big smile on mine!

The presentation was very well done with Carl Peddie playing the host and Gez giving out medals to all the players. They had a tradition of each player saying a few words on the microphone which I wasn't aware of until it started and I was frantically trying to think of something witty to say but ultimately when it came to it I just thanked them all for accepting me and said that I hoped to remain friends moving forwards. I actually got a little emotional as I enjoyed their company a lot and knew deep down it was only going to be for a limited time due to my age and knees. The day went well and the party got into full swing later on but at around 10pm Julie and I had seen enough and went to bed – it would have been a different story if I was on my own!

There was a trip to Marbella not long after this for one of the lads' birthdays and it included days and nights out with lots of entertainment available if wanted. I was always happy having a drink and a laugh with the lads and settled for that as a married man but it was always interesting to watch the younger lads change after a few drinks. It was a very rare occurrence for me to be allowed to have a weekend away and I was definitely going to make the most of it from the Friday to the Sunday which ended with an afternoon at Ocean Club in Marbella, which was full of pretentious people I really didn't like, spraying Champagne around like water! It was probably because they were all young and fit – I didn't want to show my dad bod off so my t-shirt stayed on! I got talking to Joanne Latham, the ex-page three girl, as she knew my wife from teaching her dancing when she was at school. Before long some girls she knew offered me some cake, I was a little bit peckish so I had quite a big slice. I then had to rush off to catch a taxi to the airport for my flight back home, but about halfway there I started to feel a little bit woozy. After that I remember very little apart from having an argument with the taxi driver for being charged 100 euros, which in hindsight was probably right! By the time I got on the flight I felt ill and just wanted to sleep but unfortunately I was recognised by some Wolves fans on the plane sat by me and they wanted to talk football all the way home. I hope I made some sort of sense to them!; This was the first and last time I have taken drugs, albeit unwittingly in a slice of cake! Never again!

The following season we jumped up a couple of leagues to division 2 which was obviously stronger but on our day we were capable of beating anyone and proved this by progressing well in the two main cups. The Charity Cup final was always played at Molineux at the end of Wolves' season before they ripped the pitch up to prepare for the new season. I was still being the happy sub and played occasionally when they were short or just came on towards the end if needed and played my part in the squad. We progressed to the final of both cups and were up against two teams at the top of the division 1. All the players at that level knew each other from school, football or just socially so there was a lot of banter flying around about how we were going to get our arses kicked, etc.

We managed to win the other cup final in a close game with a few flare ups and I was glad to not be on the pitch at times! In an earlier game in that cup which I did start in, I got topped by a chopsy fella in midfield as the ball dropped between us, he went right over the ball and studded me in the shin and smirked at me – I just said "Oh it's like that is it?" A few minutes later a ball was played down the line right in front of our bench and as I was chesting it down I could see him coming from the side. As the ball reached me I smashed him in the nose with my elbow and all hell let loose as he reacted and tried to get at me – fortunately all our lads on and off the pitch were involved in the melee and I just stayed quiet. Apparently a few weeks later this same lad came in The Mitre pub on a Sunday afternoon being gobby and it all kicked off again, but thankfully I was nowhere near!

Anyway, as the big final at Molineux approached I was asked by Gez whether he should pay for us all to stay at a hotel the night before the match to prepare properly! I understood how big an occasion this was for him and all the lads but I felt that this would build up an already nervous occasion for most of them even more – just due to playing at The Molineux. I felt it was important that the team prepared as normally as possible, although Gez and his pal Riad generally prepared by clubbing until the last minute possible and getting to the game late on a

Sunday morning, with Dale the manager often having to wait for them to turn up. The team was funded by Gez and Carl and part of the deal was that Gez played regardless, in contrast to me who was happy not to play!

I was asked to say a few words before the game and told each of them to play their normal game and get a good simple pass in and build from there as confidence can quickly disappear from one sloppy pass on a big occasion. The game couldn't have gone any better and the chirpy opposition soon piped down when we went 3-0 up in the first 10 minutes with some cracking goals and it ended up 5-0 at half time! As you can imagine the lads were on top of the world but I just said to keep your feet on the floor and win the second half! With about twenty minutes to go I was asked to go on and it was still 5-0. I said to put one of the other lads on who didn't get much opportunity but I was told I was going on as he didn't want the other sub to embarrass himself in front of the crowd! I went on and had a hand in setting up a couple of goals to see us run out 7-0 winners! The other team were very gracious in defeat and I don't think anyone could believe how well we played on the day – sometimes everything just clicks. Both my good friends David Wells and David Trend scored great goals that day and 'Wella' tied his boots to the crossbar after the game to hang them up and finish his playing days on a high!

There was a pre-arranged end of season do in the Jack Hayward suite which if we'd lost could have been a damp squib but as you can imagine it was a great afternoon with our wives and girlfriends in full view of the Molineux pitch.

It was decided that we would have a lads night out in celebration of our season and a bus was provided for us to get to Birmingham where Gez and Carl had booked the penthouse suite at the top of the Malmaison hotel for us to have a party. There had been lots of drinks and entertainment arranged which was on offer if wanted but I was happy having a good drink and watching the younger lads have fun. I have to say this is the only team I didn't get paid to play for yet they were living life like Premiership footballers that you read about these days – how ironic! The only financial thing on offer was a good discount on designer slim fit clothes that I couldn't fit into!

This proved to be my last team playing regularly and it was a good fun way of ending my days.

* * *

Carl Peddie (Diffusion)

It was great to have Jon as part of our squad for a couple of seasons, not only did he grace the Wolverhampton Sunday league with his silky skills but he also brought great experience which helped us in several tight games during our double cup winning season of 2003/4. Jon's calmness, encouragement and positivity made us a better team on and off the pitch.

* * *

The Diffusion winning team in the charity cup final at Molineux.

CHAPTER THIRTY

Giving Something Back in Gold and Black

Around the time I was finishing playing Saturday football at Bilston I was asked if I would be interested in playing for the Wolves All Stars, which is a team of ex-Wolves players who play charity matches a few times a year to raise much needed funds for good causes. I've never really been one to live in the past and was reluctant at first as, let's be honest, I'm not that well known and thought I would be out of place amongst some proper ex-Wolves players. After a few messages and a phone call from Mel Eves who ran the team I was persuaded to play and see how it went from there.

In the first few games I had the pleasure of playing with Bobby Thompson, Willie Carr, Phil Parkes, Steve Daley, Geoff Palmer, Phil Robinson, Andy Thompson and Steve Bull, as well as Mel Eves as the player manager.

Bobby was 62 at the time and was still as immaculate on the pitch as he was off it, he never gave the ball away and was never exposed by any younger quicker players due to his clever football brain. He was a very genial man off the pitch and lived a very clean life so it was a shock when he died at such a young age and in such good physical shape. The '70s lads could all still play and it was great to get to know them as people as they were all down to earth guys who just so happened to be able to kick a bag of wind around better than most. The '80s boys were still pretty fit and could get around the pitch still, although Bully was

Playing for Wolves All Stars recently without the mullet!

really suffering with his knees and didn't play often and gave up pretty quickly to look after himself – who can blame him.

I enjoyed this period of being a 'young' veteran as I was still relatively fit and quick in comparison to those I was playing against, and I enjoyed rubbing shoulders with some big names with the other teams. One of the early games was against a West Brom team in a game raising money for Jeff Astle and his battle with Alzheimer's, which his family had put down to heading those heavy balls that were normal back in the day. My old mate George Reilly is now also suffering with problems relating to regular head trauma caused by football. George tells the story of Graham Taylor telling his wingers, John Barnes and Nigel Callaghan, to hang some crosses up for the opposition keeper to come for and George's job was to smash the keeper to make him wary of coming off his line again. This led to George being punched and buffeted more than he would have liked and now suffers from a form of dementia sadly.

These games also gave opportunity to reconnect with the likes of Derek Statham and Cyrille Regis who I knew socially from the early days with Wolves. I remember a conversation after a game with Derek, Cyrille and Dave Bennett, we were discussing how much the game had changed in regards to the discipline involved with the young players these days. They were all in agreement that they wouldn't swap with the modern player and I was the lone voice that said "that's ok because you all made it anyway". My point being that if I had been looked after between the ages of 16 and 18 I think I could have possibly fulfilled my potential – but it's all water under the bridge and the clock can't be turned back.

We also played against an Aston Villa team that had players like Gordon Cowans, Des Bremner and Tony Morley from the

Playing in the Masters tournament for Wolves.

First game for Wolves All Stars at Molineux with Charlie and Jack.

famous European Cup winning side playing and they were all in good shape and could still play.

Around this time there was the emergence of 'The Masters Tournament' sponsored by the bookie Stan James, and I had a phone call from Phil Robinson to ask if I'd like to play and I couldn't say yes quickly enough. The first tournament was due to be played in Belfast between Aston Villa, Liverpool, Everton and Wolves. This was an all-expenses paid trip and flights, hotels, new astroturf trainers were all laid on and it was a pleasure to be involved in it. Our team was full of lads I had played with through my career: Phil Robinson, Andy Thompson, Robbie Dennison, Bully, as well as others I hadn't, such as Shane Westley, Don Goodman and Mike Stowell. Our manager was George Berry who I'd never met before. George was probably the most laid back manager I'd ever known and he just said go and enjoy yourselves lads and don't worry about anything. This was fine but we went out without knowing any of the rules and had to learn as we went along. We were playing against a lot of players who had won the First Division and European cups but we had the benefit of being the youngest team and we won all three games quite comfortably by putting a lot of energy and effort in as a whole squad and I was happy to chip in with a few goals. We beat Liverpool in our final game, much to Phil Neal's disgust and he made it obvious he wasn't best pleased and we celebrated afterwards with a few beers in the dressing room! We were really pleased with ourselves but also relieved it was over as we were all knackered as it was hard work out there. However after a few minutes an official came in and told us that we had to play the final in 30 minutes against the runners up – Liverpool, who we had just beaten easily. George Berry had no idea and just said "sorry lads" and laughed! So we had to play again reluctantly and you've guessed it we lost as we had run out of gas completely.

All four teams went out together that night into the early hours of the morning and at one stage I found myself leaning against the bar next to Tony Morley and I was very flattered when he said "you can play a bit son – what happened to you?" We had a bit of a conversation and it was a pleasure to talk to him as I still remember when I watched him rip Wolves apart when I was a schoolboy on trial at Wolves all those years before. One thing is for sure – all these boys knew how to drink as it was how we were all brought through back in the day, and we carried on the next day until I got home to Wolverhampton after a great weekend away.

This carried on for a few years afterwards and I was always involved in a successful Wolves team up until the last year when I played in the group tournament against the Midlands teams, which we won to qualify for the finals to be held in Sheffield a few months later. I kept waiting for the letter to come through the post with the information regarding the arrangements for the finals but it never came. Then a week before the tournament I bumped into Bully in a local pub and he asked if I was looking forward to Sheffield and the penny dropped that I only played in the qualifying tournament as Bully was on holiday and he was now replacing me in the finals! I totally understand that he is the bigger name and a draw for the fans but I thought I deserved my place as part of the group-winning team and I'm pretty sure I'm a better 6 a side player, but hey ho that's football and another kick in the balls was taken!

This period with the Wolves All Stars didn't last too long as the '70s boys couldn't keep playing due to general wear and tear, and the '80s lads just stopped playing, this left Mel and myself for quite a lot of games and the team was then filled with anyone we could find to play sadly. This is not really the idea and I felt it was unfair to ask the paying public to fork out and pay towards a charity to watch us under false pretences. I was also suffering after playing with my left knee that blew up to twice the size it should be and it would take a few days for the fluid to disappear which was quite painful and it became sensible to stop playing altogether.

I didn't get involved for a few years and then I read that Mel was giving up as he just couldn't get interest from ex-players. However, a chap called Jason Guy offered to help him and it has gone from strength to strength in the last couple of years with Jason getting players such as Jody Craddock, Seyi Olifinjana, Simon Osborn, Paul Jones, Tony Dinning, Adam Proudlock, Michael Kightly, Kevin Foley and Karl Henry playing recently. We also have myself amongst the old guard with Neil Edwards, Colin Taylor, Dean Edwards and my old pal Micky Holmes warming the bench and having a little run out now and again. It's a really rewarding thing to be involved in as it keeps us all in touch with each other and we have managed to raise over £500,000 for charity and I'm proud to now be on the committee to help keep up the good work.

Things have progressed so far with the organisation that we are now going on tour to Gibraltar to play a game at their national stadium, arranged with the Gibraltar arm of Wolves supporters. Unfortunately the Covid-19 outbreak scuppered this in April 2020 so it has been postponed for a year. Hopefully some of us older ones will still be able to contribute on the pitch – if not, I'm certain we will hold our own off the pitch!

* * *

Jason Guy (Wolves All Stars Chairman and friend)

As well as revering Jon as a supporter, I have had the good fortune to work with Jon during my capacity of helping to run the Wolves All Stars. Jon will always make sure he's available for a good cause and his commitment has earned him a place on our committee. Has he got 90 minutes in the tank anymore, by his own admission probably not but there are still the glimpses of magic that were schooled at Highbury all those years earlier. Class is permanent.

* * *

Recent Photo with Dean Edwards, Micky Holmes and Jackie Gallagher at Molineux.

CHAPTER THIRTY ONE

The Dark Side

I began taking my coaching badges in my mid-twenties as I always had a desire to help young players avoid the pitfalls that I suffered with and at least be in a position to advise them, whether they listen is then in their hands. I was never really helped and It's only when you look back you can realise how naive you are as a 16 year old trying to find your way in the world.

I contacted the PFA and they helped me along the way, although I chose to take the courses with anyone else starting out through the local Staffordshire FA at a school in Stafford.

Level one and two were quite simple and really for enthusiastic people looking to help out with kids teams at

The AFC Wulfrunians youth team at the Keele tournament with Charlie and Jack.

grassroots level – and there's nothing wrong with that. The only problem was that we were all used as players for the coaching sessions and they were long days and quite exhausting to be honest – not helped that I kept getting chosen to demonstrate for most of the lads and I hadn't got the heart to say no. It was part of the process to be able to take my UEFA B qualification which is what I was interested in as I knew that this is a requirement to be considered by any decent football club these days. A lot of ex-professional players moan about not getting opportunities but aren't willing to put themselves through the process of getting the necessary qualifications so won't ever be considered over someone who has put the time and effort in to meet the criteria required. Having said that I do think that ex and current professional players should be fast tracked as the level 1 and 2 was really quite basic and we should be encouraging these people to help the young players of today. Unfortunately our system is making our ex-professionals jump through too

Bilbrook Juniors U9s with Jack.

many hoops and our academies are flooded with young career coaches straight out of university with a degree and who are good on a laptop, but can they help a young player as much as someone who has been there and done it? I somehow doubt it! I also believe that the young players are protected too much and should be playing with and against experienced players as we did in the old reserve leagues instead of playing up to under 23s without real experience of what it's really like when you cross the white line in competitive football.

It took a couple of years to finally get the qualifications and although I had no driving motivation I knew that it could come in handy in the future and so it has proved.

I went through a period of just concentrating on work, looking after my lads and after a period of not exercising at all I took up playing squash purely for fitness reasons. I loved the physical aspect of the game as you get a great workout in 45

Finchfield FC U16 league winners with Charlie and Jack.

minutes. Unlike team sports you can turn up 5 minutes before you start and afterwards you can have a shower and go home or have a couple of pints if you want, although it didn't take too long for my ninth knee operation to be needed so that put paid to that avenue of pleasure!

My eldest boy Charlie was showing no interest in playing football and it took my youngest Jack to get to under 9 age group before he wanted to join a team. I found him a nice club to join – Bilbrook Juniors and was content to be a normal parent by taking him, watching him and helping him if I could in the garden or just with little bits of advice as you do as a parent. However, after a few weeks the manager – a lovely chap called Trevor Gray – held a meeting with the parents and requested some assistance as he felt he needed help. Now I'm not sure if this was a set up but literally everyone just turned and looked at me! This wasn't really the plan at all and I said that I'd think about it and let him know. I spoke to Julie about it and she basically said "you're going to be there anyway and you can help more than anyone else". So that was that and I then got involved in coaching the kids on a Saturday morning and helping with the matches on a Sunday morning. You do get the bug, and seeing the kids develop and grow is a real pleasure.

However, this was my first real experience of parental blindness – where parents can only see their child and have no appreciation for the rest of the children in the squad. This in addition to the behaviour of some of the other coaches who had a win at all costs attitude meant that I would have walked away very quickly if Jack wasn't involved and didn't love it so much. He loved the bond it gave us, and so did I. We spoke about the upcoming game all week and then did a post mortem after every game which was lovely. The team improved gradually and they progressed from the bottom division up to the top league within a few years and were competing and playing good football. Unfortunately at around the u13 age group the attitude and commitment from quite a few players and/or parents made it very difficult to sustain. Jack was given the opportunity to join Finchfield who were one of the top teams in the area and he wanted to go, which was fine by me. This happened to coincide with Charlie starting to play football too, which I never thought would happen. He was a very sensitive boy with no real interest in sport but when he went to secondary school at Stafford Grammar he grew very quickly and his co-ordination all fell into place and suddenly he was bigger, stronger and faster than the majority of kids his age and he started scoring a lot of goals for the school. The boys in his year soon got him involved with their Sunday team, Brewood Juniors, and I was then alternating between watching my boys play for their respective teams. I did miss the involvement of the coaching but for a while I settled for just watching and often suffered quietly witnessing bad coaching or angry managers on the side-lines with equally unknowledgeable parents – unfortunately, harsh but true.

Charlie was asked to join Bilbrook Juniors which was very flattering as they were the top team around Wolverhampton but unfortunately he was often an unused sub which was no good to him and it's a regret that I didn't see it coming. They were a good team and didn't need him really so I didn't see why they signed him, so I approached the Finchfield manager the year ahead of Jack, Pete Rollings, and asked if he would be interested in Charlie and he was very receptive so we quickly got him transferred. Pete was the loveliest man and he did a lot of running around picking lads up from underprivileged backgrounds to enable them to have a game of football on a Sunday.

Jack was also not having the easiest time with his team and the following season he signed for Pete a year up which was great as Julie and I could now watch them together and they trained at the same time and place. This started a three year period that was probably the most enjoyable period in my football life. Initially I just watched as a parent but before long I was helping with training and then doing the warm ups while Pete did the administration with the refs etc, and before I knew it I had somehow found myself as their coach! I wouldn't get too involved with selection as it wasn't fair, but I did try and help the lads and the team to understand their positions and get a shape in the team. I enjoyed it and the team started to do very well and competed towards the top of the first division which was great for them.

Somehow, through friends, Jack got asked to get involved in a midweek floodlit league team called AFC Wulfrunians at the u18 age group, which I felt was a bit too much of a physical jump as he was 15 and not the biggest lad but he wanted to try, so of course I supported him. Ironically this team played at the Castlecroft Stadium which used to be my training ground when I first played for Wolves and this was literally a 5 minute journey from our new home in Old Perton. They also played in the Red and White halved kit of my Kidderminster Harriers days. Both of these facts gave me an initial warmth towards the club and Jack did quite well and was soon drafted in to play men's football for Old Wulfrunians on a Saturday afternoon. It was social, amateur football which I enjoyed watching and I knew quite a few of the young lads playing and enjoyed having a few beers after the game. Jack would travel to away games and I would make my own way there and happily just watch. Then we would travel home together and chat about the game.

On one of the match days he called me and told me they were a bit short and to bring my boots in case they hadn't got a sub. I was 43 at the time and didn't really want to play anymore but when your son asks what can you say! When I got there they had kicked off and to my relief they had 12 but they still asked me to put some kit on 'just in case'. So I pulled on my favourite boots – Puma Kings, and watched hoping everyone would be ok. However, before half time one of the lads pulled up with a hamstring injury and came off so I was now the only sub left. The team weren't doing very well and were 4-0 down and then someone else said they couldn't carry on and had to come off with a bad back (it wasn't the keeper!) so I had no choice but to play for the last 20 minutes. Obviously I couldn't run around as much or as fast but I don't think your touch ever leaves you, and before long I had scored one by going through and rounding the keeper to slot home and set up two more and we were back in the game! Unfortunately we ran out of time and lost 4-3. There was a feeling of shock but respect in the bar after the game and I think Jack was amazed and maybe a little proud too. I still see some of the lads who played in this game and they always bring it up as the point they realised they weren't going to be pros!

Towards the end of the season I was approached and asked if I would like to take the youth team on the following season as the current manager didn't want to carry on. As is usual his son was going to be too old the following season and quite rightly he wanted to step aside. I agreed to take it on and Pete agreed to do the secretarial work for me which was perfect.

Charlie was coming into his final year of youth football and Jack had 2 seasons left so I felt it was the perfect time to do something serious with my coaching qualifications and put my head above the parapet and see how I got on. I put an advert in the paper to promote a trial game to be able to select an initial squad to start training with in readiness for the new season and was pleasantly surprised by the amount of interest from the local area. I requested that they emailed me with information about their positions, school, teams played for etc, so I could pick two teams and subs to be organised on the night.

It was quite an exciting night and all the boys turned up as arranged as well as about 8 lads who just showed up with their boots asking for a game! I couldn't say no to them so got them some kit and promised them a run out as you never know what they could be like. The game was 3 x 35 minutes and the majority got 70 minutes which is long enough to judge a player's touch and if they can play a bit. I took a seat in the stand well away from parents and just took numbers and made notes about each player, and the evening was very worthwhile. After the game I promised all of them that I would be in touch to let them know whether they were invited to come to training.

Over the next couple of days I emailed or text each player to either invite them for training or thank them for their efforts but let them down gently. This wasn't easy but necessary to get a squad together for me and let the boys that were unsuccessful find themselves another team to play football for, which was the most important thing to me.

We then trained every Sunday as I wanted to see who was committed and fortunately the majority that I had chosen were all very keen and training was of a decent standard. Players kept turning up asking for a game as word was getting around and I would always give them an opportunity and if they weren't what I was looking for I told them that they should find somewhere else. This was only fair on them and also the lads in the squad as one below par player can ruin a training session for everyone else.

I then had two big strokes of luck. Firstly, Carl Dwyer, my old apprentice at Wolves, got in touch asking if his son could come and train, and fortunately his son Tom was a good player with a great attitude. I managed to get Carl to help me with the training and eventually he became my coach which took some weight off my shoulders. Both Carl and Tom were great additions for me. Secondly, two lads from Sedgley, Tom Piggott and Liam Watkins, turned up asking to train and although I had enough players by now I agreed to have a look at them. Both proved to be very capable, with Piggo looking like a real find – his father Gary was a very good player who was a professional with West Brom.

So I had my squad pretty much in place and I arranged a bonding weekend at a tournament at Keele University which I hoped would get some team spirit going and also test us as a squad. This was an u19 tournament and my team were half u18 and half u17 to ensure I wouldn't lose the whole team for the second season. It proved to be a great experience for all of us, the lads really played well although it was very tiring, having to play 2-3 times a day, and they had their first experience of playing against streetwise lads from Liverpool! These boys could play a bit and could definitely talk for England and they were there to win it at all costs. We played them in a group game and one of their lads was constantly winding everyone up. I told him to shut up and concentrate on the game as he was a good player and he shouted "What's it got to do with you billy big arms!" Jack, who can be a bit fiery, was wound up by him and ended up getting sent off which got him banned for a game! To be fair to the scouse lad he came over afterwards and said he just can't stop talking and apologised! Anyway, we played against Norwegians, Americans and other English teams and we were unbeaten and made it to the final played late on the Sunday afternoon, with a very tired and depleted squad. Unfortunately we lost in the final against... yep, the scousers who funnily enough looked fresh as daisies (possibly because most of the team weren't involved earlier in the tournament!). However we had achieved our aim of the weekend.

When we first started the season some of the lads wouldn't have a shower and others wouldn't take their boxers off if they did have one. I thought that they definitely needed a shower after playing and that as young men moving into adult football they were going to have to shower with men very soon. I had to think about how to get them to overcome their fears and decided to get it all out in the open by telling them that it is important to shower because of hygiene and so that they weren't taken the mickey out of when they play in the men's league which some already were. I finished up with saying that we are like cars – we all have different models but some Minis get more mileage than a Ferrari and not to worry about it! That broke the ice and from then on they were much more relaxed about showering!

To be able to fund the season each player had to find a sponsor to pay £150 for the season which would pay for their tracksuits, the referees costs and sausage and chips for both teams after home games which they all managed to come up with. I also asked HiQ the local garage I was using to look after our family cars if they would sponsor two new kits which they agreed to thankfully. In addition to this I contacted Wolves asking if I could bring the team to play a friendly against one of their younger teams and eventually I managed to arrange a match at their Compton training ground. Again we played well and won the game quite comfortably albeit our lads were 2-3 years older, but certainly we didn't look out of place technically. After the game the Wolves Academy manager approached me for a chat and complimented me on the team's organisation and my manner and way of talking with the boys which was nice to hear. He went on to ask if I had any coaching qualifications and when he knew I had my UEFA B he offered me a coaching job on the spot! I spoke to Julie and she didn't seem to mind so I took the job – full of interest to be able to help kids make it through the system with a little help through my own experiences.

So I was now coaching at Wolves one night a week, on a Saturday morning with match day on a Sunday morning, as well as managing AFC Wulfrunians u18s two evenings a week and of course I was still working as well. By now Charlie was driving to school and back and obviously taking Jack with him but I still watched them play football together for the school and the PE teacher then asked me to help him with the school team! Of course I agreed and now I had football coming out of my ears and for a while I enjoyed it all.

At Wolves I was paired up with Ian Cranson who was a good pro for Ipswich and Stoke to coach the u14s and I learned an awful lot from him regarding coaching which was brilliant. He had been coaching for a fair few years but was also used to working within an academy system framework which I found quite suffocating to be honest. We were only allowed to play a 4-4-2 system when some games needed a change of system if we were outnumbered in midfield or the opposition had an outstanding number 10 but we had to carry on regardless. There were also players that didn't fit into this system but we couldn't help them even though it was obvious that some lads would have fared better in a midfield and front three or as a number 10. This was quite ironic as Mick McCarthy was favouring a 4-5-1 system with the first team at the time as he felt that was the best way of getting results in the premier league.

I used this platform as a learning curve and transferred the knowledge to the AFC Wulfrunians team which meant training was always interesting and challenging for them I think, well they kept turning up anyway. This Wolves connection enabled me to get a couple of benefits for the AFC Wulfrunians team as I secured the indoor Astroturf Dome for training during the winter, even though it was after the academy lads had finished at 9pm on a Monday night, it was still the best facility around. I also managed to get some training and coaching kit for us all, thanks to Ron Picken the Wolves kit manager who gave us used kit that otherwise gets replaced every year, so we all looked the part for training. I have to say I enjoyed the AFC Wulfrunians role much more than the Wolves coaching position because ultimately it was more fun and I had more control over selection, team shape, etc. Also if Wolves were releasing a young player Crannie and I weren't consulted – often a boy would come running to me crying and I had no idea it was going to happen, which was quite upsetting. We did have a couple of winter trips to Borussia Dortmund and AZ Alkmaar, which were educational, seeing how the Dutch and Germans ran their academies which turned out to be a lot more flexible than the rigidity I was experiencing at Wolves.

It also became quite obvious that most year groups possibly had only one or maybe two boys who the academy felt had a chance to be taken on at 16. This meant that there were 15 boys and their parents who were being taken advantage of in each age group from u7 to u16. All these young players and their parents believed that their son could be the next David Beckham and were committed to bringing the boys to training and following them all over the country. Obviously I understand the need to have a team to play football I just didn't think it was right to lead these people along for years and then discard them at the age of

15 or 16 only to recruit other lads from Europe as their scholars. I don't know the answer but it needs to be looked at – perhaps only starting academies at u12 like the Dutch do.

One of the final nails in the coffin for me was during a practice match in training between the u13s and u14s. One of the heads of the Academy stopped the match and pulled all the players in for a chat and told them in no uncertain terms that the standard of play wasn't good enough, which I actually thought was fair enough on the day. He then added "if you want to be millionaires and have the big houses and cars and beautiful women you will have to play better than that"! Surely that isn't what should be said to young boys dreaming of being a professional footballer! I was disgusted and pulled my u14s in after he'd gone and told them to concentrate on passing the ball to each other – nothing else!

The two seasons with AFC Wulfrunians' youth team was just an amazing time for me as I had an experience with my two sons that will last forever in our memories and also for the other boys involved I hope. They were such a tight knit group and our spirit saw us through on numerous occasions during the season when we would score late winners or hold on to a win through pure belief in each other. As an example, in the first year we went away to Kidsgrove Athletic in Stoke for an evening kick off and we had a great game with them, a very equal match with both teams giving everything and taking no prisoners. In the previous game Piggo had cut his eye quite badly but he still wanted to play but I had to look after him so compromised by putting him on the bench and said I would only use him if needed, which I was hoping we wouldn't. We found ourselves 2-1 down with 20 minutes left and I decided to throw him on and before long it was 2-2 but it could have gone either way. It was getting quite heated on and off the pitch, which my Jack and his big mate Tom Lynch were revelling in and taking care of. With a few minutes left we got given a corner and for some reason Piggo decided to take it and he proceeded in kicking the corner flag and trickled the ball to their defender who cleared to our right back – Jake Webb. Now Webby has real quality about him and he took one touch out of his feet and whipped in a great cross, and my son Charlie rose like a salmon to plant a header into the top corner 3-2 – what a feeling! The final whistle blew and it all kicked off with Jack in the middle of it all (he must get that from his mum). After a few minutes we managed to get back in the dressing room and emotions were high and the testosterone was pumping! I left the dressing room alone for 5 minutes to think about what was best to do and decided to maintain our high standards. Eventually the lads quietened down and I went in and told them how proud I was of them and that if we continue to show that spirit and determination we would be ok. I also said that every one of us was to go in the bar to have a drink and the food on offer but said that we all must stick together whatever happens. I had previously told them that if anything happens on the pitch to all back each other up without actually doing anything as this sort of team ethic is very rarely matched and it gives you a psychological advantage. So we all went in the bar and everything was fine as is normally the way. I was very proud of both my sons that night for different reasons.

On one frosty cold Saturday morning I had just come out of the Wolves training ground at Compton getting ready to take a coaching session, when one of the parents asked me if I had heard the news. He proceeded to tell me that Pete Rollings had suffered a heart attack the night before and had died. I was in total shock as this was a man I spoke to almost every day and he was such a good man – he'd do anything for anyone and life had dealt him and his family this cruel card. This was really difficult news to break to the lads at Wulfrunians, most of whom had also become good friends with Pete, but I told them he would want you all to carry on and play, and their reaction was one of determination to win the league for him. I didn't have, and to be honest didn't want, a replacement for him so I took his secretarial and kit man duties on myself. Pete's funeral was very emotional and a wonderful tribute to a really good man and his family are a credit to him.

We ended up winning the league that season at home and we had some drinks after to celebrate and the lads started giving me a bit of banter about being called 'Billy Big Arms', which I loved – so I told them to sort out their arm wrestling champion and that I'd take him on! Not long after they were back and they had decided on Ryan Bishop – Bish was a very quiet lad but 6 foot 3 and spent most of his time in the gym and I thought 'I'm in trouble here!' Anyway I couldn't back out and much to everyone's amazement, including me, I beat him and the lads went crazy! Fun times and great memories!

Carl and I had a chat with them all and thanked them all for their efforts and wished all the boys who were now too old for youth football the best of luck in whatever they were going to do and also told the ones that had another season to make the most of the following season as they would soon be in the same situation. It was actually quite emotional losing these boys as we had all become close but that was the way it was, I also had Charlie going off to university to study Law and Carl Dwyer wanted to step aside as his lad was also leaving for uni.

Recruiting players for the next season didn't prove too difficult as we had built a good reputation and lots of lads wanted to come and join us. However I needed to get some help off the pitch and fortunately Steve Palmer who I had played with at Telford all those years ago was part of the furniture in the Old Wulfrunians club. This club was originally formed by Wolverhampton Grammar school pupils and Steve had been a pupil playing cricket and football for them. He was a regular drinker in the clubhouse and I helped him move into the bungalow on the club's grounds. Palms was a little unsure to start with as he'd never been involved in youth football but after a few training sessions I think he could see the quality and attitude of the boys and agreed to help me which was great. I also asked my pal David Wells to help as he was a different character to Palms and would get on well with the young lads with his humour being the major factor.

This team were probably technically better than the first year but lacked the physical strength and perhaps weren't as streetwise as the first year. We went to the Keele tournament again and history repeated itself with us losing in the final against a team of scousers on penalties despite being by far the better team – with them yet again playing quite a few ringers in the final. This again bonded the squad and I had great optimism for the season ahead.

I was still coaching at Wolves at this time and learning all the time – I wish I knew as much as I do now about positional play and team shape when I was playing but I can honestly say I never had a coach help me as an individual at any time. The only education was from other more experienced players like Ally Robertson who wanted the best for the team so would demand that you got into a position to protect the defence.

We had a very good season but around Easter we dropped some points which meant we weren't going to win the league and had to settle for a likely runners up spot. However we were going well in the County Cup which was the most prestigious trophy as it involved all affiliated clubs to the Birmingham County FA. We drew Hednesford in the quarter finals who in club terms were a giant in comparison to us and were undoubted favourites so I went on a scouting mission to watch them play in their previous round at Shifnal Town. It was very apparent that they relied heavily on the pace of their two forwards and repeatedly got in behind the defence and won quite comfortably this way. There was no doubt in my mind that if we tried to play a high line against them we would get murdered. Fortunately I had been learning at the Wolves Academy about 'delaying' which basically means retreating into your own half with the defence staying deep, so you allow their back four to have the ball in their own half but then press hard when they play forward. We had a league game away at Telford United prior to the cup game and I was prepared to sacrifice this game to practise this tactic, although I'm not sure Palms was. Although I played at Telford, Palms had played there for longer than me and he wanted to make a good impression – perhaps for his own ambitions. I requested that everyone got there early so I could go through what I expected of them individually, as units and as a team and to answer any queries they might have, I was faced with a lot of nodding and I thought they understood after drawing diagrams and using the tactics board that I regularly used. However once we kicked off it was obvious that although the majority had got the message – one or two obviously weren't listening! We went in 1-0 down at half time and I waited until they sat down and had a little go at the individuals concerned who were letting everyone down. I instructed them that we would change back to our normal way if we were still losing with 20 to go. Then Palms stepped in and gave them the biggest rollicking ever using every expletive you can imagine! This had the desired motivational reaction and they now carried out the game plan perfectly and we kept winning the ball and breaking on them. We ended up winning 2-1 with a late goal and it gave me confidence that we had a chance in the cup match.

When we turned up at Hednesford it was quite obvious that they were very confident about winning and the arrogance of their management team was quite motivational to me personally – their manager actually congratulated me for getting this far in the competition! We produced a brilliant performance and ran out 3-0 winners and they had no idea how to play against our tactics. It was a joy to watch and I particularly enjoyed shaking their manager's limp wristed hand at the end!

We then drew Burton Albion away in the semi-final who, at the time, were a league club, a lot of these teams were now training full time alongside offering a BTEC qualification alongside professional coaching daily. So we were definitely punching well above our weight but my lads had the ability and I tried to give them the motivation and the tactics to compete with these so called better clubs. Prior to this match I tried a little psychology on the team by telling the lads that Burton had already booked their coach and a hotel for the final – this was completely fabricated but I wanted to fire them up a little bit more than normal!

The match began well and we took an early lead, but it was apparent that their winger was going to give us problems so I swapped our wingers over and got Benji Gutteridge to mark him. Benji was one of the most dedicated players I've had the pleasure to coach and he would follow instructions to the letter and he had the fitness and discipline to man mark anyone at that level – indeed at half time I had to shout at him to join us as he was still following the winger to their dressing room!

A very close game ended with us scoring a dramatic late winner by our skipper Rob Whatton – a lovely kid who very rarely scored as you could tell by the look on his face! Rob actually bought me a card with an old picture of the Molineux to thank me for the two seasons he was with me which was a lovely gesture and a testament to his character and his upbringing.

So we had made it to the final against all the odds and we were up against the biggest club of all at this level and it was against the team I had my most memorable moment against – Birmingham City!

This was another club that were training every day and offering a sports BTEC qualification and their connection with such a big club attracts a lot of the best players available outside of professional football by offering the dream of getting promoted to the professional level. The reality of this is that none of them were taken on as a pro by the club although one or two went on to play professionally elsewhere. Before long their secretary was in touch offering to host the game at St Andrews instead of playing at the normal venue, which was a decent set up at the Birmingham FA headquarters on Ray Hall Lane. I knew this offer was aimed at making them even more of favourites than they already were but I had to consider what would be the most memorable experience for my boys.

I thought about it for a couple of days and decided that I couldn't take away the opportunity for the lads to play at a top professional ground as it may well be their only chance throughout their lives to have this experience. I don't regret this decision but the whole occasion proved too much for my lads and they simply were undone by nerves and started the game terribly. We were 3-0 down at half time having been ripped apart by their impressive front two! I changed the formation to a 5-3-2 in the second half and we put in a much better performance but still lost 6-2 in the end quite rightly. I managed to get all the subs on to play and I'm still satisfied that I did the right thing for them in the long run.

I enjoyed these two years so much and it was very sad for me that they were all leaving to go onto university or simply on to men's football, with an even more notable change in my life as Jack was going to Dallas in the US on a soccer scholarship, so now both my boys would be leaving home to go to university.

CHAPTER THIRTY TWO

It's a Man's Game

After the previous two enjoyable seasons I had no firm plans about continuing to be involved in football but I had a call out of the blue from one of the committee at AFC Wulfrunians towards the end of the previous season asking if I would become manager of the first team. Now I knew absolutely nothing about football at this level and wasn't really sure if it was for me but was also intrigued enough to ask for some time to think about it. This was then followed by a call from another committee member saying that he thought Steve Palmer was getting the job! This kind of summed the place up – there is no real structure and all the committee had their own ideas and opinions.

I called Palms and just said shall we do it together as joint managers? I had no ego about it and was happy to share the responsibility with him as he knew the players at that level and above to be able to attract good players. After speaking to all parties this was agreed and we started deciding on players that we wanted to keep and to add to the squad from other clubs. Both Palms and I had contacts at our previous clubs from our playing days and we arranged friendlies against Hednesford and Kidderminster amongst others.

By now I'd had enough at the Wolves Academy after realising I wasn't going to help the 16-18 year olds as I set out to do and I'd just had enough of the system and level of commitment required in general. I told them I wanted to leave and asked them to get a replacement sorted, this didn't happen and I carried on for a month or so not really enjoying it and eventually had a meeting with Kevin Thelwall and we parted company immediately, which was a relief to me. It really was a thankless task at that level in regards to the commitment required and the unbalanced remuneration on offer at that time.

The partnership between Palms and I worked well that year with him getting the players and me being responsible for coaching them into an organised team. We generally discussed team selection and came to an agreement. The level we were playing at wasn't great but there was only one team promoted each year and there were always teams who paid their players and coaching staff decent money to have a go at promotion each year. If it became obvious that promotion wasn't on the cards most of the individuals who were throwing money at it would pull the plug and those teams would just see the season out with whoever they could find to play.

We had no budget to work with but we had a great facility at Castlecroft Stadium with the pitch being immaculate. We managed to attract a group of players who wanted to do well and were prepared to commit themselves to come training and be prepared to listen a bit. Most players at that level don't want to learn anymore and just want to play for fun at the weekends, which we understood but we just asked for a little bit more to try and be successful.

We both knew that trying to play pretty football at this level wouldn't win the league due to the state of most of the pitches during winter and also the likelihood of mistakes in your own half costing points. So we set out to be reasonably direct by playing in behind the opposition defence as often as possible although we did build up first to a point where we could play forward constructively. Initially a few of the lads showed some resistance but once we started winning games every week they accepted we were doing the right thing. Jake Sedgemore was our captain and he had played in the league with Shrewsbury, and had actually marked Cristiano Ronaldo against Man Utd in a cup match. Although he was approaching his mid-thirties he still had outstanding passing ability and his free kicks and penalties were invaluable. I think initially he was a little reluctant with our game plan but once winter kicked in he could see our reasoning and his attitude was an example to the rest of the lads.

It became apparent that the title was becoming a two horse race between Lye Town, who had a good budget, and ourselves. It was neck and neck when we played them at home and we played poorly and lost 2-0. However, they celebrated outrageously on the pitch and in the dressing room and it proved very motivational for our lads to go on and win all of our remaining games to set up an amazing climax. As you can imagine there were lots of ups and downs and memorable games throughout the season, but it came down to a final showdown with Lye only needing a draw away at our local rivals Wolverhampton Casuals, with us needing to win our game at Malvern on a Tuesday evening and hope for a favour from the Casuals which we weren't too confident of at the time.

We battled hard and took a 2-0 lead against Malvern, and then with about 20 minutes to go we heard that Casuals were winning 2-0 and if everything stayed the same we were going to win the league by a point! The minutes ticked by and the final whistle went and we just had to wait for confirmation of the Lye result, which seemed to take forever, but eventually it was confirmed and the celebrations began and never stopped all the way home and back at the Wulfrunians club until about six in the morning!

So in my 3 years as a manager/coach I had experienced nothing but good times and it was great fun and I acknowledge this last achievement wouldn't have been possible without Palms. We are very different in character but maybe that's why it worked for a while, for example I believed in trying to get the officials on our side and he couldn't help but abuse them vociferously, quite often leading him into trouble with a few dismissals along the way. But that's football – we are all different and all have our own opinions. However it wasn't without its difficulties. Earlier that year I had talked him out of resigning over something not that important in my opinion, but this was unfortunately only putting off our inevitable parting of ways a couple of months into the new season.

We drew Stamford in the FA Vase away who were 3 leagues above us and as normal we discussed team selection and we disagreed over a couple of selections but we came to a compromise as normal. However, after losing the match after a valiant effort he resigned the next day without talking to me or giving a reason and I took over as sole manager for a few games, which we played well in and were doing fine. I then got a call from the Chairman saying that I was no longer required and Palms was coming back as manager.

This is amateur football, and it's a man's game, and if Palms had said he wanted to do it alone I'd have left without a problem. After all, it was his club and his friends were there and I always felt like an outsider anyway, but to do it behind my back is unforgivable to me and it's fair to say we will never have a meaningful conversation again. I should never be surprised in football but this hurt after all the voluntary time I'd put in there, even painting the dressing rooms and barriers around the pitch during the close season, and all the success I'd enjoyed with the club.

I had a break and then had short, unsatisfactory spells with Stourport and Gornal as coach but it became obvious that the group of players and the commitment that we had at AFC Wulfrunians was very special at that level.

During the previous year I had unfortunately split up with Julie after 20 years of marriage for reasons I don't want to go in to out of respect for her and my boys. My life was turned upside down and I moved to Stourbrige and was soon asked to coach the youth team at this fine non-league club, which I did and I enjoyed it for a few months with the vision of developing players to progress towards the first team squad. However, although we had a good season and played some lovely football, the reality was that none of them were going to be strong or good enough to be considered to play in the physical league that the first team were in, managed by Gary Hackett – ex-Shrewsbury, Stoke and Albion. Gaz was very successful with the first team and knew what he wanted and what was needed. Unfortunately that meant 17 and 18 year olds weren't in his thoughts, which is fair enough. I do feel however that kids need to be given opportunity to succeed or fail, and I felt that having two youth team players on the bench out of five substitutes wouldn't hurt and they could get a run out if the team were either winning comfortably or losing heavily. Ultimately, my opinion didn't matter and before long the opportunity arose to try my luck as a manager in non-league again, this time at Bilston Town who I had played for previously and I wanted to see how I could do on my own. Unfortunately the standards of commitment I expected proved unrealistic at this level as most of the players wouldn't come to training and I ended up in a constant cycle of turning over players and it was like an unpaid full time job which just didn't make sense. I even had to be sub myself once and around February I'd had enough and offered my resignation. I offered to stay until the end of the season but the board decided to let the youth team manager take over immediately and sadly they didn't win a game for the rest of the season, but thankfully avoided relegation.

During this period I had reconnected with Darren Heyes – my England schoolboy teammate, through Facebook and he invited me to play in a charity game for Help the Heroes. I was happy to oblige as it came with an invite to stay with Darren and have a couple of days catching up on old times. When I arrived at Darren's house we were enjoying a glass of wine when he got a phone call from an old friend who was running a veterans team in Harrogate and they had a cup final in Nottingham the next day and he was short of players. Darren put me forward initially but there was no way I was going to play in a cup final ahead of someone who was a regular with the team so I agreed to be a sub and only play if necessary. I ended up playing the second half and we won the cup and I played well. It transpired that the manager was also the manager of a touring England representative side who went to Thailand every year to play in a tournament. Darren Heyes said don't be surprised if you're invited and sure enough a few weeks later I received a phone call and was invited to represent England in the over 50s category!

CHAPTER THIRTY THREE

The Land of Smiles

After a turbulent relationship with a girlfriend following my divorce I found myself being single with some money in the bank. I was able to do exactly what I wanted and I just fancied taking any interesting opportunity that came my way as I now had no obligations to stop me. Once I had agreed to go on the trip to Thailand, I contacted Ricky Muir who was an old friend that I played football with and against during my schooldays 35 years previously. Ricky was a very good player all those years ago and like a lot of Corby boys could have done a lot better with more guidance and support. However his life took another direction which I only found out after reconnecting with him and it saddened me to hear that he became a drug addict and lived on the streets in Corby and then Amsterdam doing anything he could to get his next fix. I'm very proud to say that he is now 17 years clean and he's very much on the straight and narrow with his own family that he worships. Ricky drove a long way to visit me in Thailand with his wife and we have become firm friends, he's always there with an ear when needed, and our friendship has certainly taught me about the seriousness of addiction which I had never really been subjected to previously.

When I first contacted him to let him know about the tournament he asked what I was doing and I explained I'd just not long been divorced and recently split up with my girlfriend, and was at a bit of a crossroads not knowing which path to take.

He then asked if I would be interested in coaching in Thailand and I could only reply that I had no idea as I'd never been there. It was agreed that I had nothing to lose by sending him my CV and he forwarded it on to a few clubs that he knew of in and around Thailand.

Subsequently I was contacted by a club called Samui United which is on a paradise island off the south of Thailand. After a few emails I agreed to meet the owner in London for a lunch meeting just to see whether I was suitable for him and vice

Playing for England over 50s with Ricky Muir in Thailand.

versa. The meeting went well but I didn't hear anything from them for a few weeks and thought it was a dead end, and then I received an email offering me a contract and to pay for me to visit them directly after playing in the tournament for the England select team, which I agreed to as I had nothing to lose by visiting for a few days.

Prior to the tournament itself I had been running quite a bit to build my fitness up, but a couple of weeks before departure I felt a twinge in my calf which I hoped I would recover from before having to play – so I just iced it and rested. Once we arrived we enjoyed a couple of crazy nights in Bangkok which is an experience in itself! If you've never been it's worth a visit but a weekend is probably enough before going somewhere beautiful like Koh Samui, Krabi or Phuket.

The manager arranged a training session once we arrived in Ubon Rattathani in northern Thailand, and my calf held up fine and I enjoyed the football and I think I impressed the lads who I really didn't know at this time apart from socially. When we got back to the hotel I could feel my body stiffen up and suggested going for a massage with my roommate to try and help our recovery. So we went for a walk and found a place that looked professional and not an excuse for a knocking shop! However as it was our first experience we had no idea what to ask for so just agreed to a Thai massage – an hour later I felt like I'd gone through 12 rounds with Mike Tyson! I'd been stood all over, turned inside out and afterwards I felt worse than when I started!

Match day arrived and I was still struggling from the after effects of the training and the massage but found out that I was starting in the game in central midfield, which is fine but then the dreaded formation was announced as 4-4-2! Not an ideal formation against Asian players in 35 degrees who carried no weight and buzzed about like 18 year olds! This proved to be accurate and we were outnumbered and overrun in midfield, and to say I was blowing out of my arse would be an understatement. It was obvious to me that we needed to change the system but that wasn't forthcoming so at half time I asked to come off and let someone else have a go. I know when I'm being ineffective and I couldn't get on the ball to use my passing ability and was about as useful as a chocolate teapot defending!

As the game progressed the lads started dropping like flies and I offered to go back on at right back to help out – this lasted for about 5 minutes as my suspect calf went completely and I limped off with my tournament over as a player. I helped out as a coach for the rest of the tournament but felt a bit useless as that wasn't what I was there for – but such is life. All in all it was a good experience and I've met up with this group for another tournament a couple of years later. So we headed back to Bangkok as the team prepared to fly back to Manchester, but I met up with an old friend from Wolverhampton, Jim Carty, and

Samui United U12s at a tournament in Suratthani.

we flew to Phuket for a couple of nights before moving on to Koh Samui to meet up with the owner and people from the football academy.

When I arrived in Koh Samui the first thing you notice is just how quaint the airport is, and I'd certainly say it's the most beautiful I've ever experienced, which was a wonderful start to the trip. The people at the club were very friendly and after a couple of evenings observing training, there was no doubt in my mind that I could help the club and would improve the standard of coaching. In addition to this the weather was wonderful, the beaches are the best I've ever seen, and the people are all very welcoming. Before I left for home I agreed to come back for an initial three months to see how it went for both parties. So I literally went home for a couple of weeks to get ready for a new life on a new continent and I was excited and nervous in equal measure.

On my last night before flying home I popped into a pub called 'The Irish Times' close to the football academy and met the manager Derek Watson. We spoke about football long into the night and it transpired that Derek had played in the same Northern Ireland youth team as George Best and Pat Jennings, but was very modest about it which I liked. The pub was literally underneath the apartment block that had been recommended as one of the living accommodations suggested to me by the club. After this evening I had no hesitation in agreeing to stay there on my return, as at least I had someone to talk to after training over a beer or two.

When I returned on the 1st November the weather had changed and I experienced flooding like I'd never seen before with the cars trying to get through 3-4 feet of water, and on my first training night after torrential rain there were only three lads at training, which is a challenge for any coach for two hours!

I had been given the u16 team and the u12 teams to coach for different reasons. The u16s as they had lost interest under the previous coach as they didn't warm to him and I think he was far too serious for them, so I set out to make training enjoyable with the ball always involved and plenty of small sided games. These lads wanted to enjoy their football and have fun and within a few months our numbers went up to around the 20 mark and they were competing well in tournaments with an A and B team. Some of the A team have gone on and done well and secured scholarships in Phuket and Bangkok. These boys were all from different nationalities varying from English, Australian, Russian, French and Thai obviously – with some having one Thai parent and one Western one. These boys could speak three languages generally, which was really so impressive and they were all so respectful to me and indeed to anyone in authority. I was known as Coach Jon by them all and they would 'Wai' me as a mark of respect (hands together and bow). This was in direct contrast to my last coaching job at a Birmingham inner city Community Football Academy where there was absolutely no respect shown and I couldn't wait for every session to end.

Although the A team were a pleasure to coach and they played some fantastic football, my biggest achievement was with a lovely intelligent French lad called Lucas who was 15 and 6 foot 6, but unfortunately had no co-ordination at all to begin with. Initially I paired up with him as the other boys just got frustrated with him, however after giving him encouragement and plenty of practise his improvement was really very rewarding for me. This culminated when we held a tournament and he made the B team squad, and during one of the games he scored a cracking left foot drive and he turned and looked at me in amazement and I could have burst with pride for him – it was worth everything just to see his face. All these boys were pretty self-sufficient and turned up for training on small motorbikes, like I did, and the ones that didn't were just dropped off and picked up so there was very little parental involvement, which was great. Unfortunately the u12s were a different story…

Understandably the u12s parents were very supportive of their kids and we had a decent team. However they had expectations that were far higher than their kids' capabilities as a group, and they refused to understand the ethos of the Academy, which was for all of the boys in the squad to get equal game time which impacted on results at times. I couldn't win either way as some parents would be disgruntled if I made the required changes to play all the boys, and the others would be if I didn't give the subs enough game time. Practice is the only way that children improve and it doesn't happen overnight, but every parent only thinks of their child and not the collective unfortunately. They all had their opinions but none of them had played or obtained any of the coaching qualifications like I had, and my job was to care for all of the boys not just theirs. This problem was highlighted at tournaments that we would travel to on the mainland, including Phuket, Krabi, Suratthani and Bangkok, the expectations placed on the boys by most of their parents were ridiculous, especially as most of the Thai teams would blatantly play boys a couple of years older and do anything to win. I came to the stage where I dreaded a tournament coming up as it became a stressful experience and not an enjoyable one for the boys as it should be. However I must have been doing something right as I was asked to become Academy manager, which included a 50% pay rise as well as the extra responsibility of looking after the other coaches and just generally being involved with the Academy management generally. I did have another success story with a boy called Bastien, who when I arrived was very timid and sometimes bullied by the other boys at times. However his attitude was excellent and his willingness to listen, learn and practise meant he developed very well in comparison to the more naturally talented lads – and the fact that I was willing to persevere and give him plenty of game time meant that his confidence gradually grew to becoming a regular starter for the team. When I finally left the club he sent me a message to thank me for believing in him and that he will be forever grateful. It was wonderful to hear that he had been offered a scholarship in Phuket a couple of years later and I'm happy if I played a small part in his development.

At the end of my initial 3 months in Samui I decided I wanted to stay and continue with the football academy. In order to do so I had to go on a Visa run, which entailed going out of Thailand to go to an embassy and get my Visa renewed to enable me to stay for another three months and this has to be done every quarter repeatedly. The club arranged this trip with one of the island's renowned organisers, an Austrian chap called Herbert, who ran his operation in a similar fashion to another Austrian dictator! Firstly I had to be at a bus stop to be picked up at 4am and was taken to Herbert's office where he had about 20 of us all stood outside while he barked instructions at us! Now I was 50 at this point and I don't really like being shouted at, especially when I'm half asleep and when he said "is there anyone English here?" I raised my hand and he said "you will be the trouble!" – I felt like telling him where to go and heading straight back to bed! I had never known anything like it and just stopped listening to this madman, but I just heard him say "make sure you are all on the back of the boat ready to get straight on the bus as we have no time to wait!" So I sat on the back of the ferry while we crossed the sea to mainland Thailand to then get the bus to Malaysia which is a good 8 hour journey at breakneck speed. Apparently during the crossing I was supposed to give him my papers and the money for him to process the Visa when we got to Malaysia, but I had missed this vital piece of information and he revelled in belittling me before we left the ferry. I tried to apologise several times on the way and he could easily have taken my documents at any point on the way to Malaysia but he refused like a spoilt child. I just presumed he enjoyed seeing me suffer. Once we got off the bus we had to get a small long tail boat to the border and then go through customs into Malaysia. At this point he turned to me and said "you are on your own now – good luck!"

He basically abandoned me on the border and I had no idea where I was or where I was going to! Fortunately I managed to jump into the last taxi and went to the hotel with a couple of other people in the group, I then checked into the hotel so at least I had time to think and contacted the football club to ask what I should do! I was in a place called Kota Burra and it was hammering down with rain and really not a nice place to be under the best of circumstances. It was agreed that I would try to get my Visa the next day and I duly got a taxi to the embassy and gave my papers in to be told to return the next day. I literally lived in my room feeling the worst I had ever felt in my life, and only popped out for something to eat. The rain poured down non-stop and to make matters worse my Visa was declined the following day, which I'm pretty sure was down to Herr Herbert's influence there. It was agreed that I would catch a plane back to Samui but there was no flight for another couple of days! I can honestly say that this is probably the worst few days of my life and it really put me off Visa runs from then on, which some expats really look forward to for a few days off the island but definitely not me. From then on I always flew to Penang which was a much nicer place, although I'm sure it cost the club more money.

There were other benefits of being in Samui as my working hours were 4.30pm – 7pm, and I generally spent a couple of hours a day by the pool or visiting one of the beautiful beaches before getting ready for training, although the heat during the summer could be over 40 degrees in the shade. I became a bit restless in the apartment and wanted some outside space as I felt a bit claustrophobic. As I was doing well I decided to move to a lovely place with a shared pool with 11 other houses in the block. Fortunately these were mainly holiday lets and 80% of the time they remained empty so I generally had the pool to myself which was bliss. However, I did find one friend in the form of a street dog called Charlie (coincidentally also my eldest son's name!) and I started to feed him outside of the entrance gate and he took a liking to me. Now in Thailand it's normal for dogs to live on the street in packs and they forage for themselves but Charlie was a bit of a loner and had this area to himself. I shared the feeding of him with a neighbour who was a bit of a busybody, and Charlie soon made it clear who he preferred as he would be waiting outside my door in the morning. Before long he worked up the courage to come inside the house and lie underneath the ceiling fan to keep cool. This was quite unheard of as Soi (street) dogs normally won't go into a house. He also insisted on having a ride on my scooter before I left to go to work by jumping into the foot well and refusing to budge! So it became my ritual to leave 10 minutes early taking him for a ride, let him jump off to do his business and then take him back before I went to work, he was the happiest dog ever. I would also bring him back any leftover food and he would literally eat anything – rice, egg, lamb shank bones, you name it he'd devour it gratefully. I'd never had a dog before and I now understand how people get so attached to their dogs. Sadly, after a few months of this friendship I woke up to the unpleasant sight of my busybody neighbour outside my door with no shirt on, and he broke the news that he had found Charlie outside my neighbour's door and when he called him he didn't move, and it turned out that he was dead. Although I wasn't keen on this neighbour to be fair to him he had buried Charlie just outside the gate in the jungle and made a cross for his grave. After the initial shock, when I was alone, I unashamedly cried my eyes out. Although I don't know how it happened there were two possibilities – either he'd been bitten by a poisonous snake or he'd been poisoned by a Thai protecting the territory of his dog, which was relatively normal there. Either way it was terribly sad.

I had been enjoying my life there and decided that I wanted to stay long term so I started looking at other business ventures so I wouldn't end up reliant solely on the football club for my income. As coincidence would have it I was trying to find a pool table, table football or table tennis table for the Academy – to give the kids something to do while encouraging the parents to stay for a drink after training to help the income of the club. I had a meeting with an English guy called Steve who supplied pool tables to the local bars in the area. Steve was in his late sixties and during the meeting he let it be known that he was ready to retire and wanted to sell his business. So we began talking and eventually we agreed on a deal and I was about to become the owner of a pool table rental business, to provide me with additional income for not too much hassle. However, before I officially owned the business there was to be another turning point in my life.

CHAPTER THIRTY FOUR

One Night in Bangkok

As an Academy we were invited to one of the most prestigious tournaments in Bangkok which the owners wanted to attend, the only problem to overcome was the cost of the trip. The options were to take the train, hire buses or to fly. After speaking to a few parents they were reluctant for their kids to travel in buses, which I understood as the driving over there has to be seen to be believed, and the train would be a logistical nightmare for our staff to look after 40 kids. So we decided to attempt to raise the funds to fly everyone together. The Academy was split between wealthy families and Thai kids with very little money so we had to try and find a fair way of getting everyone there in the age groups invited. I suggested that we try and find business sponsors for the club and we would put advertising around the Academy pitches and on the website. I also set about writing a letter to all the parents to encourage them to find a business to sponsor their child.

This was a similar way in which I funded the youth team at AFC Wulfrunians a few years before and before long we had quite a bit of interest from the people of Samui. This was quite a big occasion there and good press for their businesses to help the kids get to Bangkok as a lot of them had never been that far away from home before. Before long we were on our way and we all boarded a flight from Samui, which takes an hour, with a very excited group of children with all of us looking forward to a great weekend.

I had been on a few tournament weekends before in Thailand and I had to sort a particular problem out, which was that they think it is normal and acceptable for the kids to share rooms and even beds with the coaches on these trips. There was no way I was leaving myself in such a vulnerable position and I objected very strongly after the first trip when I slept on the sofa. After this, the coaches generally had separate rooms and the children slept together. I even offered to pay for my own room if that was necessary as I felt so strongly about this – it would be unheard of in Europe. However, when we arrived at the hotel they had booked a large 3 bedroomed room with 6 kids and 3 coaches to share. I either had to sleep with 2 children or a large Dutchman and neither appealed to me particularly! The Thai coach was happy to sleep with the two Thai kids as he didn't know any different and I gave the bed to the Dutch guy. The other four kids all slept together and I took the two seater sofa with a towel as a cover. As you can imagine I didn't get much sleep but preferred this to the other options available and tried to get on with it as best I could. The football went pretty well on Saturday with my team winning all their group games despite the heat in early June, which was stifling. The sweat was pouring out of me – I had a small towel wrapped around my shoulders constantly to wipe the sweat away and a cap on to protect my under threat scalp!

When we got back to the hotel the kids all went swimming or played on their phones and gadgets and we could have a couple of beers and relax until we had to get the kids to bed. Whilst having these beers I got chatting to one of the parents who spoke perfect English and we were invited to go out in Bangkok for the night as this person had friends there from her time at university and from living there afterwards. Well, I had the devil on one shoulder as I knew I wouldn't get a good night's sleep on the sofa anyway, and this alternative opportunity seemed quite appealing to be honest. I explained that we had to make sure the kids were all asleep so we could meet up later in the night, but that didn't create much of an obstacle at all.

So the Dutchman and I waited until the kids eventually fell asleep and then ordered a taxi and quietly left the hotel into central Bangkok. We met up with a few people in a lively area and we enjoyed ourselves and then moved onto a nightclub – not really my scene but I went with it! Afterwards a couple of us decided to do what you do in the early hours of the morning after a few drinks in Bangkok, we went for an Indian curry! It was now light and I knew I had to get back before the kids woke up in the morning and managed to get back to the hotel around 6am hoping for an hour's sleep before another long day ahead of me. However when I arrived back one of the bosses of the club was waiting for me and it transpired that some of the other parents had grassed on us having spotted us leaving the hotel the night before. I carried on the day as normal with my team getting knocked out in the quarter finals in a bizarre version of a shoot-out where at the end of full time they drop the numbers from 7 v 7 to 3 v 3 and the first team to score wins!

After the event, it was obvious that the boss wasn't happy and he said he wanted a couple of days to think about things and he would get back to me. Fortunately I had arranged a week off to stay in Bangkok with a friend anyway. We hired a motorbike and I somehow ended up driving around Bangkok with my friend on the back, which was an experience in itself. I now have no fear about driving anything, anywhere in the world!

After a few days I had a call from the boss of the academy saying that he didn't think it was going to work and that was that

– I'd lost my job over one night in Bangkok! I saw my holiday out and then flew back to Samui as planned, aiming to push through my purchase of the pool table business, to enable me to have an income and also be able to have the necessary Visa and work permit to stay in Thailand. Prior to this point, I was quite happy with life there but I didn't realise how much I was going to miss the football club and the social aspect it gave me. In hindsight I rushed into buying the business but it seemed to be my only option at the time.

After a stubborn month or so it dawned on me that the pool table business wasn't going to be enough either financially or in terms of it being busy enough to keep me occupied, and I hit a downward spiral that really wasn't good for me either mentally or physically. I literally had 6 hours work a month which consisted of cleaning the pool tables and collecting the money due. I was spending far more than I was earning and I was also definitely drinking too much. The only people I knew at this time were ex-pats that managed bars and I either visited their bars or waited for them to finish work and went out with them afterwards until the early hours as I had nothing to get up for in the morning. On one occasion after a drinking session watching the rugby internationals all day I went out into town and stupidly tried to drive home on my motorbike and the next thing I knew I was surrounded by Thai people trying to bring me around. Fortunately there was a friend amongst these people and he managed to get me home in a taxi. I still don't know what happened but I think I must have blacked out. If my friend wasn't there I would have been taken to hospital and the police would have become involved – both of which would have proven very expensive over there. I was really very lucky to come away with a very deeply bruised chest, a few cuts, and I bit through my tongue – nothing in comparison to the injuries and deaths suffered over there every day. At this juncture I had two options available to me – either invest more into trying to make a life over there or accept my time was up and go home. The problem was I had no idea what I would do if I came home.

I thought about opening a jazz bar with live music at weekends, as there was nowhere on the island with a bit of class, and there were plenty of people with money and nowhere really nice to go apart from the top hotels, which were very expensive and not really open to the general public. However finding premises that were available and affordable was difficult and this idea fizzled out. I then looked at a small hotel in a good area but when I got down to the nitty gritty the books didn't match up with the owners claims on income and again I felt it best to walk away. Once I'd left the football academy my social life was very limited and I only really knew a handful of people and ironically a couple of these were a father and son from Willenhall which is about 10 miles from where I lived in Wolverhampton. The son is a Wolves fan called Dean Bryant and his father Paul who is a West Brom fan which led to some interesting banter as you can imagine. However, I was becoming increasingly lonely and unhappy, and felt it was time to come home.

I don't regret the experience of living in Thailand and it has made me a much more rounded, accepting and understanding person. I like to think that I've always treated people as I find them but to learn about another culture certainly opened my mind. For instance, before I went to Samui I didn't really think I could have a proper female friend but on one occasion a lesbian friend I had met out there called me and asked if she could talk to me over a drink. When I arrived she had also invited some other of her friends and it seemed she just wanted to get drunk!

Her other friends consisted of three other lesbians and three ladyboys who were all bigger than me! I had no option but to go with it and it was just an evening of pure innocent fun playing pool and drinking albeit a little unusual compared to my normal nights out!

There is a lot of stigma attached to people who visit Thailand and I understand why, but it's just down to supply and demand really. The government support is minimal for the Thai people so if they aren't wealthy enough to provide a good education for their children they become farmers at home or they leave to become prostitutes in one of the tourist areas. I'm not saying I agree with that way of life, but they see it as a way of earning good money and regard it as normal, and in contrast to our culture they often link sex with money and not always love. I heard many stories of Western men falling for a pretty girl in Thailand and being fleeced by her either after marriage or on an ongoing basis – one very attractive lady had numerous men sending her £200 a month believing that she was their girlfriend and she would spend time with them on their annual vacation to appease them. She was driving around in a top of the range Mercedes and living in a Penthouse apartment and was investing their money in businesses locally so I'm not sure who was being exploited!

Ultimately I mainly enjoyed the Thailand experience but it was time to come home.

CHAPTER THIRTY FIVE

Back to Blighty

When I arrived home I had no idea what I was going to do and took some time at my parents to consider my options. It took a little while to decide on a new career and I have now built a new life for myself living in a beautiful town called Bridgnorth in Shropshire. I'm working as an Estate Planner for a solicitor's practice in Stourbridge called KingsGuard Legal covering all of the Midlands area and beyond. I find the work very rewarding as I'm mainly providing Trusts to protect people's property from being taken to pay for care home fees in addition to providing Wills, Lasting Powers of Attorney and Funeral Plans. The company also offer conveyancing for house sales and purchases and probate services too (jp@kingsguardlegal.co.uk).

I am also coaching on a part time basis with Eddie McGoldrick in the Crystal Palace Foundation based at Northampton College, which I enjoy and find it rewarding to help the boys improve as footballers and young men generally. Being close to Corby three days a week enables me to help my parents as they become older which is the least I can do for them and being at home means I can be in touch with my boys and get to see them on a more regular basis which is great.

At weekends I enjoy watching Bridgnorth and Shifnal FC and I hope to be able to watch the local Bridgnorth rugby team too when the Covid restrictions are over and I will also hopefully see Wolves play occasionally. I'm still involved with the Wolves All Stars as a committee member and regular substitute and I enjoy raising money for Charity and also keeping in touch with the lads.

Joining Eddie McGoldrick as a coach in his Crystal Palace Foundation Academy.

* * *

Eddie McGoldrick (Corby boy, Crystal Palace, Arsenal, Man City & Republic of Ireland)

Both Jon and I grew up in Corby, a real hotbed for talented footballers in the late 70s and early 80s and we were no different. As I was two years older our paths rarely crossed in school or Sunday football but Jon's name was on everyone's lips at the time. He was a precocious talent that had flair and could score and assist goals with his youthful confidence in his own ability. His ability rightly attracted admirers and his performance at Wembley for England Schoolboys v Holland made our whole town very proud and gave Jon the pick of England's top clubs to choose from and he chose Arsenal – a fantastic achievement for a little boy from Corby. We have become good friends and I'm delighted he is now helping me with a new generation of budding footballers at my Crystal Palace foundation academy.

* * *

Celebrating my 50th birthday with Charlie and Jack.

Footnote

I have read quite a few ex-footballers books and recently listened to lots of podcasts and the one thing that is always said is that they have no regrets and wouldn't change anything. Well I've got loads of regrets in regards to my football career as you can probably recognise if you have read the content of this book, but the truth is that I'm not bitter about the way things have turned out for me. I have been far more successful outside of football than I ever was in it and who knows how I could have ended up if I'd have signed the contract that was offered to me at Arsenal! Perhaps I'd have played for England or maybe I'd be an alcoholic or perhaps my knees wouldn't have stood up to full time football for very long! I believe that I had the ability to do much better but perhaps not the mental strength or self-belief that is needed to get to the top. I regret not being more committed when I had the chance at Arsenal and Wolves but don't believe I was given much help and despite a few sleepless nights I've realised that there is no point in looking back in any aspect of life. I'm a very proud father of two young men and I'm looking forward to the future whatever it may bring. I have found writing this book quite painful at times but wanted to give an insight into the realities of life as a journeyman footballer, although I am aware that I've achieved what a lot of boys dream of. I also wanted my sons to have something to remember me by and pass down to the future generations of Purdies.

I hope you have enjoyed the book and I thank you for reading.

Purds